Psychology in
Education

UNDER THE EDITORSHIP OF GARDNER MURPHY

PSYCHOLOGY IN EDUCATION

Sidney L. Pressey
Francis P. Robinson
John E. Horrocks

Ohio State University

HARPER & BROTHERS · PUBLISHERS · NEW YORK

Pressey, Sidney Leavitt, 1888–
    Psychology in education ₍by₎ Sidney L. Pressey, Fran-
cis Robinson ₍and₎ John E. Horrocks.   New York,
Harper ₍1959₎
    658 p.   illus.   25 cm.
    "Parts of this book were previously published under the title,
Psychology and the new education, revised edition."

    1. Educational psychology.   I. Title.

LB1051.P72   370.15   58–13965 ‡

Library of Congress

Contents

v

Preface

PSYCHOLOGY IN EDUCATION IS AN ATTEMPT TO RECOG-
nize and draw on four features which the writers believe are now of
major importance as regards contributions of psychology to education.

First is the broadening and what might be called the coming-of-age of
research in child development. Initially often preoccupied with infancy and
the preschool years, child development is now tending to combine with
the earlier somewhat separate work on adolescence; thus the growth years
are seen in larger and more consistent perspectives. Understanding of development has been variously enriched, as by minutely detailed studies of
physical growth, and the use of methods and material from sociology and
cultural anthropology. And longtiudinal studies that follow the growth of
individuals, sometimes from infancy into adulthood, have revised certain
earlier concepts—as in showing personality correlates of "early" and "late"
maturing, and the possible substantial influence of environment on growth
of ability. Part I of this book attempts a compact summary of our present
knowledge regarding development in the first twenty years.

A second feature of the psychoeducational present is the seemingly heterogeneous mass of material on learning. Some educators have proceeded
from recognizing individual dynamics in learning to advocating curricular
content and methods that are sometimes so highly personal to each pupil
in each class and for each teacher that, except when teachers have been
especially adaptive and clever, the public and even the schools have been
confused as to just what was or should be happening. Increasing emphasis
has been put on the social aspects of learning. There are both advocacy and
rejection of the position that the somewhat special types of learning involved in the building of social competence, leisure interests, character
traits, and ideals are major concerns of the school. Meanwhile, somewhat
in contrast, much of the extraordinary amount of recent psychological research on learning has become remote from classrooms and indeed from
any other environment than the psychological laboratory. Part II of this

volume attempts some coördination of various types of pertinent research and thinking regarding learning, and their application to school work.

A third feature of the current educational scene, to which psychologists have been major contributors, is the trend toward greater individualization of educational work, so that optimal stimulation is provided for each pupil in an effort to foster his total development. Such individualization is primarily the function of the teacher. At times, however, certain youngsters have problems that go beyond what she has time or training for; so she needs help from such specialists as school psychologists, counselors, speech and hearing therapists, etc. These specialists aid in three ways: by consulting with the teacher on psychological problems, by dealing directly with youngsters who have serious difficulties, and by arranging educational experiences of types not ordinarily provided by the curriculum. When such specialists are available, the teacher should know what services they can render, and how to coördinate her efforts with theirs. In case these specialists are not available, a teacher should know enough about these types of services to enable her to do at least something for such pupils. Part III of this volume attempts to indicate in concrete detail how she can better understand and help each youngster.

A fourth feature, although of increasing potential value to teachers, can be touched on only briefly. Longitudinal studies of individuals are being continued from childhood into their twenties and beyond. Special phases of adult life are being investigated, often in relation to childhood and youth —Kinsey's famous work, for example, and Lehman's studies on age of achievement. Gerontologists are studying old age and seeking antecedents of problems that arise during this period. Adult education is an important and growing movement. In the research on adult life and its problems, teachers should find help in understanding themselves, as well as other adults—colleagues, parents, community leaders. Valuable perspectives may then be gained on the total of human development and change, and the outcomes and goals of education. The final chapter of this volume looks briefly at certain of these topics.

In 1933 the senior author of the present volume published a book which he called *Psychology and the New Education,* a title kept, though the book was almost completely rewritten, in a revision published in collaboration with F. P. Robinson in 1944. Not only is the present volume greatly changed from the 1944 edition, but the "new education" is no longer new, and the psychology related to it is greatly expanded. The title has therefore been changed, for *Psychology in Education* seems best to indicate the content and orientation of the treatment attempted, and it suggests a largely new treatment.

In the present volume, the first six chapters and the last have been the primary responsibility of Dr. Pressey, Chapters 7–11 and 13 of Dr. Horrocks, and Chapters 12 and 14–18 of Dr. Robinson. But there has been extensive collaboration throughout.

THE AUTHORS

Columbus
December, 1958

Psychology in
Education

Chapter 1

The Basic Importance of Psychology in Preparing for Teaching

SOMEWHAT AS PHYSIOLOGY IS BASIC IN PREPARING TO practice medicine, so certain major topics in psychology, the writers believe, are basic in preparing to teach. In particular, three large areas of psychological investigation—development, learning, and individualization of educational programs—seem of great potential value to teachers as a means of understanding educational problems and suggesting ways of dealing with them. Recent work in all three areas has contributed greatly to such understanding and to possible improvement in our schools.

DISTINCTIVE CONTRIBUTIONS OF RECENT WORK ON HUMAN DEVELOPMENT

Of first importance in understanding the task and the opportunity of our schools is consideration of the recent substantial reconstitution of concepts regarding development in childhood and youth.

Detailed investigations that follow the development of the same individuals, in some instances from early infancy into adult life, have shown important differences in patterns of physical growth which are related to body build and growth rate. These studies are of major importance in helping a teacher understand problems involving her pupils' physique and vigor. More important, they have presented correlative information on personality growth, thus illuminating hitherto obscure problems concerning social maladjustment, boy-girl relationships, and leadership and social status through childhood and youth. If the schools would adjust their practices to this new knowledge, they could largely solve certain major problems of adjustment and of discipline.

1

From these same studies, and also from a variety of other investigations, have recently come major modifications of earlier concepts regarding abilities. Individuals differ in their patterns of mental as well as physical growth, and in their comparative strengths and weaknesses in different abilities. Some abilities may continue to "grow" well into adult life. A variety of such factors as the family's socioeconomic status may be related to mental growth. Fascinating recent evidence suggests that, much more than was suspected a few years ago, subtle conditions at home and also in school may influence the rate of growth and the intellectual level finally attained. If our schools took such findings into consideration, the level of general ability might conceivably be raised somewhat, and the careers of the very able be fostered.

Mass media of communication—especially radio and television—have provided an extraordinary richness and even surfeit of vicarious experiences, and have artfully fostered wants and desires, and ideas regarding social behavior. The interests of young people are thus developing under the stimulation of influences which often seem grossly artificial and possibly conducive to irresponsibility or delinquency, but which could be used constructively and in forceful supplementation of educational efforts.

A third contribution of recent years to the understanding of human development concerns emotional dynamics. Not intellectual but emotional growth and change are now seen to be of central importance in many respects. Not the young person's understandings but his feelings, which he himself usually does not understand, are the forces that really move him and determine the direction he takes. Usually these feelings are quite as poorly understood by the adults who have contact with him. But if a teacher can understand them, she gains invaluable insights into her pupil's problems. However, recent work is stressing not problems of emotional frustration, but the emotional satisfaction to be found in the realization of interests, and the cumulative effects of such satisfactions on the building of attitudes and competences. Largely new concepts regarding emotional health and the dynamics of positive personality growth are resulting.

In the fourth place, there is increasing emphasis on and understanding of social development through childhood and adolescence, and also the effects of the total social and cultural environment on development. The distinctive fact about a human being is after all not that he is a biological organism, but that he is a social being. His growth is not so much physical as social, and the world he lives in is not so much a physical as a social world. Therefore the newer studies of what may be called the social

psychology of childhood and youth are important not only for their origi-
nality and their remaking of that topic, but even more for the light
they throw on the growth and change of interests and ideals and of the
total personality.

In successive chapters on growth in physique, abilities, interests, emotions, and social life, Part I of this book attempts to give an integrated
view of development through the first twenty years that will be especially
helpful in understanding young people and fostering their education.

ENLARGEMENT OF CONCEPTS REGARDING LEARNING AND TEACHING

Somewhat as concepts regarding human development have in recent
years been substantially reconstituted, so also, in part as a result, have
understandings regarding learning in its relation to teaching.

As indicated in the preceding section, abilities not only increase but
change during the growth years. More than was realized earlier, this
growth may be affected by certain factors, and a good school program may
even be able somewhat to increase functioning "intelligence." A 14-year-
old boy with an "interest age" of 12 presents a different learning-teaching
problem than another lad of the same chronological age but whose "interest
age" is 16. The mass media and especially television may strongly influence
interests and attitudes, may create unprecedented educational problems,
but may also be of great value as educational aids. Social development is
a major feature and should be a major educational responsibility during
the growth years; school tasks and methods should be appropriate to pupils'
social maturity. Emotional maturing and emotional distresses and enthu-
siasms are of vital influence on learning.

The above comments suggest a broadened concept of learning and of the
task of the schools. The learning provided by the traditional school was
largely apart from the pupil's real life. Certain facts and skills do need
to be learned, but there is evidence that they are learned more efficiently
in modern schools. And other learnings may be of far greater significance
to the learner—health habits, good taste in dress, skill in reading newspapers and judgment in appraising what they contain, knowledge and
appraisal of jobs toward which education may be directed. The modern
school is rightly concerned that pupils should learn to get along with other
people and work coöperatively. It also recognizes recent criticisms, and
knows that it should be more effective in the more conventional tasks. A
psychology of learning designed to aid teachers must take account of

these varied learnings. It must also recognize and allow for individual differences in learning.

With these broader modern concepts regarding both child development and learning should come recognition that the learning situation is not simply the child hunched over his desk under the threatening eye of the teacher. The total situation in which the learning takes place involves the other members of the class and their relations with one another and with the teacher. Both teacher and pupils are members of the community and are constantly affected by its customs, attitudes, and ways of living. All live in a culture which shapes their thinking. Hence, among the important learnings to be sought are easiness and coöperative effectiveness in working with others. Teaching must stress learning in a social context and bring out the special values inherent in social learning.

With these broadened concepts of the school's tasks and of learning come more inclusive concepts regarding desirable results of schooling. It is not enough to learn to remember until the next quiz. Presumably much that the student learns in a first course in chemistry should be kept in mind when he begins a second course in that subject. Some learnings—how to read and study effectively, to keep one's own accounts accurately, to have good manners—should be permanent. Learnings should also transfer; thus the study of Latin *should* increase English vocabulary, and the study of hygiene lead to improvement of health habits. A country boy's high-school work in agriculture should help him in his farm work. Certainly any discussion of learning should include consideration as to how long it lasts and how effective it is.

If information about learning is to be useful in teaching, it should be not only general, but applied to specific school subjects. Intensive consideration is therefore given to reading—that most basic of all subjects from the first grade through college—to indicate the practical problems of school learning that have been investigated, and to show how illuminating many of these investigations have been as far as teaching difficulties are concerned. Since many college students are slow or inefficient readers, this material may be of value to them.

Part II thus summarizes a variety of material on learning that will be helpful to a person who is preparing to teach. Concrete data on the progress of learning in school, effects of school social situations on learning, ways of improving retention and application, examples of special inquiries on the learning of a particular school subject—these are some of the topics dealt with.

WORKING WITH THE INDIVIDUAL STUDENT

A major contribution of psychology to education has been the devising of means of making mental measurements that are useful in the schools. Not only are there now a great variety of tests of general and special abilities, there are even more varied means for appraising progress in learning. Carefully constructed tests, many of which can be scored by machine, make it easy for a teacher to appraise the standing of her class in reading or history or science, and to compare her pupils' scores with averages based on large numbers of pupils in different parts of the country. Diagnostic tests help her find the special difficulties of pupils who are not progressing satisfactorily. There are clever means of discovering whether a pupil actually applies outside of school what he has learned in class and how he rates with his classmates.

All such methods of studying youngsters emphasize the extent to which each pupil is unique and must be known as a person. There are the fascinating children of superior abilities, until recently too often neglected, who are capable of outstanding school work and, later, outstanding careers. There are the very dull, many of them potential delinquents, who are capable of usefulness in humble ways, with wise guidance. A handicapped child likewise presents special problems. Every teacher needs some understanding, in terms of concrete instances, of the great variety of young people with whom she must deal, and the variety of backgrounds from which they come.

But once these children who vary so widely have been identified to some extent, how are they to be better understood and helped? Efforts to solve these problems may well be called the most distinctive psychoeducational development of recent years. All such work is now being widely stressed. For example, the President's Committee on Education Beyond High School recommends "that school systems greatly increase their emphasis on developing sound guidance and counseling programs" and recognizes "that all teachers must complement and assist the professional counselor as part of a team."[1] The writers believe that some orientation in working with individual pupils should be part of teacher education, and that it can best be provided as part of a larger view of child development and learning. Efforts to understand and help individual youngsters may be the most fascinating and most rewarding phase of a teacher's work.

How, for instance, does one go about helping a girl with a special

[1] *Second Report to the President,* July, 1957, pp. 55, 42.

difficulty, as in reading? How may a good interview with her be conducted? How may such work be made not merely remedial, but part of a broader effort to bring out each pupil's potentialities? How may counseling and classroom methods and also the total school situation be used for such purposes? And what may be done with superior students—not alone the "problem" students—to lift them above mediocre performance and inadequate goals?

Also largely individual are problems of the hygiene of work. Certain factors, such as illumination, are general; but interest and emotional health are more important. A teacher needs to consider possible fatigue in her own work. What are the health hazards of teaching and what can be done to reduce them? How can teaching be made more pleasant and satisfying?

Part III of this book includes a rich variety of data, case summaries, excerpts of interviews, that show how pupils can be appraised, known as persons, counseled, guided wisely in their school work and in their larger plans.

CONTINUING PSYCHOEDUCATIONAL PROBLEMS

Research regarding certain psychological problems of teachers was mentioned above. But research is broadening its scope, for increasingly a great variety of problems of adult life are being investigated. Biographical and autobiographical materials are bringing out trends in life patterns. Changes in abilities, interests, attitudes, purposes are being followed through the individual's life. Because a considerable portion of all this material concerns teachers and is significant in possible forecasts for teachers-to-be, it is touched upon briefly. More broadly, there are indications of educational outcomes and needs in adult life, and hints as to how the adult world and the school may more effectively coördinate and coöperate.

In summary, this volume attempts to overview development in the school years, with a glance at the years after school; to consider a wide variety of research on learning in relation to the work of the schools; and to note various educational problems and services with which psychologists have been especially concerned. The range of topics is indeed wide, but they are so interrelated that their consideration together should be helpful.

PART I

Development Through
Childhood and Youth

Chapter 2

Physical Growth and Change,
and Health

THE MOST IMPORTANT, HELPFUL, DECEIVING, CONFUSING, and neglected fact in education is growth. Most important, because the first requirement through the school years should be that healthy growth be achieved; most helpful, because the plasticity and vigor of the growth period greatly aid education; most deceiving, because education frequently mistakes as its own accomplishment what is actually the result of maturing; most confusing, because growth involves constant change; most neglected, because growth is so usual and yet so complex and often subtle.

Growth in intellect, personality, and character can be adequately understood only in relation to physical growth. To appreciate the fundamental biological character of growth in abilities, the similarity between the curves for growth in "intelligence" and those for growth in physique should be noted. Only in relation to the physiological changes going on in childhood and adolescence can we interpret changes in interest and attitudes during this period. Anomalies of physical development explain many a "problem child."

For a child, to be constantly growing and changing is indeed an experience, often puzzling, frequently presenting problems, sometimes pleasing. During adolescence, physical growth may cause manifold embarrassments and anxieties for the youngster of either sex. In a boy's world, physical size and prowess are so important that his rapid or slow growth as compared to that of his associates may determine his position and prestige among them. Oddly enough, advantages of early versus late maturing are largely reversed for girls, as will be seen shortly. The grown person can hardly realize how bewildering growing may be; some problems of his childhood and youth may have caused him so much unhappiness that he does not wish to remember them.

The concrete significance of differences and changes in physical size will be clearer if you will recall their bearing on your own childhood and adolescence. You may remember how very big adults—and even children in the fifth grade —seemed when you were in the second grade; how awkward and immature you felt as a high-school freshman in comparison with the seniors. There are also the cases in which growth factors were pervasively important. In your high school there were probably the big, early-maturing boy whose prominence in sports and masculine assurance made him a featured leader, and the slight, shy youngster whom most of you hardly knew. There may have been one girl, small for her age, who became the pampered pet of both the teacher and the other girls in the class, and another girl, big and raw-boned, who was acutely un-happy because she was so tall that most of the boys did not want to dance with her. If you look back critically at your own adolescence there will probably emerge unpleasant recollections of bewilderment and anxiety over the changes of puberty.

To begin the study of educational psychology by considering physical growth is, then, of great value, for knowledge of the basic biological and physiological factors is seen at the outset as essential for understanding psychological development. Furthermore, the numerous psychological problems the child has to meet because he is physically a growing and changing organism can be better recognized.

GROWTH IN SIZE

Most elementary of all data regarding growth are measurements of height and weight. Size is only a rough indication of the stage of growth of a given child, but massed data on height and weight tell much about the course of growth and the relation of various factors thereto.

Curves of Growth in Height and Weight

The total sweep of the growth process is well shown in Fig. 2.1, which shows growth curves in average height and weight. Growth is rapid in infancy, slower in middle childhood, upsurging at adolescence—this is more noticeable on the curves for weight; an adult leveling off begins around 20 for the boys, earlier for the girls.[1]

[1] Many books dealing with child development or adolescence treat growth only through 18. Wherever possible, this volume presents data showing growth through 20 or 21, partly because many American young people now continue school through 20, and partly to include the average undergraduate so that he may see his place

The magnitude of the total growth process through the years, especially in adolescence, is of great importance. Thus during the twelve years from 6 to 18, boys increase over one-half in height and over three times in weight. The powerful nature of the forces of growth and the insistency of the individual's demands as regards food, exercise, sleep, and the other factors involved in physical well-being can hardly be overemphasized.

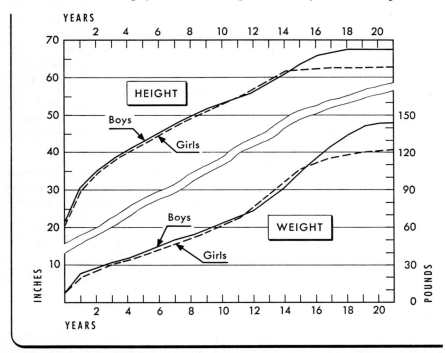

FIG. 2.1. Growth in height and weight from birth to 21 years. Although American children now are a bit heavier and taller than before the Second World War when these data were gathered, these curves still give an exceptionally valuable picture of average height and weight through the first two decades. "Longitudinal" studies are too selective to show averages. (Adapted from Baldwin [1], Davenport [15], and Burgess [10].)

Little wonder that there are times when—very likely to the distress of their teachers—many children seem to be preoccupied with merely growing. Moreover, the rate of growth varies at different ages, as is brought out in Fig. 2.2, which shows not the height and weight at each age, but the gain each year. Growth increases rapidly in the early teens. Boys have

in the developmental picture. Moreover, inly by such extension can the attainment of the adult level be shown, with the sex differences clearly apparent and the growth phase of the total life span really covered.

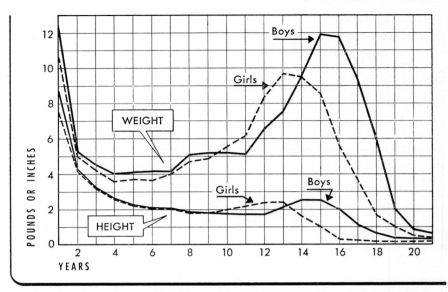

FIG. 2.2. Average gains each year in height and weight for boys and girls. One division equals 1 pound, 1 inch, or 1 year. The figure shows that from birth through the first year boys average 12.2 pounds gain in weight and 8.7 inches in height. They gain 5.2 pounds and grow 4.4 inches during the second year, etc. (Adapted from Baldwin [1], Davenport [15], and Burgess [10].)

a later and greater maximum and keep growing taller until about 19 years, as compared to 16 for girls.

Physical Size and Social Status

The great significance, for "child society," of these marked differences in physical size from age to age must be stressed. Childhood and youth are rough-and-tumble periods, and a youngster's position among his fellows is determined in large part by his physical size, strength, and vigor. In proportion as a child can associate and compete physically, he achieves confidence and the ability to get along with others and has a happy or a miserable childhood. These differences in height and weight from one age to the next thus give chronological age special significance in the associations of childhood.[2]

[2] It is interesting to note that the boxing world considers the weight increase of the average boy between 14 and 15—about 15 pounds—as more than sufficient to move a man from one boxing class into another, as from featherweight to lightweight. Between the ages of 14 and 17, the average boy puts on enough weight to move a man all the way from a lightweight to a heavyweight. And 15 pounds is proportionately more in the youth than in the man.

The pervasive effects of differences in physical size are well illustrated by a study of two brothers, the older unusually large for his age, the other not only a year younger but smaller than average. As far back as the younger one could remember, his brother had imposed on him, teased him, made him do the unpleasant chores. By adolescence, the younger was so thoroughly cowed that he did not dare drive the family car, have a date, or wear the kind of clothes he liked. He did poorer work in school, largely because of his feelings of inadequacy, and withdrew from the social life of his fellows into a dream world in which he was the successful person he might have become had he only been large. Not until his senior year in college did the younger brother come to understand his difficulties; he still remains shy and unsure of himself, and is frequently harassed by his earlier feelings of inferiority, the basis of which was being a few inches shorter and a few pounds lighter than his brother during his childhood years (4).[3]

Often neglected in discussions of the psychology of childhood is the pervasive importance of the child's physical inferiority to adults. In their relations with one another, shrewd adults recognize differences in physical size and vigor as of subtle but substantial significance. Thus the small man feels inferior and becomes either submissive or defensively aggressive; the man of powerful physique may be either domineering or patronizing. But physical differences between children and adults are even more marked (and are accentuated by multiple other differences in intellectual and emotional maturity and prestige).

The young child is a pygmy among adult giants. Childhood attitudes of dependence, submissiveness, fear, or resentment, and adult protectiveness or domineering could hardly develop as they do if it were not for the crude animal fact of the child's physical inferiority. And it may be a very important factor in a child's attitudes in school. Whatever the relations between a 100-pound boy and a 200-pound principal, the mere difference in physical size is for both a fundamental factor in the situation. Some of the most obstinate cases of discipline in high school seem to have their root in the youngster's feeling that he has at last grown to the point where he can fight back.

Sex Differences in Growth Rate

As already mentioned, Fig. 2.2 made clear that girls reach the maximum adolescent growth rate about two years earlier than boys—around 13 to 14, as compared with around 15 to 16 for boys. Fig. 2.1 showed that from about 12 to 14, girls average both taller and heavier than boys. Shrewd

---

[3] Figures in parentheses or brackets refer to readings at the end of the chapter.

observers of children know that there are interesting consequences as regards the social relations between the two sexes. The vigor and physical superiority of many girls during this period frequently bring participation —as never before or later—in boys' sports and amusements, and the development of a splendid physical confidence and poise. As a result, the boys either admit the girls to comradeship or else draw away from them and assume a scorn which seems in no small part a defense reaction; the girls respond by a great show of independence.

Throughout childhood girls appear to be on the average more mature physiologically than boys; even at 6 they are already about a year in advance of boys, as is shown by such evidence as the replacing of certain cartilage by bone. Girls reach puberty on the average over a year earlier than boys. As already mentioned, girls attain adult height at about 16 or 17, as compared with 19 for the boys (the outcome being that by 20 men average over 4½ inches taller and 22 pounds heavier than women). In secondary school, girls seem to show a greater sex-social maturity, compared with boys of the same chronological age. All these facts have manifold significance for the schools; they involve social, moral, and educational problems, the full import of which the average high school seems not to realize.

Individual Differences

So far, the discussion has dealt with averages. But in physical growth, as in every other important trait considered in this book, individual differences from the average are as important and much more neglected. Thus 2276 boys, all 15 years of age, were found to vary in height from 4 feet 8 inches to 6 feet 2 inches, and in weight from 80 to 161 pounds (1). Of difficulty to the schools in regard to such matters as size of seats and playground groups is the fact that different ages greatly overlap in size. Thus some 12-year-old girls may be taller than the average 16-year-old, whereas others are almost as short as the average 8-year-old girl, as is brought out in Fig. 2.3. This figure shows the standing heights of the *same* 167 girls at four-year intervals, as determined by a "longitudinal" study, one that followed the development of each girl from childhood through adolescence. The figure brings out a further important and surprising fact: the girls differ more in height at 12 than they do at either 8 *or* 16. Why is this?

Fig. 2.4 gives a hint as to the answer. Based on another very careful longitudinal study, it shows height and weight curves for four girls, measured at regular intervals from early infancy into the twenties. The shortest and lightest girl was so from early infancy on; similarly, the tallest girl was tall throughout, with good weight, though her weight fluctuated after age 13, perhaps in part because of dieting. But the weight curves clearly exhibit a feature that is less evident for height. The girl who was biggest in childhood reached the marked pubertal increase in growth first, and the

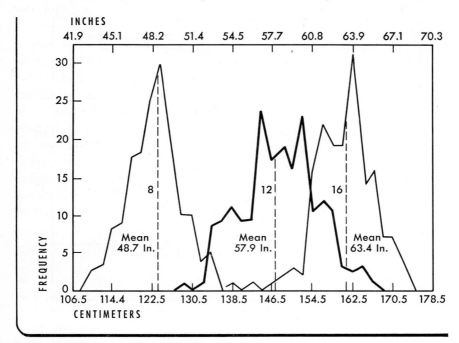

FIG. 2.3. Standing heights of 167 girls at ages 8, 12, and 16. (Adapted from Dearborn and Rothney [16].)

smallest child was slowest in reaching that upswing; that is, the girl represented by the dotted line in Fig. 2.4 began gaining weight rapidly soon after she was 8, but the one represented by the line with the dash and the dot did not begin this growth till after 14, and then it was slower. These are not special cases; careful research has shown that bigger children typically reach this period of rapid growth, and puberty, earlier than smaller children. In size and developmental status, children differ more in the early teens than before *or* after, and are more heterogeneous in both physique and personality—as harassed junior-high-school teachers can testify!

As a matter of fact, Figs. 2.3 and 2.4 probably do not adequately show the full range of differences in either height or growth pattern because they include fewer of those with less adequate physique and health than there are in the general population. It is important to keep in mind the fact that continuing coöperation of parents and children is necessary for longitudinal studies, so they tend to be made in good neighborhoods. And the young people whose families remain in the same community, and who are available for and coöp-

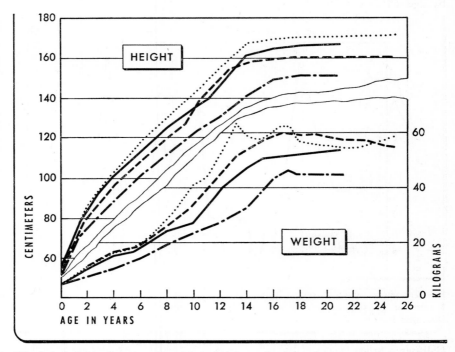

FIG. 2.4. Individual curves of growth in height and weight of four girls. (Adapted from Bayley [7].)

erate in the long investigation, are likely to be from families who are prosperous and intelligent and actively interested in their children's welfare. Accordingly, one of these studies reports for the middle and later teens average heights some 4 inches more, and weights 10 pounds more, than those shown in Fig. 2.1, which was based on cross-sectional surveys, that is, measurements of all the children in certain communities at a given time. The data in Fig. 2.1 are a bit old (cross-sectional studies are apparently not being made now); as will be seen shortly, better nutrition and similar factors seem to be increasing the size of our children a little. And there are regional differences. But the special selectiveness of long-continued longitudinal studies should be kept in mind.

The decided differences in total growth curves and in height and weight at a given age, indicated in the preceding figures, should be understood as in large part normal. Thus one study (*10*) found differences between the 10th and 90th percentile in height (between the 10th and 90th child in 100 children) of 5 inches at age 4; these differences reached a maximum of 8 inches for girls at age 13 and 9 inches for boys at age 15, but dropped by age 18 to 6 inches for girls and 7 inches for boys. A long-continued

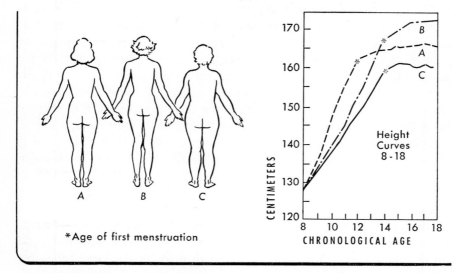

*Age of first menstruation

FIG. 2.5. Three girls at the age of 18, who matured differently. A was accelerated, B retarded, and C irregular in growth. The graph shows their increase in height. (Adapted from Bayley [7].)

California study (*45*) showed the age of maximal growth ranging from 9 to 14 for 80 girls and from 11 to 17 for 86 boys; the mean was 11.5 years for girls and 13.7 for boys. In consequence, care must be exercised before deciding that a given youngster is overweight or underweight or growing too slowly or rapidly. The fundamental question is this: What is normal *for him?*

Thus the mother of a rather short, slight child was very worried, and stuffed him with food. Inquiry showed that both parents were short and slight—but in excellent health—and had also been small and developed slowly as children. This mother was told to stop worrying, that her son was normal and healthy for his particular build and constitution. As already said, slender children tend to grow more slowly and to reach their pubertal rapid growth period later than the average child, and broad-built youngsters tend to grow faster and reach puberty earlier. The need to consider each child's body build and type in appraising his growth has led to the construction of various charts—for example, the Wetzel Grid—for plotting growth in relation to such factors. Fig. 2.5 shows relations of growth rate, final height, and body build for three girls.

GROWTH AND CHANGE

To triple his weight and add 50 percent to his stature during the years from 6 to 18, the average child must obviously do a lot of growing. But mere increase in size is not the most important feature of his total growth process. Every proportion of his body alters; there are changes in the internal organs and body processes, and subtle alterations in the composition of the tissues. Not merely does the individual become bigger; he is transformed. It need hardly be added that there are concomitant changes in abilities, interests, personality. And these last changes, which are of vital importance for a teacher to understand, will be best understood if the more determinable and depictable physical changes are first brought to mind.

Changes in Proportions of the Body

Changes in body proportions from infancy to maturity are admirably pictured in Fig. 2.6, made up of photographs of the same boy at 15 and 30 months and 6, 11, 14, and 18 years, all made to the same height for comparison of proportions. From these photographs it is very evident

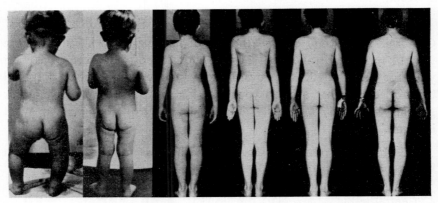

FIG. 2.6. Changes in proportions of the body, as shown by photographs of the same boy at 15 and 30 months and 6, 11, 14, and 18 years, all the photographs being made the same apparent height. (From Bayley [7].)

that "the head makes up a steadily diminishing part of the total; the legs grow relatively longer to 15 years, and then the stem length increases slightly; the whole body is broad at 15 months, then slenders down, to broaden again later, mostly in the shoulder girdle. The same patterns hold for the girl, except that as she approaches maturity, it is her hips rather than her shoulders that become wide" (7).

The changes are not confined to gross proportions, however. The baby has a small, flat nose, a tiny chin, and large eyes. The nose grows, often becoming so prominent in adolescence that, as one writer put it, sensitive youngsters may regard themselves as being "veritable Cyrano de Bergeracs." The feet may attain full size before many other parts of the body, and so seem unduly and embarrassingly large. Secondary-school teachers should be aware of such facts.

Changes in Organs and Tissues

During the growth years, changes occur not only in body size and proportion but in every organ and tissue, and the various changes take place at varying rates. As Fig. 2.7 indicates, the nervous system has almost reached its final size by age 12, the lymphatic system grows rapidly and then after about that age becomes proportionally smaller, and the genital organs grow hardly at all until after that year.

The heart is four or five times as large at age 6 as at birth; it grows more slowly until puberty, but from then till 17 or 18 it doubles in weight and volume, though the arteries increase in cross section by only about 15 percent. The blood pressure rises accordingly (56). However, the average pulse rate drops from around 79 at age 6 to 60 at 18, the respiratory rate from 22 to 16 for the same ages (25). The bones increase not only in size, but in number—from 270 at birth to 350 at puberty; their chemical composition also changes, for their mineral content increases. Their greatest weight, however, is not reached until around age 35. The "baby" teeth begin to emerge around the age of 6 months and the first permanent teeth at about 6 years; all of these teeth have emerged at about age 13, except for the wisdom teeth which may come as late as the 25th year (56). Muscle has been reported as constituting 23 percent of the total body weight at birth, 27 percent at age 8, and 44 percent at age 16. Moreover, the composition of muscle tissue changes.

Central in the total complicated process of growth and change is sexual maturing. Age of first menstruation of girls is the most generally recognized event. Table 2.1 summarizes results of five investigations regarding

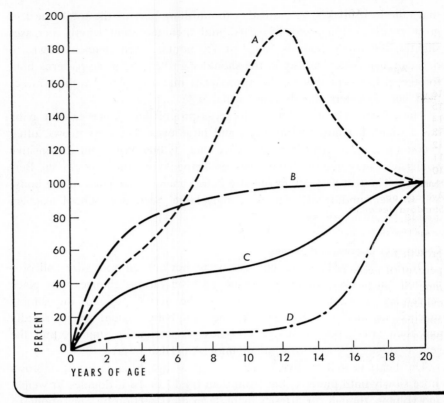

FIG. 2.7. Major types of postnatal growth of the various parts and organs of the body. The several curves are drawn to a common scale by computing their values at successive ages in terms of their total postnatal increments (to 20 years). (From Harris and others [22].)

A, Lymphoid type: Thymus, lymph nodes, intestinal lymphoid masses.

B, Neural type: Brain and its parts, dura, spinal cord, optic apparatus, many head dimensions.

C, General type: Body as a whole, external dimensions (except head and neck), respiratory and digestive organs, kidneys, aorta and pulmonary trunks, spleen, musculature as a whole, skeleton as a whole, blood volumes.

D, Genital type: Testis, ovary, epididymis, uterine tube, prostate, prostatic urethra, seminal vesicles.

its time of occurrence; the most important feature is the age range from 10 to 16, the most common being from 11 through 14.

Though there is no such generally recognized event for boys, various evidence indicates their slower rate of maturing. Thus the longitudinal study by Nicolson and Hanley (45) reports that the age of maximal

TABLE 2.1.   Age of First Menstruation of 1312 Girls[4]
(In percentages)

Age[a]	Shuttleworth	Abernathy	Investigator Engle	Boas	Nicolson
16 up	1	2	1	2	
15	3	6	7	7	4
14	11	25	27	13	9
13	36	35	35	31	28
12	34	23	22	32	37
11	12	8	8	13	18
10	3	1		3	4
Number	248	487	250	236	91
Average age	13.0	13.5	13.5	13.1	12.8
Standard deviation	1.1	1.1	1.1	1.2	1.1

[a] Age 15 means from the 15th to the 16th birthday, etc.

growth for girls was 11.5 and for boys 13.7, and the age of reaching 99 percent of adult height was 14.6 and 16.4 respectively. In boys the beginning of sexual maturing (appearance of hair in the pubic region) was evident at an average age of 11.8 years, the range being from 9 to 15, and the process was largely completed at an average age of 15.2, the range being from 13 to 19.[5] The shoulders broaden, hair grows under the armpits

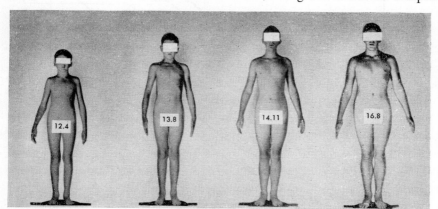

FIG. 2.8. Differences in physique. These boys are all 14.2 years old chronologically, but vary in "skeletal" or developmental age from 12.4 to 16.8. (From Greulich [21]. Pictures from Dr. J. R. Gallagher, The Adolescent Unit, Children's Hospital, Boston.)

[4] Data in first four columns from Shuttleworth (49); data in last column from Nicolson and Hanley (45).

[5] Indexes for appraising maturation, and phases of the total process, are discussed in Nicolson and Hanley (45), Greulich (21), Shuttleworth (51), and Stolz and Stolz (52).

and on the face, the voice changes, and the sweat glands under the arms become much more active and also odorous.

As already mentioned, in larger children the pubertal increase in growth tends to begin earlier than in small and slight children, and it involves all the above various features of maturing. As a result, a slow-maturing still prepubescent youngster may be strikingly different in total appearance from a rapid maturer of the same age; this is brought out well in Fig. 2.8.

Development of Strength and Quickness

Strength and quickness increase markedly through the growth years. Fig. 2.9, which summarizes early cross-sectional data on rate of tapping and strength of grip, shows that during the school years from 6 to 18 there is a continuing increase in both speed and strength. On both, except for tapping at ages 6 and 7 (this irregularity in the curve is probably

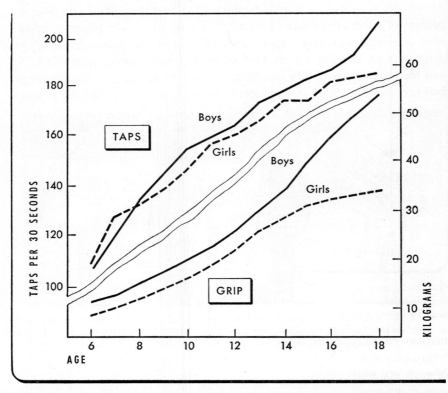

FIG. 2.9. Increases in rate of tapping and strength of grip, ages 6 to 18. (Adapted from Jones [29].)

of no consequence), the boys are superior, and this superiority increases after 14.

What further details might be brought out by longitudinal studies of the same youngster over a substantial period of time? Fig. 2.10 sum-

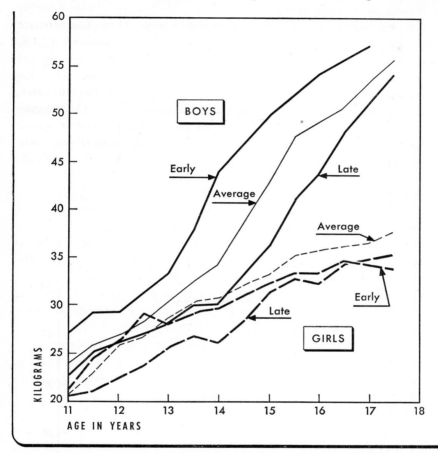

FIG. 2.10. Strength of right-hand grip of early-maturing, average, and late-maturing boys and girls. Maturation based on age of menarche in girls, on skeletal development in boys. (Adapted from Jones [31].)

marizes results of repeated tests of grip in 16 early- and 16 late-maturing boys and the same number of girls, out of a total of some 70 individuals of each sex who were studied from ages 11 through 17. The boys clearly gain much more rapidly through the adolescent years than do the girls. What is more, the early-maturing boys are superior at all ages; their acceleration begins around 12, whereas for the late-maturing it does not begin until 14. As a result, these two groups of boys differ about twice as much in strength of grip at the age of 14 as at either 11 or 17—14 kilograms at 14 as compared to 6 at 17! Both early and late maturers are still increasing in strength at 17.

The girls contrast with the boys in several respects. They show relatively little increase in grip after age 13 and seem to reach a level by 17. But most striking is the finding that after age 13 the early-maturing girls actually fall below 24 girls whose rate of maturing is average. This drop is not statistically significant but is congruent with the fact that these early-maturing girls were also below average height at age 13. "Physical precocity in girls appears to be associated with an early arrest in growth; the same is not true of boys" (*31*, page 63). The late-maturing girls were below average in strength of grip at all ages.

Physical Growth and Change, and Personality

That such findings are of decided significance with reference not only to physique but also to personality is made clear in other data from these same studies. Fig. 2.11 summarizes three of a considerable number of measures of various personality traits. The first two sections show that early-maturing boys were rated distinctly above late-maturing boys in physical attractiveness and relaxation by three staff members observing these youngsters in small free-play groups of the same sex. According to the third pair of curves, the late-maturing boys were judged more animated and, indeed, somewhat overactive. This animation seemed partly persisting childish exuberance, and partly somewhat defensive—an anxious effort by the smaller and less vigorous boys to get attention by noisiness and excessive activity because they were otherwise not noticed.

The above data concerned behavior in small groups of the same sex, as judged by members of the research staff. Table 2.2 gives somewhat different evidence on the same general problem. It presents ratings of these same boys, but by their classmates, in situations including both sexes. The early-maturing boys tend to be leaders and to have older friends; the late-maturing tend to be restless and attention-seeking. The evaluations are quite similar to those made by the research staff and shown in Fig. 2.11.

"Among adults it is often difficult to realize what it means to an adolescent when through illness, late development, or other factors, he is unable to play a usual part in the physical activities of his fellows. Such a boy may turn his interest to other goals. It is a critical question whether, in so doing, he rejects

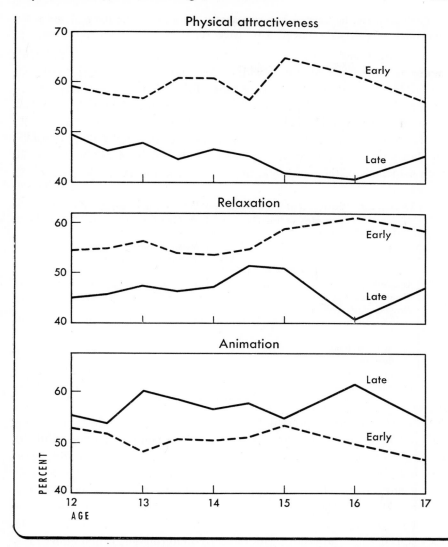

FIG. 2.11. Ratings by three staff members on certain traits of early- and late-maturing boys as observed in small free-play groups of the same sex. (Adapted from Jones and Bayley [32].)

the sphere in which he has been unsuccessful and loses effective contact with his classmates, or whether he finds a socially adequate use of such favorable traits as he may possess. When it becomes feasible for the teacher to provide guidance in such situations, the child must be helped in making an adjustment to his own resources. If he is unable to meet his classmates' standards in physical achievement, he must at any rate accept these as among the realities of his immediate social environment" (*31,* page 162).

In interest and behavior with reference to the other sex, the late-maturing boys showed "their widest deviation from the early maturers during the period when they were most different in physical respects; in senior high school the apparent differences diminished, but the development of a more mature pattern in the late maturers does not necessarily imply a prompt change in their status in the peer culture" (*32,* page 143). In short, late-maturing boys appeared handicapped as regards relations with associates of their own and the other sex in the same age group, and

TABLE 2.2.   Early- and Late-Maturing Boys as Judged by Classmates in the 10th and 11th Grades[6]

Traits	Mean Standard Scores	
	Early-Maturing	Late-Maturing
Leadership	51	47
Humor (about self)	53	49
Having older friends	56	42
Good appearance	54	49
Attention-getting	48	52
Restlessness	45	53
Talkativeness	48	53
Bossiness	47	53

on the whole were appraised less favorably by adults who knew them well. At least, this holds true for the American culture of today, with its emphasis on athletics and on association with the other sex during adolescence. In strange contrast, girls seemed to have an advantage by maturing late, and to be handicapped by maturing early—at least, in our culture. The girl who matures late does so at about the average age of the boys with whom she associates, and she tends to have the slim build they consider most attractive. But the early-maturing girl is first embarrassingly bigger and stronger than the boys of the same age, is embarrassingly early in development of heterosexual interests, and tends to become stocky and overly plump.

Special situations in the culture may affect the early-maturing girl. Thus in a university town where dating of high-school girls by college boys was approved, the early-maturing girl sometimes secured companionship and even increased

[6] Adapted from Jones and Bayley (*32*).

status. But such a girl in a town with no college had to date older lads who were employed and often of lower social status, and such dating was frowned upon.

HEALTH, AND PSYCHOLOGICAL PROBLEMS OF THE GROWTH YEARS

A physical handicap or chronic illness may be the dominant factor in the development of a child's personality and abilities. As will be seen shortly, the number of such cases is substantial. Incipient illness may first be manifest to a teacher as irritability or disinterest. Even though the child recovers from the accident or illness, not only his school work but also his companionships may be interrupted, and various emotional readjustments may be required. These situations are chronic in every classroom. As a later chapter will stress, sundry physical indispositions and illnesses are largely psychological in origin, products of emotional stress. Therefore some mention of psychological problems related to health seems called for, in any adequate educational psychology.

The first distressing fact is the possibility of death even in these most healthy years of life. In 1950 the annual death rate per 100,000 children aged 5 to 14 was 56; for ages 15 to 24 it was 112 (13). Almost half these deaths were the result of accidents; 30 boys in the first age group and 92 in the second died in this way. The importance of safety campaigns and driver education is clear. The next most frequent causes of death were leukemia and other malignant or cancerous conditions, and cardiac diseases; these are major threats in youth as well as age. The third-ranking cause of death for males 15 to 24 was suicide (7 cases per 100,000); homicide was seventh. Obviously these last causes involve sundry psychological factors often related to school. The lingering fatal illness of a student may be the occasion for educating his classmates in considerateness—and awareness of mortality. Sudden violent death, accidental or with intent, causes shock, morbid gossip—and distressed pondering of the steps which might have been taken to prevent it.

An extensive health survey (12) involving over 80,000 persons visited at intervals of one to three months showed 1114 illnesses per year per 1000 children aged 5 to 14, of which 734 were sufficiently severe to prevent such usual activities as going to school a total of 10 days a year. Youth aged 15 to 24 had 826 illnesses per 1000, of which 430 were disabling for a total of 5 days. A careful continuing record of the illnesses of 126 normal California children from infancy to age 18 showed that the youngster least often ill had 13 colds and other respiratory infections,

4 gastrointestinal upsets, 3 communicable diseases, 1 accident, a tonsillec-
tomy, and 4 other minor ailments. A robust athlete had over 70 such
items in his health history. Fig. 2.12 shows the frequency of various types
of illness in this group during these years. Colds and upper respiratory
infections are common throughout, but especially so in the nursery-school
and primary-school years. Gastrointestinal disturbances are most common

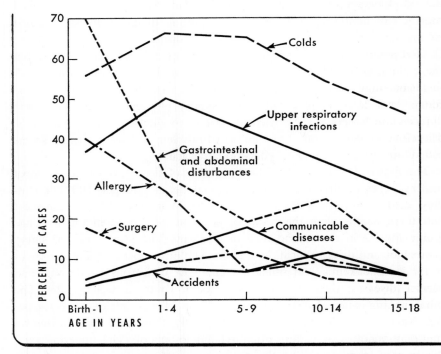

FIG. 2.12. Relative incidence of various categories of illness in a group of 126 normal
California children from infancy to age 18. (From Bayer and Snyder [5].)

in infancy, decrease in the primary-school years, but increase again around
puberty. Communicable diseases such as measles and mumps are most
common at ages 5 to 9. These 126 youngsters were probably better than
average as regards their families' socioeconomic and educational status,
and the attention given to health.

Obviously a child who is running a temperature because of a cold or
is in physical discomfort from hives may be irritable or inattentive; after
an acute illness, lassitude may be expected. Longer or more severe illness
may cause more difficulties. A boy was out of school much of the winter;

he had had a good school record up to that time, but because he disliked asking for help or admitting any difficulty it took him two years of academic stumbling to catch up. Another boy was in a hospital for some time because of a near-fatal automobile accident. When he went home he at first was shy with his family, seemed afraid to go out into the neighborhood, hung back from play at recess, was timid about reciting in class. He made a good physical recovery, but not until he entered a largely new group in high school did he get back confidence in his relations with other youngsters.

That physical defects may present psychological problems seems evident; the total number of children hampered by some defect is larger than might be supposed. For example, a survey of a Kansas county (2) found 5.9 percent of all children physically disabled in some way ("generally perceived in his cultural group to have a physique that prevents him from participating in important activities on a basis of equality with normal individuals of his own age"). Speech, visual, and orthopedic disabilities were most common. For the United States in 1950, some 750,000 persons under 21 years of age (5 out of 1000) were reported crippled in some way; 2 to 3 percent of all school children were estimated to have serious speech defects, and possibly 4 percent some defect of hearing; perhaps 1 in every 1000 should be in a sight-saving class, whereas 20 percent had correctable eye defects (23).

Psychological problems resulting from physical defects vary but are almost always difficult (3). A seriously crippled lad should learn to do what he is capable of doing; he should prepare for a vocation that is feasible for him. Less serious handicaps or blemishes are more common and may present more difficult adjustmental problems, since these children are in contact with other children but are handicapped in their relations with them. If a defect may be somewhat lessened or by-passed, accepted, or compensated for by some special prestige-giving skill or ability, an essentially normal life may be possible. A boy with a crippled right arm learned to do things with his left hand, became an exceptionally good left-handed pitcher, and was popular with his group. Another with much the same handicap was overprotected, learned no special skills, avoided social occasions where his defect might be noticed. A slightly deaf child may seem inattentive and dull in school, and tend to play by himself because he cannot follow the other children's chatter. If his teacher seats him near her so that he may not only hear better but watch her expression and lips, he may be appreciably helped; if she speaks especially slowly and clearly when he is involved, brings him into things rather than lets him be left out, and has the other children do likewise, she may help him even more.

A teacher should be concerned with establishing and maintaining desirable health habits. A nursery school may try to provide a sensible lunch for its tots and insist on unhurried and well-mannered eating, but an elementary school frequently must struggle with children who are chronically torpid or restless because of inadequate and poorly prepared food hastily gulped at home. An adolescent girl may come to high school without breakfast, and lunch on sweets at the candy store rather than sensibly in the school cafeteria. Another girl who needs glasses may refuse to wear them because of vanity; the teacher may need to comment on glasses as becoming, thus fostering a class attitude favorable to them. A boy may nod in class because he stayed up too late watching television or got up very early to deliver papers. The teacher who finds such causes for her problem pupils will be more charitable and may, with patience and tact, be able to do something about them.

In short, illnesses of various types are part of life in the school years; their effects on behavior should be recognized, and behavior episodes and absences from such causes should be taken in stride. Health factors may explain some problem pupils. For example, a girl's persistent intractability may be an encephalitic residual; another's grimacing and dropping of books may be incipient chorea; a boy's unresponsiveness may be due to deafness; another's withdrawing may be due to his desire to minimize notice of a deformity. To understand and adjust to these various problems, help the children affected, and foster habits favorable to health should be an important part of every teacher's job. Maximal health and vigor should be her goal. Physical well-being and ill-being are related to every major topic discussed in this volume, and affect the group as well as the individual. A class of healthy, well-nourished, well-rested youngsters is more interested, alert, and ready to learn than a group that is physically not as well.

FACTORS INVOLVED IN PHYSICAL GROWTH

The first two decades of life are a period of extraordinary change in size, proportion, biochemical constitution, strength, and skill. What factors influence this development? The preceding section has stressed psychological problems resulting from physical illness and handicaps. But to what extent may they affect growth? What can be done to foster desirable growth?

Biological Constitution

Indubitably the most important factor is the marvelous biological constitution which brings it about that individuals do develop in an ordered, coördinated, and basically similar fashion. Certain deficiencies, as of nutrition, may hamper this development; but under ordinary conditions growth goes forward in its own way and in its own good time. Weight increases, proportions change, strength and quickness increase in accordance with these fundamental patterns of growth; educational programs can proceed only as these patterns permit. It is not possible, for instance, to train babies to walk before their neuromuscular systems have developed to the point where they are ready for this activity. Somewhat as extra food will not make a baby grow faster than the "normal" rate, so extra practice will not bring progress in such skills beyond what the baby's own maturation processes permit. No matter how much doting parents try to teach their baby to talk, he does not (cannot) learn until he is "ready." A certain stage of maturation must be reached before a child can learn to read. This problem of maturation will be discussed later.

In gross, human beings are alike and develop in similar fashion, in line with the basic constitutional influences mentioned above. Nevertheless, individual differences are relatively great. The first factor to be mentioned as causing these differences is individual variations in constitution. Some people are "naturally" tall, others short; some fortunate individuals can eat all they wish without growing stout, whereas others take on fat with even a relatively moderate diet. As already mentioned, some girls menstruate as early as age 10, others not till after their sixteenth birthday. Those who menstruate early tend to be bigger as children, but the late maturers are slim through childhood as a result of constitutional differences in body build and growth pattern.

Racial or national groups may show individual differences. A comparison of ten-year-old children in different parts of the world (40) found native Okinawa children averaging 50 inches in height and 55 pounds in weight; French children in Marseilles averaged 51 inches in height and 58 pounds in weight; for Mexicans in Los Angeles the corresponding figures were 53 and 66; for poor urban whites in North America 54 and 64; for children of American business and professional men, 56 and 72. The range from smallest to largest was some 6 inches and 17 pounds respectively. These differences were presumably partly socioeconomic but also partly racial in origin. A comparison of around 1000 boys of Finnish parents and about the same number of Italian origin, all living in Minnesota, showed the first group consistently to be about 1 inch taller and 2 pounds heavier. Clearly different national and racial groups and subgroups differ in size and other physical characteristics (38).

Living Conditions, Nutrition, and Health Care

Growth is not completely determined by inherited organic constitution, nor is individuality. The environment in which growth takes place is also of major importance. Before the child is born the mother's body, the fetus' environment, may be so affected by injury or disease as to affect the child's development. A birth injury may affect both physique and intellect. Later injuries and such diseases as syphilis, tuberculosis of the spine, and poliomyelitis may very obviously affect growth.

Presumably, as a result of general improvement in the health of children, as through the elimination of diphtheria and the reduction in severity of other childhood diseases, many children are in better physical condition and develop more rapidly now than was true fifty or a hundred years ago; and the sum of all such improvements may be general enough to affect the average. From 1900 to 1952, the death rate in the school years has been reduced markedly—from 3.9 to .59 per 1000 children 5 to 14 years of age, and from 5.9 to 1.3 for those 15 to 24 years old (13). Even in the ten years from 1939 to 1949, the death rate per 100,000 children 1 to 14 years of age dropped from 24 to 9 for influenza and pneumonia, from 8 to 3 for tuberculosis, from 9 to 4 for diseases of the heart and rheumatic fever. Indeed, the drop in the total death rate for these ages during this decade was from 166 to 93 (46).

The disturbances and deprivations of war have been shown repeatedly to affect child growth. During the First World War, young French children were found to be retarded one or two years in growth, and older children more, with marked delay in pubescence. In 1941–1942, the early part of the Second World War, 13 percent of a large group of Parisian children lost weight and 21 percent did not gain at all, although normally no more than 2 percent would fail to gain (33, page 996). Measurements of large groups of German children beginning in 1910 showed height and weight down during both these wars but otherwise tending upward (24).

The many improvements in medical care, diet, recreation, and general living conditions over the past fifty years have brought about widespread improvements in children's physique and increases in rate of development. Data from such various places as Brisbane (Australia), Toronto (Canada), and London (England) show that children now are taller and heavier than they were earlier (*26, 27, 41*). Thus Toronto children were taller in 1939 than in 1892 by 2 inches at age 6 and by 3.5 inches at age 12; some of this increase was apparently due to a greater rate of growth, since after adolescence the differences dropped 1 inch. In the United States both white and colored boys were 6 to 8 percent taller and 12 to 15 percent heavier around 1940 than a half century earlier (*39*). Muscular strength seems also to have increased somewhat (*31,* page 99). The height and weight of British children increased from 1880 to 1947 except during the war years; the average 6-year-old in 1947 was as tall as the average youngster of 7½ in 1880. Increases were greatest in later childhood, and in the lower socioeconomic classes, presumably as a result of improvements in their living conditions, diet, and health care. Several studies (*20, 26, 27*) indicate that puberty tends to occur a little earlier now than formerly.

Psychological Outcomes and Influences

As was said earlier, not only freedom from disease and malnutrition but abounding physical vigor and well-being should be the goal of educational programs. And there may be psychological results—livelier interests, greater alertness and readiness in learning, happier dispositions, more rapid maturing of abilities and personality. Psychological factors may also affect physical condition. Although a war or a great depression may retard growth because of inadequate food or living conditions, emotional stress and strain also may interfere with digestion, circulation, sleep. The stresses incident to war may affect the health of children and their growth; but the stresses that are less intense but ever present in life—the miseries of slum living, the constraints and rough discipline such as were practiced a hundred years ago and are found even today—may hamper the physical growth of a sensitive youngster. The present more sympathetic furthering of happy child life, the freer recreation, clothing, and comfort, may facilitate growing—at least a little. Conceivably today's less repressed and more informed attitude toward sex may play a part in earlier maturing. A very repressive, hostile home might conceivably restrict the development not only of a child's personality, but of his health and physique. If his school can help this child, it may perhaps hope for improvement in his emotional and also his physical well-being.

PHYSICAL GROWTH AND CHANGE AS BASIC PHENOMENA FOR EDUCATIONAL PSYCHOLOGY AND EDUCATION

Sweeping, dynamic growth with change—this is the basic biological phenomenon of the school years. Consideration of physical growth and change in this early chapter has a threefold advantage. Because these readily measured and pictured increases and changes in physique have an integral relation to the growth and changes in psychological traits which are the major topics considered in this volume, they may emphasize the magnitude and variety of these correlative psychological growths and changes. The magnitude of the individual differences found at a given age, especially in the early teens, in the maturation of interests and emotionality, cannot be fully appreciated until the differences in physique are considered. And since psychological growth and differences may be thought of as products of each individual's physical growth and variations, initial consideration of these last topics is logical.

Moreover, the crude facts of the great differences in size and strength and physique, especially between child and adult and between early and late maturers, present psychological problems often little understood by parent or teacher or the youngster himself. To the child, his growth now in this, now in that part of his body, especially the changes inherent in adolescence, may be awkward and puzzling and often anxiety-causing. Both teacher and parent may not make adequate allowances for the small child's physical limitations, and may fail to realize how much their greater size and strength affect both his attitudes and their own.[7] They may have no appreciation of the almost all-pervading influence which early or late physical maturing may have on a youngster's activities and status and self-regard. They may not adequately allow for residual weakness after illness.

Finally, all this presents or is related to a variety of educational issues. The facts summarized above should be known to teachers and sometimes be discussed in parent-teacher meetings. Many of them may well be discussed with pupils; for example, a late-maturing boy may be reassured by being told that his comparative immaturity is not only usual but a passing phase of growth. School tasks and recreation should not be too difficult or taxing for the immature physique—or too uninterestingly easy. The

---

[7] The restlessness of a four-year-old boy on a lovely drive in the country suddenly became very intelligible to his mother when she slumped down to his eye level and realized that all he could see was bits of sky and an occasional treetop (55).

most serious fault of most schools is their failure to take account of the great individual differences in size and strength and physical maturity, especially in the early teens. A few high schools have special sports programs or other activities for boys whose weight is below average. Though of some value, such devices are inadequate. There should be such flexibility in recreational and social grouping that the boy of 15, who developmentally is 12, may easily and without shame associate with 12-year-olds; and the girl who is 12, but older developmentally, may associate with older boys and girls. The largely unsolved problem of educational adaptations to individual differences will be repeatedly referred to.

One further point must be mentioned for a perspective regarding physical growth through the school years, and as partial explanation of the difficulties adults have in understanding children. The growth years are a special phase of the total life span. After around 18 or 20, growth largely ceases, and the individual establishes himself in his adult size and status and settles down; the adult is in a different life stage than the child or youth, the physical functioning differs in many way. The adult's understanding of youthful problems is therefore more difficult, and various new problems of physiological functioning and change arise. "My most difficult problem," remarked a high-school principal, "is due not to the pubescence of a pupil, but to the menopause of a teacher." These and other issues of adult life, and of the "psychology of the teacher," will be considered later.

SUMMARY

Basic for an adequate understanding of the development of abilities and personality throughout the school years is an understanding of physical growth and change through these years. This growth and change is also "psychologically" important, but largely neglected by most schools.

In the twelve years from 6 to 12, the average boy increases over 50 percent in height and more than three times in weight; obviously, such growing must be a major physiological task and psychological experience for him. The young child is a pygmy among giants; attitudes of dependence or fear on his part, and of protectiveness or domination on the part of parent or teacher, readily develop. Individual differences at each age are marked; one 10-year-old may be twice as heavy as another; some 12-year-old girls may be taller than the average 16-year-old and others almost as short as the average girl of 8. In play and physical competition and in various social situations, such differences between older and younger children are of great importance.

The various parts and organs of the body grow at different rates, and its total proportion and constitution change markedly during the growth years. The 16-year-old is not simply larger than the 10-year-old; in proportion and internal constitution he is physiologically a different person. Individual differences in amount, rate, and age of change may be marked; thus the same high-school class may have a preadolescent boy and a youngster of the same age who is sexually mature and probably also much heavier and taller. Such situations create many psychological problems.

The average boy triples his strength of grip in the ten years from 7 to 17 and doubles his quickness as shown by tapping. At a given age, the strongest boy may be as much as three times as strong as the weakest. Obviously such individual differences in physical effectiveness are of great importance in athletics and in any activity involving strength or skill, and are highly significant in relation to the individual's total personality.

Illness and accidents are so much a part of childhood and youth that they should be so recognized. That fatal accidents are the major cause of death in these years emphasizes the importance of safety education. The interruption of school work and classroom association caused by illness and accident is so common that the teacher should take these difficulties in stride and help the youngsters involved. That illness and accidents are now less frequent than fifty or even twenty years ago is both encouraging and presumptive of increasing vigor and potentiality for effective schooling.

Growth goes forward under the impulsion and control of biological determiners which remain mysterious. Individual differences are in part the product of individual differences in constitution which are also largely unknown. Research has shown that growth is also affected by living conditions and by nutrition and disease. American children today are bigger and stronger and probably grow faster and mature earlier than was the case fifty years ago. Hence the community and the school have a responsibility for healthy physical growth, which may be assumed to further the growth of personality and ability. Not merely freedom from handicap, but abounding healthy vigor, should be the goal of education, and the result should be not only healthier but also more alert and happier children.

Early consideration of physical growth has three values. (1) It makes vivid the sweep of the growth process, which involves psychological as well as physical traits. (2) Physical growth and change through the school years give rise to important psychological problems. (3) Growth and the problems involved therewith, especially individual differences in the teens, should be considered by teachers and parents and adjusted to far more than is true at present. The biological differences between the growing youngster and the stabilized adult individual should also be recognized. The psychology of adult life is especially important as an aid to the teacher in understanding herself.

BIBLIOGRAPHY

1. Baldwin, B. T., The physical growth of children from birth to maturity, *Univ. Iowa Stud. Child Welfare*, 1921, *1*, No. 1.
2. Barker, L. S., Schoggen, M., Schoggen, P., and Barker, R. G., The frequency of physical disability in children: A comparison of three sources of information, *Child Devel.*, 1952, *23*:215–226.
3. Barker, R. G., and others, *Adjustment to Physical Handicap and Illness. A Survey of the Social Psychology of Physique and Disability*, New York: Social Science Research Council, 1953.
4. Barker, R. H., The effect of an unsatisfactory relationship of brother to brother on the development of personality, *Social Forces*, 1930, *9*:85–91.
5. Bayer, L. M., and Snyder, M. M., Illness experience in a group of normal children, *Child Devel.*, 1950, *21*:93–120.
6. Bayley, Nancy, Some increasing parent-child similarities during the growth of children, *J. Educ. Psychol.*, 1954, *45*:1–20.
7. Bayley, Nancy, Individual patterns of development, *Child Devel.*, 1956, *27*:45–74.
8. Bayley, Nancy, and Espenschade, Anna, Motor development and decline, *Rev. Educ. Res.*, 1950, *20*:367–374.
9. Boyd, E., Pictorial and graphic analysis of the body build of one boy, *Amer. J. Dis. Child.*, 1955, *89*:332–340.
10. Burgess, M. A., Construction of two height-weight charts, *J. Amer. Statist. Assn.*, 1937, *32*:290–310.
11. Clements, E. M. B., The age of children when growth in stature ceases, *Arch. Dis. Childhood*, 1954, *29*:141–151.
12. Collins, S. D., Lehmann, Josephine L., and Trantham, Katharine S., Sickness experience in selected areas of the United States, *Public Health Monog. No. 25*, Govt. Printing Office, 1954.
13. Collins, S. D., Lehmann, Josephine L., and Trantham, Katharine S., Major causes of illness and of death in six age periods, *Public Health Monog. No. 30*, Govt. Printing Office, 1955.
14. Cruikshank, W. M., The relation of physical disability to fear and guilt feelings, *Child Devel.*, 1951, *22*:291–298.
15. Davenport, C. B., Human metamorphosis, *Amer. J. Phys. Anthrop.*, 1926, *9*:205–232.
16. Dearborn, W. F., and Rothney, J. W., *Predicting the Child's Development*, Cambridge: Sci-Art Publishers, 1941.
17. Dreisen, S., Currie, C., Gilley, E. J., and Spies, T. D., The effect of nutri-

tive failure on the growth pattern of white children in Alabama, *Child De-vel.,* 1953, *24*:189–202.

18. Fried, Ralph I., Socio-emotional factors accounting for growth failure in children as measured by the Wetzel grid procedure, *Assn. Res. Nerv. Ment. Dis.,* 1949, *29*:317–325.

19. Garn, S. M., Physical growth and development, *Amer. J. Phys. Anthrop.,* 1952, *10*:169–192.

20. Gould, H. N., and Gould, M. R., Age of first menstruation in mother and daughter, *J. Amer. Med. Assn.,* 1932, *98*:1349–1352.

21. Greulich, William W., Skeletal aspects of maturity, *Child Devel.,* 1950, *21*:33–44.

22. Harris, J. A., and others, *The Measurement of Man,* Minneapolis: Univ. of Minnesota Press, 1930.

23. Heck, A. O., *The Education of Exceptional Children,* New York: McGraw-Hill, 1953.

24. Howe, P. E., and Schiller, M., Growth responses of the school child to changes in diet and environmental factors, *J. Appl. Psychol.,* 1952, *5*:51–61.

25. Iliff, A., and Lee, V. A., Pulse rate, respiratory rate, and body temperatures of children between 2 months and 18 years of age, *Child Devel.,* 1952, *23*:234–245.

26. Jensen, Kai, Physical growth, *Rev. Educ. Res.,* 1952, *22*:391–420.

27. Jensen, Kai, Physical growth, *Rev. Educ. Res.,* 1955, *25*:369–414.

28. Johnson, W., To help the child with a speech handicap, *Child Devel.,* 1950, *15*:12–14.

29. Jones, H. E., Development of physical abilities, *Yearb. Nat. Soc. Stud. Educ.,* 1941, Part I.

30. Jones, H. E., Physical ability as a factor in social adjustment in adolescence, *J. Educ. Res.,* 1946, *40*:287–301.

31. Jones, H. E., *Motor Performance and Growth,* Berkeley: Univ. of California Press, 1949.

32. Jones, M. C., and Bayley, Nancy, Physical maturing among boys as related to behavior, *J. Educ. Psychol.,* 1950, *41*:129–148.

33. Keys, A. B., and others, *The Biology of Human Starvation,* Minneapolis: Univ. of Minnesota Press, 1950, 2 vols.

34. Kinsey, A. C., and others, *Sexual Behavior in the Human Male,* Philadelphia: Saunders, 1948.

35. Kinsey, A. C., and others, *Sexual Behavior in the Human Female,* Philadelphia: Saunders, 1953.

36. Krogman, W. M., The physical growth of children: an appraisal of studies, 1950–55, *Monog. Socy. Res. Child Devel. No. 20,* 1956.

37. Latham, A. J., The relationship between pubertal status and leadership in junior high school boys, *J. Genet. Psychol.,* 1951, *78*:185–194.

38. Matheny, W. D., and Meredith, H. V., Mean body size of Minnesota school boys of Finnish and Italian ancestry, *Amer. J. Phys. Anthrop.,* 1947, *5*:343–355.

39. Meredith, H. V., Stature and weight of children of the United States, *Amer. J. Dis. Child.,* 1941, *62*:909–932.

40. Meredith, H. V., Body size in infancy and childhood; a comparative study of data from Okinawa, France, South Africa and North America, *Child Devel.,* 1948, *19*:179–195.

41. Meredith, H. V., and Meredith, E. M., The stature of Toronto children half a century ago and today, *Hum. Biol.,* 1944, *16*:126–131.

42. Michelson, H., Studies in physical development of Negroes; onset of puberty, *Amer. J. Phys. Anthrop.,* 1949, *2*:151–160.

43. Mussen, R. H., and Jones, Mary C., Self-conceptions, motivations and interpersonal attitudes of late or early maturing boys, *Child Devel.,* 1957, *28*:243–256.

44. Newman, H. H., Freeman, F. H., and Holzinger, K. J., *Twins—A Study of Heredity and Environment,* Chicago: Univ. of Chicago Press, 1937.

45. Nicolson, A. B., and Hanley, C., Indices of physiological maturity: derivation and interrelationships, *Child Devel.,* 1953, *24*:3–38.

46. Price, B., and Hunt, Eleanor, *Main Causes of Infant, Childhood and Maternal Mortality 1939–1949* (6th rev.), U.S. Dept. of Health, Education and Welfare, 1953, No. 15.

47. Rapaport, H. G., Psycho-somatic aspects of allergy in childhood, *J. Amer. Med. Assn.,* 1957, *165*:812–815.

48. Schonfeld, W. A., Inadequate masculine physique as a factor in personality development of adolescent boys, *Psychosom. Med.,* 1950, *12*:49–54.

49. Shuttleworth, F. K., Sexual maturation and the physical growth of girls age 6–19, *Monog. Socy. Res. Child Devel.,* 1937, vol. 2.

50. Shuttleworth, F. K., Physical and mental growth of girls and boys aged 6–19 in relation to age at maximum growth, *Monog. Socy. Res. Child Devel.,* 1939, *4*:1–291.

51. Shuttleworth, F. K., The adolescent period: a graphic atlas and a pictorial atlas, *Monog. Socy. Res. Child Devel.,* Nos. *1* and *2,* 1951.

52. Stolz, H. R., and Stolz, L. M., *Somatic Development of Adolescent Boys,* New York: Macmillan, 1951.

53. Tuddenham, R. O., and Snyder, M. M., Physical growth of California boys and girls from birth to 18 years, *Publ. Child Devel.,* 1954, *1*:183–364.

54. Wenar, Charles, The effect of a motor handicap on personality: II. The effects of integrative ability, *Child Devel.,* 1954, *25*:287–294.

55. Wishik, S. M., The importance of "timing" and child health supervision, *Child Devel.,* 1950, *21*:51–60.

56. Zubek, J. P., and Solberg, P. A., *Human Development,* New York: McGraw-Hill, 1954.

Chapter 3

The Nature and Nurture of Abilities

I T IS COMMON IN EVERYDAY SPEECH TO SAY THAT SO-
and-so is an able fellow, that another person is about average in ability, and that a third individual is not very bright. It is evident to everyone
that people differ greatly in their competence in meeting the problems
which arise for them. It is obvious that a 20-year-old man has much more
ability than a 6-year-old boy. Ability is something that increases during
the years with which this book deals, and its increase may be furthered
or hindered by various agencies including the school.

This practical and obviously important topic must now be considered.
What factors are involved in a person's general level of effectiveness? How
do abilities develop? Is it possible to increase an individual's effectiveness
—one's own, for instance? Can a school increase the abilities of its pupils?
If so, how? This is a central problem for every ambitious person, and a
major issue in educational theory and practice.

A FIRST OVERALL ANALYSIS

Evidently the everyday concept of abilities is very broad and concerns
the individual's effectiveness in various real-life situations. Many factors
are involved. Which are most important?

Factors Involved in Realized Ability

The first factor in the adequacy with which a person meets a situation
is the information and skill he has that will help in dealing with it.
Where the task and the necessary information or skill are very specific,
as in repairing a piece of electrical equipment, this factor is well recognized. Its lack may be specific but unrecognized in a school subject. For
example, a high-school pupil may have trouble in a French class because

in his earlier study of English he never learned grammatical terms that are assumed to be known.

A second factor is more general. Almost any task involves certain methods of attack or procedures, which will be more or less adequate. A student needs to know how to look up information in a dictionary or encyclopedia, and how to use a library. Methods of study and of work are so important that they are given special consideration in a later chapter.

A third factor concerns interests and emotional involvements. Everyone knows that a person is likely to do something well in proportion as he is interested in doing it. Continuing interest and effectiveness depend on the extent to which the individual is successful in the particular task, as well as in more general projects. A person with good intellectual capacity may be ineffective because of emotional distractions or blockings. Another individual, with less intellectual potentiality, may react with easy confidence in a crisis and "excel himself." In everyday life people thus show themselves able in dealing with a situation in proportion as they (1) have the information and special skill required for it, (2) have efficient methods of attack and of work on problems, and (3) are stimulated by interest and successes, or disinterested and distraught by failure.

There is another basic factor—constitutional capacities or potentialities. As we saw in Chapter 2, poor nutrition and health may slow a child's rate of growth and perhaps make him shorter as an adult than he would have been under more favorable circumstances. However, no combination of favorable conditions can result in a height or body build above an individual's potential. Some people are naturally short and others tall, some are slim and others heavy-set. Furthermore, some individuals are constitutionally slow and others fast developers. Somewhat analogously, people differ in their natural rate of mental growth and in their constitutional potentialities for certain types of intellectual "body build." But most people do not develop their potentialities up to the limit.

Special Abilities

Some youngsters show special abilities along a particular line; one boy has a knack with mechanical gadgets, another is especially musical, a girl is particularly skillful in sketching and painting. A special ability may have much vocational importance, particularly if it is marked and is based on some special constitutional potentiality. However, if a special knack is simply the result of some special circumstance (perhaps even of undesirable circumstances, as when a boy turns to a mechanical hobby because he is not getting along well with other youngsters) or if it has minimal vocational potentialities, any attempt to foster and base career plans on it will be unfortunate. Examples will make clearer both possible causes and possible problems.

Ellen's father was killed in a tragic accident shortly before her birth. The mother was left with a good income and had done a good deal of painting and designing as a hobby; in her bereavement she devoted herself entirely to these interests and to her only child. As soon as Ellen could hold a pencil she was helped to use it for drawing, and her efforts were constructively guided and the results admired. When Ellen entered school she gained the admiration of teachers and of the other children by her knack in drawing, but was mediocre in her other work. As she grew older, her associates called her a coming young artist. Her mother's small fortune and their common interests led to the continuance of their close association. . . . Ellen is now a woman of fifty who does some commercial illustrating, designing, and painting. Some of her pictures have been exhibited but have taken no prizes. Financially comfortable, she is a conventional amateur in art. Whether her failure to have a real career was due to her lack of special talent or to the absence of strongly motivated ambitions is hard to say.

Will's special ability was different, but the special factors involved were somewhat analogous. His father was a carpenter, but the family lived in a "white-collar" neighborhood and felt slighted. Although Will did not do well in school, he made the best airplane models and was better at repairing things than any other youngster in his class. His chum was another boy with somewhat similar background and interests. Both boys had a genuine interest and adeptness in matters mechanical which stemmed naturally from their home background. And these interests and abilities obviously had a vocational value which made them well worth encouragement, as in plans for entering a vocational high school which might be expected to lead later to vocational opportunity.

Special Disabilities

A special disability may have even more diverse origins. Thus one girl's difficulty in reading was due to visual defects and a boy's poor spelling to a slight deafness which prevented him from hearing certain sounds clearly and led to his odd spelling of them. A very bright boy did poorly in sports because a visual defect made it impossible for him to hit a baseball as accurately as the average child. Disability may be the result of emotional aversion or even panic. One of the present authors well remembers a very severe fourth-grade teacher whose class exercises in "mental arithmetic" he never could keep up with, and whose sarcastic remarks gave rise to malicious delight in the other children. Arithmetic has remained for him a disliked and difficult subject.

Perhaps there are some genuinely innate special handicaps—an ineptitude in music or mechanical manipulation or mathematics. However, neither teacher nor student should yield to temptation and assume that a special constitutional disability is involved about which nothing can be done. Rather, an analysis should be made to see whether remediable factors may be found. At least, this will alleviate the student's distress to some extent and enable the formation of educational plans that are better adjusted to his capacities.

A Practical Approach to Problems of Ability

A person's special disabilities and abilities, and his general effectiveness or general ability, are thus complex products of his total self and total experience. His physique and physical vitality, his equipment of information and skills, his work methods, his integrations or conflicts of interests, his constitutional intellectual capacities—all are involved in the ability he shows at a particular time or on a particular task. Although the last factor is obviously most important, practically it can never be isolated from the others. A major thesis of this chapter is that only by keeping all these factors in mind can either psychological theory or educational practice regarding abilities be kept straight.

THE APPRAISAL OF ABILITIES

What contributions does this broad approach make to a consideration of methods for appraising abilities? It suggests first of all that any practical appraisal of the abilities of a particular child should not overlook any of these factors. And it aids greatly in understanding the nature and limitations of tests of abilities. First will be mentioned certain methods of appraisal which are sufficiently broad to include most of the various factors mentioned above.

Methods for Obtaining Judgments Regarding Ability

If appraisal is to be very broad, some method of obtaining the judgments of persons (such as teachers) who know the individual is of value. Most informal is a general statement, such as the following report from a small high school in a well-to-do suburb to the parents of a tenth-grade boy:

"Ronald has been doing well in the industrial arts laboratory and has spent much extra time there. His more academic work is mediocre, however; his French in particular is unsatisfactory. All his teachers feel that his accomplishment is distinctly below his capacities. In class he is listless and often day-dreams. He doesn't seem to know how to use time or study effectively. We would appreciate an opportunity to talk with you about your son's work."

This statement evidently sees the boy's abilities in something of the broad perspective suggested above. It pictures a lad with mechanical ability but difficulty in verbal subjects. His potentialities were felt to be distinctly

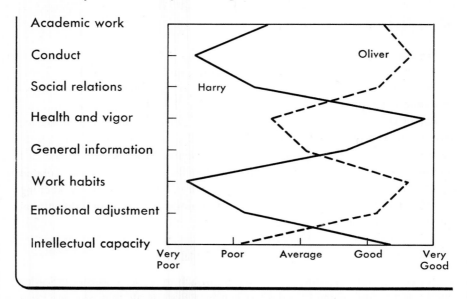

FIG. 3.1. Profiles showing abilities and traits of two boys, as indicated by ratings made by their home-room teacher.

above what he was doing. But when the principal went over a number of unsystematic impressionistic reports such as this one, he was uncertain whether the same points had been considered in judging each pupil; he could not compare the different students to see which ones presented the most serious problems of a given type. A rating scheme was therefore made part of the report on each youngster so that each would be judged on the same general traits and the judgments expressed in somewhat the same fashion. Fig. 3.1 shows the profiles for two tenth-grade boys. The home-room teacher was asked to check, on a blank form, where Harry stood in academic work, in conduct, and so on. She then made the ability profile by drawing a line from one check to the next. She rated Oliver on another blank. The profiles for these two boys are shown in the same figure for contrast and convenience.

The figure shows that Harry does poorly in school and is a conduct problem. His relations with other people are not good; there is conflict in his home, he is not liked in the neighborhood, and is shunned by other pupils. He has no real habits of work. His sour expression, surly manner, and erratic behavior give constant evidence of the conflicts and frustrations in his life. But the teacher was inclined to believe that he really has good intellectual potentialities, though they are unrealized. In contrast, Oliver is doing good work, gets along well with everybody, is notably systematic and dependable, and enthusiastic about what he is doing. But his health is not very good. The teacher feels that his intellectual capacity is distinctly below Harry's.

Harry and Oliver are somewhat extreme cases, and their home-room teacher knew the boys well. But often a teacher does not know her pupils. She may be prejudiced, rating the docile child too high and underestimating the lively youngster who is impatient of books and a sedentary educational program. Frequently an appraisal is wanted at the beginning of the school year or for a new pupil, whom teachers cannot thus judge. Also such judgments are hardly definite enough to enable comparisons to be made of one school and another or one year and another so as to consider and plan possible changes as a pupil progresses through school. Clearly the most important and most difficult factors to judge are constitutional capacities. To separate these more clearly from the other factors and to meet these various difficulties, special devices known as tests have been developed. These are now considered.

Individual Tests of General Ability

Some tests of ability are so designed that they can be given to an entire class or other group at one time; this is true of tests in arithmetic or spelling and the usual class examination. But historically most important, and most distinctive and significant with reference to problems in the field, are the tests of "general intelligence" planned to be given to one child at a time. Of these, the first and still most important are the Binet scales, the first of which was issued by the French psychologist Binet in 1905. The form best known in this country is the Stanford revision developed by Terman at Stanford University; it was first issued in 1916 and revised in 1937 in two equivalent forms (56).

The test consists of simple questions and tasks presented so informally that the test seems more like an interesting game or a chat with the examiner than a test. For example, the child is asked what he would do if he were on his way to school and saw that he was in danger of being late, or if another child struck him without meaning to; such questions are aimed at detecting good sense in dealing with everyday minor emergencies. He is given simple things to do, like repeating a series of numbers which are said to him, or reconstructing a sentence whose words have been mixed up; he is also asked questions requiring practical generalizations, such as telling in what way wood and coal are alike or defining pity and charity.

In short, an effort is made to include in the test knowledge the child should have from his everyday experience or from the minimal essentials of schooling which everyone is supposed to have had. In attempting to measure the fourth factor—constitutional mental capacity—the first factor, relevant information, is made unimportant by having the information called for such that all children presumably have about equal opportunities to learn it. The second factor, methods of work, is supposedly controlled by having the test tasks so short that hardly any systematic sustained study is needed, and by having the examiner constantly watch the youngster to make sure that he is applying himself. The third factor, interest and emotional blocking or facilitation, is dealt with by the examiner's making a special effort to make the child feel at ease and confident, and by having the materials and tasks so varied and interesting that the test has the appeal of a game.

The Terman-Merrill book and the blanks and materials for the revised scales may well be examined so that their general nature is known. The sets of problems or "tests" are for age groups from age 2 to superior adult; in making the scale, each test has been put at the age where from half to two-thirds of all that age pass it. The usual procedure is to give a child six tests in each group beginning with an age at which he can comfortably pass them all, and proceeding to one at which he can pass none. The score is figured by considering the age at which he passed all the tests as the "base" (it is assumed that he would pass all tests below this age had they been given), and adding to this "basal year" two months for each test passed in any higher year (each test of the six counting as one-sixth of a year, or two months).[1] The total score is the sum of these values, or the "mental age," which is commonly abbreviated as MA. Suppose a child passes all the 5-year tests, four of the 6-year, three of the 7-year, and two of the 8-year, and fails all of the 9-year tests. His total score will be 5 years plus 8 months plus 6 months plus 4 months—or a total of 6 years and 6 months. This is his mental age, and it shows that his mental development

[1] As a matter of detail, in the earliest years the tests are in half-year groups in order to provide more adequate testing in those first years of most rapid growth. There are three "superior adult" groups for the better measurement of very bright older children and adults. The month equivalents of each test at these two extremes will thus be given different values than "two months." The Terman-Merrill book should be consulted for details.

is approximately that of the average child of about 6½ years of age. But whether this indicates "normal" intelligence cannot be determined until his chronological age is considered with reference to it. If his chronological age is 6 years and 3 months, he is approximately an average child, since his mental and chronological ages are so nearly the same. However, if his chronological age is 8 years, he has apparently not grown mentally as much as he should have; he is mentally under par. The usual way of expressing a child's intellectual standing with reference to his age is to show the result as a percentage. If a child is 10 years old chronologically but tests 7 years old mentally, he shows 70 percent of the mental growth that should be expected of him; he has an "intelligence quotient" or IQ of 70. If a child's chronological age is 8 years and 3 months and his mental age is 10 years 8 months, his IQ will be 128 months divided by 99 months, or 130.

The MA is thus a statement of a child's *intellectual maturity* without respect to the number of years he has lived, whereas the IQ is a statement of the relationship between the length of time he has lived and the ability he has developed in that time—his brightness. A 6-year-old boy with an IQ of 150 and a 12-year-old with an IQ of 75 both have an MA of 9. They can do tasks of roughly the same difficulty. But their potentialities are very different. Four years later the mental age of the first child will probably be around 15; that of the second, about 12.

As the years pass, a child's MA increases at a rate usually indicated quite closely by his IQ. That is, his IQ tends to remain about the same. But how constant is the IQ? Is it possible to predict with assurance that a 5-year-old boy with an IQ of 140 will show about the same superiority at 15? Numerous studies of this problem have been made by retesting the same children at different intervals. The IQ as determined by a Stanford-Binet test given by a trained investigator appears likely to vary an average of three points one way or the other on a second test within a few days; for about one child out of five it varies more than six points (56, page 46). But over a longer period, and especially if the first test was given at an early age, the variations may be much greater, as shown by continuing or longitudinal studies to be reported later in this chapter. Does ability, like height, cease to increase around 16 or 18 or 20? The revised Stanford-Binet assumes so and puts the age at 16 for the average person. But the longitudinal studies question that assumption; this will be pointed out later.

The Stanford-Binet scale has been the most widely used and generally recognized individual "interview" test for use with one child at a time. But other examinations, such as the Wechsler scale for children, are also used,

and there are various special individual tests for special purposes. The
Binet test is largely verbal. For a child who has a speech defect, who
comes from a home where English is not spoken, or who appears to be
much more "thing"-minded than "word"-minded, "performance" tests
are available—simple puzzles to be solved, or other things to *do*. Thus
the widely known Pintner-Paterson and Arthur scales consist chiefly of
various formboards and picture puzzles.[2]

The various individual tests have important distinctive values. The test
not only yields a score; it affords an excellent opportunity for the examiner
to observe how the child works and to get acquainted with him. Interest
can be maintained, any special circumstance affecting his work noted,
and some adaptation made (within the rules) to each child. But there are
important disadvantages. Testing one child may take an hour or more.
Only after intensive study and experience can a person use these tests
adequately. It is clearly not possible to give such time-consuming tests that
require such expert testers to anywhere near all the children for whom
some measure of ability is needed. Tests which can be given to a class
or other group at one time, and whose administration and scoring are simple enough so that the average teacher can use them, are necessary.

Group Tests of General Ability

Various group tests have been devised to meet these needs. Those for
the middle and upper grades and high school consist of blanks which contain such questions as:

The day before Thursday is (1) Wednesday (2) Tuesday (3) Friday (4) Sunday.
Cheese comes from (1) milk (2) plants (3) eggs (4) butter.
What is iron never without? (1) coldness (2) polish (3) weight (4) rust.
Head is to hat as hand is to: (a) foot (b) glove (c) shoe (d) coat.
What is the most useful thing physicians can do? (a) cheer up patients, (b) pre-
vent disease, (c) give medicine, (d) perform operations.

The pupils are told to underline or check the answer to each question
which they consider correct, or to write its number or letter in an answer
space. Some tests have a separate sheet for the answers. In any case, the
directions are so simple that any teacher can give the tests; usually the di-

---

[2] Tests for very young children are necessarily largely individual performance tests
—handling a cup, piling blocks, playing peek-a-boo, and so on. The reader interested
in nursery school will find of distinct interest the little stunts of the Merrill-Palmer
scale, the Minnesota Pre-School tests, and the California Pre-School schedule. As already mentioned, the revised Stanford-Binet begins at two years and uses sundry
performance items in the early ages.

rections are printed on the blank. Since the pupils answer by checking, writing a number, or underlining, a large number of questions can be covered in a short time—as many as 200 in 40 minutes; such a range is very necessary in attempts to measure such a complex trait as general ability. And checking the pupils' answers against a key is so simple that a 200-question test can be scored by a clerk in as little as three or four minutes. Many tests are now scored by machine.

Group tests require the ability to read. But the questions are somewhat like those in the Binet in that they deal primarily not with material taught in school, but rather with material the child should be familiar with from his everyday experience. The examiner cannot control the pupil's attention or make sure that his emotional attitude is favorable as well as he can in an interview examination. However, the usual group test contains many more questions than the Binet, methods of administering and scoring are more clear cut, and the test is sufficiently interesting so that it usually holds the pupil's attention well; consequently in certain respects the results are more reliable.

Group tests are even more verbal than the Binet and somewhat "schoolish" in character, since they involve reading and information partly of a rather academic nature. Therefore the results may be influenced by any reading disability. Inferences based on such tests as to probable vocational success must be made with caution. It is probably best to say that these tests measure general academic ability.

Children in the first two or three grades cannot read well enough to take tests like those just described. For these pupils simple blanks are available that present problems by means of pictures and similar devices. Thus one such test contains pictures one part of which is wrong (for example, an envelope is shown with a stamp in the wrong corner); the pupil is asked to find this wrong part and put a cross on it. Another test consists of a series of pictures, each showing several similar objects and one that is different from the others (such as four dogs and a cat); the pupils are told to mark the object that doesn't belong with the others. Here again the aim is to present familiar material and simple tasks that permit each child to show the extent to which he observes well or sees the relationship between objects.

Scores on these group tests are often most helpfully used by noting, for example, that Mary, in the fourth grade, scores highest and is above median for sixth grade and hence may deserve special opportunities or be considered for rapid advancement, whereas Tom is below the third-grade norm and is likely to need special help. If age norms have been established, the tester may say that since Mary scores at the norm for age 13 her "mental age" is roughly 13, whereas Tom's score is only at the norm for age 7. The score may be expressed as a percentile of the results for each child's age; thus 9-year-old Mary may be at the 91st percentile or in the top tenth for her age, 11-year-old Tom at the 9th percentile or in the lowest tenth. Some tests provide for a "standard score"; each such test has its own norm and way of expressing results. Sample tests with their directions booklets and other materials, and perhaps a recent book on tests— for example, that by Anastasi (2) or Cronbach (21)—may be examined.

Tests of Special Aptitudes; Differential Aptitude Batteries

Tests of special abilities—mechanical, linguistic, and so on—usually present a youngster with typical problems involving the special abilities being investigated. For example, a test of mechanical ability may require the pupil to put together the pieces of a bicycle bell so it will ring; a test of musical ability may ask which of two chords he hears is more dissonant; a test of linguistic ability may present a sample vocabulary in an artificial language which he is to use in various ways. The test may also include necessary background material, such as the grammar needed in studying a foreign language. A test in art may ask the pupil to choose the more attractive of two pictures that are largely the same except that the balance or some other feature is less satisfactory in one than in the other.

A good school will seek to discover the various types of abilities in its pupils and it will use a variety of means for doing so (24). Capacities for leadership may be located by having teachers note instances of this ability in pupil groups or asking pupils to name, on "Guess Who" tests, those they think good leaders. Pupils with talent for creative writing may be located by having the teacher list in a "roster workbook" each child who typically "gives a refreshing twist even to old ideas" or who "uses only necessary details in telling a story," and so on (24). Both interest and talent in science may be evidenced by the type of questions pupils asked in class, the types of pupil hobbies and the amount of free time given them, the nature and amount of leisure-time reading (10).

An early ingenious test of appreciation of poetry not only measured but also significantly analyzed that special ability. Each page contained a stanza by a well-known poet and three changed versions of it; in one the meter was spoiled, in another the diction was commonplace, and the third was excessively sentimental. The student was to mark the version on each page that he considered best. Fig. 3.2 shows the results, for one such stanza, from the fifth grade through college. From the seventh grade on, few pupils liked the matter-of-fact and metrically damaged versions. But from the sixth to the eleventh grade the excessively sentimental form was preferred—apparently an adolescent reaction. Only from the senior year of high school and after was the original version preferred. The total scores also indicated that ability to judge good poetry usually did not appear until well into high school, and often not then.

Differential batteries consist of sets of tests designed for the comparative appraisal of a person's abilities of various types, these usually being differentiated statistically on the basis of factor analysis. For example, the eight Differential Aptitude Tests developed by the Psychological Corporation

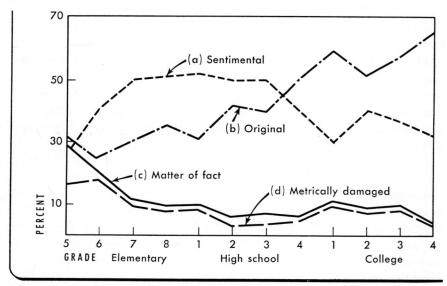

FIG. 3.2. Percentage of students in each grade marking as best (a) the sentimental variant of one stanza, (b) the original stanza, (c) the commonplace, matter-of-fact version, and (d) the metrically damaged version. (From Abbott and Trabue [1].)

are in the following fields: verbal reasoning, numerical ability, abstract reasoning, space relations, mechanical reasoning, clerical speed and accuracy, spelling, language usage. Extensive norms for Grades 8–12 and follow-up data provide means for various interpretations. Thus in high school, students who later went into engineering showed special strength on tests of numerical ability, space relations, and mechanical reasoning. Clearly such batteries of tests should be useful in vocational and educational guidance. Their greater range emphasizes that the older tests of "general ability" were really primarily tests of verbal and numerical ability; the first two tests of the DAT appear to serve fairly well in place of the older "intelligence" or scholastic aptitude tests (2, pages 351–386).

Desirable Methods of Appraising Abilities

Every teacher forms judgments of her pupils' abilities on the basis of their alertness and the quality of their school work. She may obtain judgments from other teachers about certain youngsters, may go over their school record to date. Many schools give all pupils a group test of "general ability." However, it is increasingly being recognized that these tests, involving reading and scholastic verbal and numerical skills, primarily measure academic ability. And this may be largely sufficient for many educational purposes. For example, if on such a test Harry scores as high in "intellectual capacity" as his home-room teacher rated him (Fig. 3.1), she will be justified in expecting better work of him; and telling him about his good score may stimulate him to do better. Similarly, if Oliver scores as low in "intellectual capacity" as she rated him, she may be doubtful about his hope of going to college. And the higher average score made by students in the Hill School across town suggests that those children have greater readiness and aptitude for schooling than the pupils in the Valley School where Harry and Oliver are.

It is desirable that a differential test battery be given in these schools to see whether, for example, Ronald has the special mechanical abilities suggested by his strong interest in industrial arts. A school psychologist, skilled in administering the Binet or Wechsler and tests of special abilities and disabilities and in methods of case study, is much to be desired. But before the various needs of different youngsters can be adequately understood, data regarding the growth of abilities and the influences that affect them must be considered.

THE GROWTH OF ABILITIES

As mentioned at the beginning of this chapter, the growth of abilities is about as well recognized a phenomenon as physical growth; everyone knows that a 10-year-old child can do many more things, and more difficult things, than a 5-year-old. But there are important questions about which more definite information is needed. Do abilities grow at a regular rate like height, or is there an increase in rate of growth at adolescence, as there is in weight and strength? Growth in height ceases around 18 or 20; do abilities also stop growing, perhaps at about the same age? The human body is different in proportion and tissue composition at 18 from what it is at 8, and different at 4 from what it is at 8. Are abilities similarly different at various ages? How do dull people differ from bright people in rate and nature of intellectual growth? Do the bright continue growing in abilities longer, and reach an adult level later? These are all questions of decided importance for education. Although general observation suggests certain answers, the more exact evidence derived from systematized observations, and especially from measurements obtained by careful testing, should carry understanding much further.

Growth of Abilities as Shown by Cross-Sectional Data

A distinction was made in Chapter 2 between cross-sectional and longitudinal studies. Data on growth of abilities from cross-sectional studies

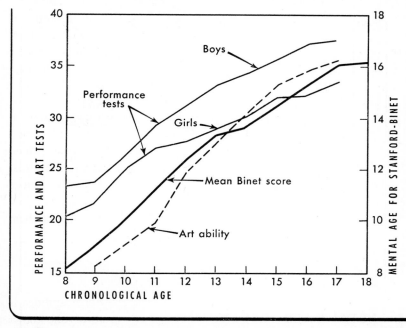

FIG. 3.3. Growth in abilities as shown by total scores on the Stanford-Binet scale and by scores on performance and art tests. (Adapted from Anastasi [2], Wood and Kumin [65], and the normative data of the Lewerenz tests.)

have been obtained by testing at a given time all the children of certain ages in certain schools or communities. Data from longitudinal studies have accumulated from repeated testing of the same individuals, preferably over many years and with much supplementary information about each person so that influences affecting growth might be intimately understood. Obviously the cross-sectional data can be obtained most easily and quickly. Fig. 3.3 combines results obtained in standardizing the 1937 edition of the Stanford-Binet scale (the heavy line) and normative data for several tests of special abilities.

The heavy line indicates a fairly steady growth in capacity to deal with the varied tasks of the Binet over the years covered in this figure, with some continuing of growth up to 18. Since the scale was constructed so

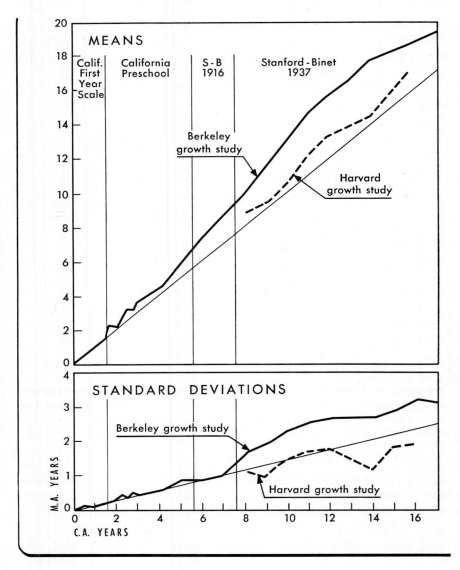

as to show such growth, that it does so is hardly surprising but is nevertheless indicative that probably increase in general ability is roughly at the rate indicated. The increasing superiority of boys over girls on the performance tests is to be expected, because of the boys' greater relevant experience. But the important fact is that all these lines indicate the growth years to be a period of growth in abilities as well as in physique. However, they do not answer the question as to whether there is an adult level, and they obviously give only a general contour of growth, since they were made from scores of different children at different ages. More adequate information on these and other questions might be expected from longitudinal studies which follow individuals over many years, can be related to any special influences in the person's life, and are continued into the adult years. Fortunately, such material is now available.

Growth of Abilities as Shown by Longitudinal Studies

Both the special values and the difficulties of longitudinal studies can perhaps best be considered in terms of a particular investigation. The solid lines in Fig. 3.4 show results of the repeated testing from infancy through age 17 of some 40 youngsters in the Berkeley growth study. In infancy they were tested as frequently as every month; but later on, tests were given every year. Special tests (the California First Year and Preschool scales) devised in connection with the investigation were used up to age 5½, and after that the 1916 and then the 1937 forms of the Stanford-Binet scale for the most part. The solid line in the upper part of the graph shows the mental growth (the mental age in months) of these youngsters from early infancy through 17 as expressed in mean or average mental ages at these dates (coördinated to make scores on the various tests comparable).

FIG. 3.4. (*Opposite page*) Curves of means and standard deviations of mental ages, 1 month to 17 years, Berkeley and Harvard growth studies. (Adapted from Bayley [8].)

The diagonal straight line shows where the mean would have run if the group at each age had tested exactly according to the norms—those chronologically 14 years old had had a mean mental age of 14, and so on. The Berkeley children (solid line) were substantially above this. The dashed line shows the Harvard growth study results, another longitudinal study carried on in Massachusetts over a shorter range of time.

The Berkeley results were obtained with a special infant scale for the first year and a preschool scale for ages 1 to 5½ developed in connection with this study; from 5½ to 7½ the 1916 form of the Stanford-Binet was used; from 7½ Forms L or M of the 1937 edition of the Stanford-Binet, and occasionally the Terman-McNemar and the Wechsler-Bellevue adult intelligence test. A number of group tests were used in the Harvard study.

The lower section of the graph shows that standard deviations of the Berkeley study are decidedly larger from 7 on, and especially around ages 10 and 11. A somewhat similar bulge around 10 and 11 was found in the Harvard study.

The dashed line shows results obtained by the Harvard study, another longitudinal study in the Boston area, using a variety of group tests and covering a shorter age range. The straight diagonal line indicates where the curve would have fallen if every mental age had been the same as the chronological age. The Berkeley and Cambridge groups are above this theoretical average line, as might be expected because their socioeconomic status was probably somewhat superior. And the fact that their parents remained in the same community over such long periods of time presupposes that they were economically competent and established, and also of such intelligence and with such interest in their children that they were agreeable to these long-continuing studies. Furthermore, the continuing measurements might give such familiarity with the tests that a little of their superiority might be due to practice effects. However, the investigators believed that the lives of these youngsters were full enough of other concerns, and that such various tests were used, that practice effects were not predominant.

The lower part of the figure, showing standard deviations or variations from the average at each age, indicates greater variation in scores around ages 10 to 12 than at any other time in both the Berkeley and the Harvard groups. Bayley concluded that this "reflected a true state of increased variability in intelligence during adolescence" (8, page 810). This same investigator found a similar greater variation (not evident in Fig. 3.4) around the age of 1 year, and concluded that growth in the abilities tested at these ages—largely involving coördination of movement—was especially rapid, so that differences in rate added to individual differences made the variations especially great at these times. A second increase in variability was found around ages 4 and 5, and careful inspection of the various test items for these ages suggested that they were measuring especially growth in oral speech and acquaintance with the immediate environment. The marked increase in variability around ages 10 to 12 may similarly be related to the growth in abstract intelligence and to some extent in social intelligence that occurs at that time, and which the tests for these ages seem particularly to involve. The investigator draws the following conclusion: "I see no reason why we should continue to think of intelligence as an integrated (or simple) entity or capacity which grows throughout childhood by steady accretions. Intelligence appears to me, rather, to be a dynamic succession of developing functions with the more advanced and complex functions in the hierarchy depending on the prior maturing of earlier simpler ones" (8, page 807).

The curves in Fig. 3.4 end at the age of 17, and are still going up. Fortunately, the Berkeley study is being continued. Fig. 3.5 shows scores for five boys in this group tested to age 25. They differ greatly in rate of development; thus case 5 grew much more rapidly in ability all through

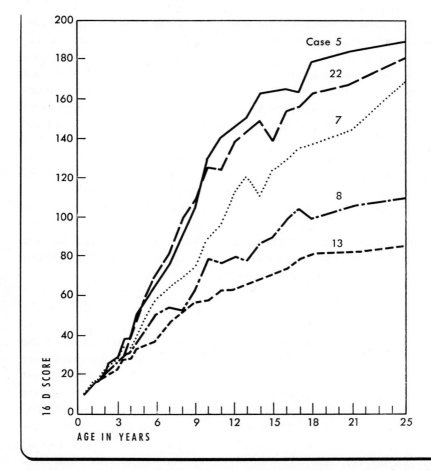

FIG. 3.5. Growth in general ability of five boys, as indicated by tests given from infancy to age 25. Scores are expressed in terms of the standard deviations of the scores for the group at 16 years. (From Bayley [8].)

childhood and adolescence than case 13. And even at 25, ability seems to be still increasing a bit, and somewhat more for the brighter than the duller boys. Again it might be argued that familiarity with the tests might account for these continuing increases to some extent, and that the nature of many of the tests at these higher levels—involving as they do mostly reading and vocabulary which should increase with more education and experience—might account for these gains. But clearly we must not conclude, as was formerly assumed, that an adult level is regularly reached around 16 or 18.

Fig. 3.5 shows differences in the test scores of these boys increasing with chronological age. It also indicates some irregularities in growth; thus case 8 seems actually to have tested a bit lower at age 8 than at 7 and to have made no gain from about 10 to 12. And cases 7 and 22 both show test score drops around 14 and 15. Some of these variations may have been due to a different test being used—for example, the Wechsler in place of the Binet; possibly others resulted from indisposition on the day of the testing.

As mentioned earlier, it has been supposed that rates of growth and the IQ remain relatively constant. What is the specific evidence, from this and other longitudinal studies, regarding consistency in rate of growth?

For a general statement of the extent to which tests at earlier ages indicated later ability, the scores obtained at ages 1 and 2 and at certain other ages up to 15 by 27 youngsters, for whom most complete data were available, were correlated with their scores at age 18 on the Wechsler test for adults (1939 edition). These correlations were as follows:

Age	1	2	4	7	9	11	15
Correlation	.14	.39	.52	.68	.80	.87	.84

The test given at age 1 correlated practically not at all with the score made at 18. It seemed clear that such tests could not be used (as for instance in trying to estimate the ability of babies considered for adoption) to forecast probable ability in later childhood. However, by age 7 relationships are fairly high. To obtain still more stable scores in studying these relationships, the scores at 17 and 18 were averaged, and earlier tests were averaged and correlations made. Average scores of the tests given at 10, 11, and 12 months correlated .41 with an average for tests at ages 17 and 18. Tests given at 42, 48, and 54 months correlated .62 with the 17 to 18 average. The average scores for ages 5, 6, and 7 years correlated .86 with the averages for ages 17 and 18 (7). Evidently tests given in the primary grades are likely to indicate fairly well the probable standing of these children if tested in the last year of senior high school. But the correlation is still low enough for considerable variations to occur, as shown in Figs. 3.4 and 3.5 and even more fully in a later figure.

Differentiations and Potentialities of Growth

The more recent longitudinal studies thus suggest that ability increases not only through the growth periods of childhood and adolescence but to some extent into the adult years. Individuals differ in their curves of mental growth. Certain individuals in Fig. 3.5 appear indeed to have lost, but others gained comparatively; hence the question is raised as to whether abilities can be increased in any real sense by educational or other means. This fascinating topic will be discussed later.

As was mentioned above, certain longitudinal studies suggested also that growth in intelligence was not merely an increase, as in height, but rather "a dynamic succession of developing functions." Moreover, through the growth years, a youngster's mental traits tend to become more diverse and independent. Thus, one investigator (30) found that average "intercorrelations on tests of memory, verbal, and number abilities for ages 9, 12, and 15 were, for boys, .30, .21, and .18, and for girls, .27, .30, and .10." Other investigations have yielded similar results.

DISTRIBUTION OF ABILITIES

As was mentioned at the beginning of this chapter, everyone recognizes that people differ in abilities. But how great are these differences? What differences may a teacher expect to find in a typical class? Between different schools? Between country and city? Evidence on such questions will now be examined.

Range and Classification of Abilities

Various features of the results obtained with tests of general ability are well brought out in Fig. 3.6, from the Harvard longitudinal study. It shows the distribution of mental ages of 167 girls at the chronological ages of 8, 12, and 16—the same girls whose height was shown in Fig. 2.3. Clearly, at each age these girls differ greatly in general ability, as measured by several group tests. Thus some of the 12-year-olds are no brighter than the average 8-year-old, whereas others are as able as the average 16-year-old. It is also clear that, like height and weight, ability is distributed in a bell-shaped or "normal" curve. Most girls are around average in ability. But there are many who are sufficiently above or below average to present distinct educational problems. Thus at age 12, an appreciable number of these girls had an MA of 16 or higher, but several had an MA of 10 or lower. It is obvious that the latter pupils cannot be expected to do anywhere near as well in school as the superior group; programs as well as expectations should probably be different for people who differ so in potentialities in school.

Note that when these girls had a chronological age of 8 they averaged nearer 9 in mental age; when they were 12, their MA was around 14; when 16, their MA was around 18. This superiority might be expected because, as was said earlier, the families of these girls presumably were sufficiently prosperous to

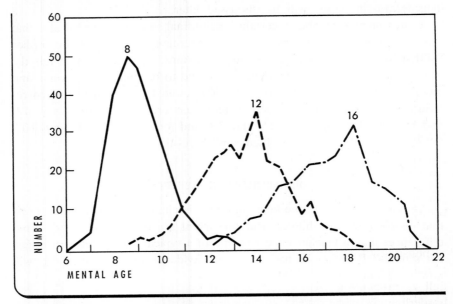

FIG. 3.6. Distribution of mental ages of 167 girls at ages 8, 12, and 16. (From Dearborn and Rothney [23].)

remain in the community over the period of the study, and sufficiently interested in child welfare to have their daughters continue the study. Moreover, the 12-year-old group seems to have a greater range in ability than both the 8-year-olds and the 16-year-olds, a finding similar to the greater dispersion in height for these same 12-year-olds (Fig. 2.3). However, the tests may have had too little material at the upper end and in consequence the ablest 16-year-olds did not score as high as they could have; they may have hit the test ceiling.

Fig. 3.6 brings out well the impossibility of saying that one child is in a distinct group of dull children and another in a distinct group of bright children; rather, the distribution of ability is continuous. Nevertheless, for practical purposes it is useful to make some classification, even though this is arbitrary. Table 3.1 summarizes two of many attempts to classify children according to general ability. The first column of percentages shows the classification in terms of IQ on Forms L and M of the 1937 revision of the Stanford-Binet scale. The second column shows a similar classification by Wechsler in terms of a somewhat different but nevertheless largely analogous IQ on his scale for measuring the general ability of children. According to this table, in a typical group of children, between 2 and 4 percent might be considered very superior, and 7 to 8 percent superior, in general ability; a total of between 9 and 12 percent of these children have such fine intellects that the schools may be thought to have a special

TABLE 3.1.   Levels of General Ability in Children as Indicated by Standardization Samples of Two Intelligence Tests[3]

IQ	Verbal Characterization	Percentage of Children	
		1937 Binet	Wechsler
130 up	Very superior	4	2
120–129	Superior	8	7
110–119	Bright	18	16
90–109	Average	46	50
80–89	Dull	14	16
70–79	Borderline	7	7
Below 70	Mentally defective	3	2

responsibility for helping them realize their potentialities. At the other extreme, between 2 and 3 percent of the children might be considered so dull as properly to be called mentally defective and another 7 percent borderline. Though all the categories in this table are in terms of test results only, the tests have been so extensively used and the results viewed in terms of school success and other evidence of ability, that each group may be considered to be as characterized; the children with IQ's of 130 and up can be considered very superior not alone on their scores on these tests but in capacity for school work, expectation of success in a career, and like criteria. Those with IQ's of 70 or below are so limited in all these respects that they are likely to present special educational and vocational problems.

But caution is necessary in interpreting a particular youngster's score in terms of this table. Some circumstance may affect his score on a particular day; furthermore, a few children show long-term trends up or down, as will be emphasized shortly. Tests of "primary abilities" might show that

[3] Adapted from data of Merrill and of Wechsler in Anastasi (2).

a boy poor in the largely verbal abilities called for by the usual tests of "general intelligence" has good mechanical aptitude. The composite of abilities of a bright 12-year-old with a mental age of 16 is probably not the same as in the case of an average 16-year-old youngster. But the fact remains that the potentialities for education, career, and contribution to society of children with IQ's of 70 and of 130 are vastly different.

Physique and Abilities

Careful studies have shown that, on the average, intellectually superior children are superior physically. Most substantiating are the appraisals of Terman's large group of gifted youngsters that were begun in childhood and continued into adult life (57). These subjects averaged taller and heavier at all ages; their height as adults averaged two inches above that for the general population and their weight averaged ten pounds heavier. The common misconception that bright children are physically smaller and inadequate may have arisen from comparisons of "accelerated" children with older classmates, from failure to differentiate unhappy average children who try to compensate for maladjustment by intensive school work, and perhaps from jealousy of the bright. Dull children have been found to average two or three inches shorter and five to eight pounds lighter than the norm, but their physical inferiority may not be noticed because their dullness holds them back with younger children. Feeble-minded individuals in institutions tend to be below normal in height and weight; the more defective they are mentally, the more inferior they are likely to be physically.

Furthermore, bright children tend to develop physically a bit more rapidly than the average child, and to reach puberty a little sooner (57), but the physical growth of the mentally inferior tends to lag. However, correlations between measures of intellect and of physique are so low (usually around .10 to .20) that no inferences regarding a particular child's mental abilities should be based on his physique. Similarly, physical defects are more common among dull than bright children, but the correlation is so low as not to warrant inferences regarding brightness based on the presence of physical defects.

Family, Race, Sex, and Abilities

Chapter 2 indicated that physical traits tend to run in families. Many investigations have indicated that general ability or the lack of it similarly tends to be constitutional. Over eighty years ago Galton reported that an eminent man was 130 times as likely to have an eminent male relative as was an average man. Among 643 children with IQ's of 140 or higher, Terman found that their family trees included six signers of the Declaration of Independence and two Presidents of the United States, as well as many other notable people (57). At the other extreme, one investigator reported that 44 percent of the children of a group of mentally defective mothers were mentally defective (31). Table 3.2 summarizes various find-

TABLE 3.2. Correlations Between Related Pairs of Persons, Northern European Stock, in Twelve Different Investigations[4]

	Physical Measures	Mental Measures
Unrelated children		−.19 to .09
Cousins		.27
Parents	.00 to .15	.46 to .49
Parent-child	.42 to .53	.45 to .55
Siblings, same home[a]	.42 to .53	.45 to .55
Nonidentical twins	.58	.53 to .70
Identical twins	.91	.88 to .97

[a] A correlation of only .25 in intelligence has been reported for siblings who spent at least four years in different homes, the correlation dropping to .19 when the homes were of different socioeconomic levels. And the longer the siblings were apart, the greater the differences tended to be. For identical twins in the same home Binet mental ages correlated .92, but .64 for identicals reared apart; for the Stanford achievement test battery the correlations were .96 and .51. For weight they were .97 and .89; for height, .98 and .97.

ings indicating an increase in similarity with increasing close family relationship, in both physical and mental measurements.

The table shows that mental as well as physical traits involve constitutional elements, and the high correlations for identical twins suggest that these constitutional elements are very important. However, it should be recognized that identical twins in the same home, who look so much alike that they are mistaken for each other, are probably subject to such similar influences that some similarity in abilities may thus result. All the people in one home live under largely similar physical, socioeconomic, and cultural conditions. Two children of the same intellectual potentiality presumably would develop somewhat different abilities if one grew up in the home of a professional family in California, and the other lived half-starved in the shack of an illiterate southern sharecropper. The highly privileged English upper-class families whom Galton was largely concerned with gave their members many advantages. This topic will be discussed again later.

[4] Adapted from Greene (31).

Are there racial differences in intellectual capacities? Eight studies of Negro children indicated an average IQ about 10 points below that of white youngsters. But other studies must be considered before conclusions are drawn. American-born children whose foreign-born parents were Polish Jews or Swedes have been reported to average 103 in IQ, whereas children of French-Canadian and Italian parentage averaged 87. Selective migration may be a factor in many of the differences found in national and racial groups in the United States. On a nonverbal test battery designed especially for international comparisons, Danish Americans scored higher than Italian Americans, but Italian children in Rome tested slightly above Danish children in Copenhagen (3). Differences in educational advantages and experience may affect scores on tests of general ability. For example, a New York study found that Negro children who had moved there from the South within one or two years of the time of testing averaged 72 in IQ, whereas those who had been in the North nine years or more averaged 94; moreover, the school records before migration averaged about the same for all these children (36). Subtle cultural differences may be a factor in racial comparisons. Thus on certain formboard tests a group of Indian children took more time but made fewer errors than white children; to the Indians, time meant little, but a mistake distressed them. Another Indian group considered it improper to try to score high (3).[5]

It is conceivable that there may be some differences in average abilities between certain racial groups, though none have been established, and such factors as the above have always seemed dominant. And always the most marked features of the comparative data have been the great individual differences in every group and the great overlappings of each on every other. There are able and stupid people in all these groups; hence discrimination against an individual on the assumption that his race is of some significance as regards his ability is clearly without scientific justification.

A hundred and more years ago it was generally assumed that women and girls were less able than the male sex. However, intelligence tests show that girls average the same or a bit higher than boys, as might be expected in view of the girls' more rapid growth, and have the same variability. There do appear to be some differences in special abilities. Girls begin to talk earlier and seem to maintain some verbal superiority;

[5] "Cultures differ in the specific activities which they encourage, stimulate and value. The 'higher mental processes' of one culture may be relatively useless 'stunts' of another. . . . Each culture selects and stimulates certain abilities, skills and fields of knowledge as the most significant" ([3], pp. 782, 824).

they also show greater finger dexterity but usually less big-muscle skills and mechanical aptitude.

Socioeconomic Status and Ability

As will be emphasized shortly, the relationships between socioeconomic status and abilities are very complex. Table 3.3 summarizes the reports by three studies on the average scores on certain tests of general ability made by youngsters whose fathers were in various occupations.

Not only do college students from professional homes average highest on a test of general ability given on entering college, but the Wechsler

TABLE 3.3. Relation of Fathers' Occupation to Their Children's Scores on Three Tests of General Ability[6]

| Father's Occupation | Binet IQ | | Wechsler IQ | Percentile College Group Test |
	Age 2–5½	Age 15–18		
Professional	116	116	110	59
Clerical, skilled worker	108	110	103	54
Farmer	99	94	97	47
Unskilled	94	98	94	37

and the Binet give similar findings for such children. The Binet shows that children from professional homes are about as superior, compared to youngsters whose fathers are unskilled workers, in the preschool as in secondary-school years. Perhaps most of the influences that foster the development of abilities such as would be found in the home of a professional man as compared to that of a wage-earning father are about as active in the preschool years as later; these influences include stimulating contacts with fond adults, as well as good nutrition and health care. Or the superiority of children from better-class homes may be understood as constitutional—the parents are constitutionally superior and the children hereditarily so. Both factors may be operative.

Anyhow, the fact seems to be that a smaller number of bright children come from homes of upper than of middle or even lower socioeconomic class, the basic reason being that there are many more and larger families in these latter two classes. For example, the Elmtown survey found 8 youngsters with an IQ of 120 or more out of a total of 35 children of professional and business families; but there were 19 with this IQ out of

[6] Adapted from Terman and Merrill, (56), Anastasi (2), and Smith (53).

a total of 152 youth from middle-class homes, and 11 out of 229 in the lower middle class (the fathers being mostly unskilled or semiskilled workers). The percentage of these adolescents with an IQ of 120 and up was much higher in the first group than the last (23 percent as compared to 5 percent), but there were more (11 as compared to 8) bright youngsters in the last group than in the first (*34*, page 175). And probably there were still more bright children in the lower socioeconomic groups, since

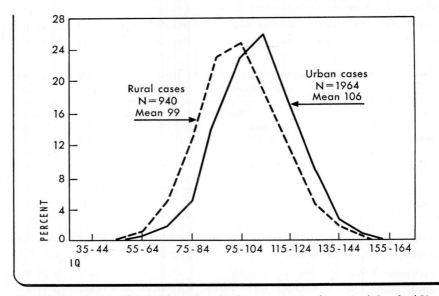

FIG. 3.7. Distribution of IQ's of rural and urban groups on the revised Stanford-Binet scale. (From Terman and Merrill [56].)

most tests of general ability are probably subtly weighted in favor of the upper and upper-middle classes because the makers of these tests come from these classes.[7]

The comparison of country and city children shown in Fig. 3.7 brings out two major facts regarding practically all such comparisons: the differences are slight, and there is much overlapping; there are very bright and

[7] For example, an elaborate investigation that compared children of different socioeconomic status on nonverbal and verbal tests found substantially greater differences between socioeconomic groups on the verbal tests. Detailed analyses showed that children from the poorer homes did especially poorly on certain items that were probably unfair to them—as for instance on a question about fireplaces, which in that city would be more common in an upper- than a lower-class home. When a special test was constructed that included only items not substantially class-weighted, many lower-class children did comparatively better (*25*).

very dull children in both country and city, and a boy from the country cannot for that reason be assumed to be dull. Again a detailed analysis showed that many items were so urban in nature as to be unfair to a country child. In fact, on a special test made up of items found to be somewhat rural in nature, country children averaged above city youngsters (Shimberg, in [3, page 827]).

In short, healthy children of good family coming from good homes in good urban neighborhoods tend to score somewhat higher on tests of general ability than children less favored in these various respects; however, dull children are found in favored groups, and bright children in poor families in poor neighborhoods. Two considerations prevent acceptance of these comparative test scores as essentially indicative of constitutional intellectual capacities. (1) The tests more or less favor upper-middle-class urban American children; and (2) health, home, socioeconomic status, and schooling may affect abilities. This second possibility will now be examined.

EFFECTS OF CERTAIN INFLUENCES ON ABILITIES

Will improving a child's health improve his abilities? A child suffering from malnutrition or a chronic infection may show greater energy and interest if his physical condition is improved, and both his temperament and his school work may be better, but numerous investigations largely agree that there is no appreciable increase in his general ability. Improved nutrition and health might to some extent overcome an earlier retardation of mental and physical growth caused by illness or related handicap.

Socioeconomic Conditions and Ability

As implied above, poor socioeconomic status and other unfavorable conditions of living may be associated with poor ability, conceivably in part a cause of it. But will improved conditions indicate any improvement in abilities? Fig. 3.8 presents a variety of evidence bearing on this total issue of the relation between ability, as measured by typical tests of general ability, and social and economic conditions.

The top curve shows that Massachusetts children whose fathers were in upper occupational groups scored higher in IQ than children whose parents were of a lower occupational status, presumably partly because the latter children were constitutionally somewhat less able mentally, had homes offering fewer advantages, were less familiar with some of the test content as mentioned above, and perhaps were handicapped in other ways. The differences were about the same from ages 8 to 18, presumably because the factors involved operated to about the same extent over this age range. However, children from very underprivileged homes showed a decrease from the younger to the older ages, as did the mountain children

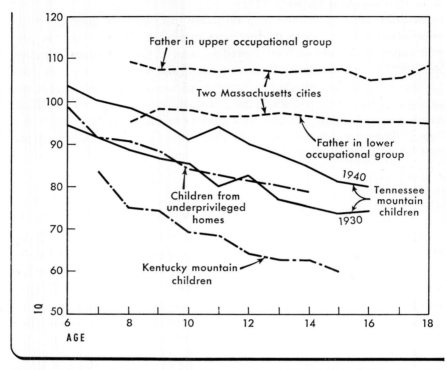

FIG. 3.8. Relations to IQ of urban differences in socioeconomic conditions (top two curves), very meager rural environment in 1930 and 1940 after ten years' improvement (heavy lines), an even more limited condition (bottom curve), and a city slum area of underprivileged homes. (Adapted from Asher [4], Skeels and Fillmore [52], and Wheeler [62].)

(the solid lines and the lowest line). These decreases may be thought of as in part indicative of a cumulative "mental malnutrition" of the children with very meager environments, and in part as the result of test content that was less and less familiar to such children. The most interesting feature of this figure is the high curve for the Tennessee mountain children tested in 1940 in contrast to the curve in 1930. During this decade, better roads, better schools, and various other favoring conditions presumably made the mountain communities more stimulating places in which to live—and perhaps the test content more appropriate. As a result, the children scored higher in general ability in the 1940 tests.

A fascinating account (*39*) of a teacher's experiences, first in a nursery school in the Greenwich Village section of New York City and then in a little school in the Tennessee mountains, gives glimpses of the variety and subtlety of the factors involved in such contrasting environments. The Manhattan youngsters were mostly aboundingly healthy and very active. They were confident and even aggressive, perhaps overstimulated as a healthy child there might well be, full of ideas. Their parents were mostly ambitious and successful young professional and business people who lived in comfortable apartments. Various other adults were seen daily. In contrast, the diet of the mountain children was inadequate and their crude homes lacked warmth in the winter and were too crowded to let them have enough sleep. Many seemed to suffer chronically from respiratory or other ailments. That these back-country youngsters seemed to lack energy and alertness was to be expected. Many families were on relief, the parents ignorant and discouraged. The children were so much a part of their big family group and so unacquainted outside their own little world that they were shy in contacts with other people, things, and ideas. There was inbreeding culturally as well as biologically. Biologically, these mountain children may well have been somewhat below average in constitutional intellectual potential. At any rate, their total environment was so meager that they could hardly fully realize whatever potentials they might have.

As Fig. 3.8 brought out, when general conditions in a community are improved, the children in it may make higher scores on tests of general ability. Will a planned change in a child's environment bring demonstrable gains? A considerable number of experiments have attempted to determine the effect of moving children from very poor homes, or homes broken by death or divorce, to foster homes. Table 3.4 summarizes one of

TABLE 3.4. Effect of Quality of Foster Home and Age of Placement on Change in IQ of Foster Children[8]

	Number of Cases	IQ Before Placement	IQ After 4 Years	Gain
Foster home rating				
Good	33	95.2	100.5	5.3
Poor	41	88.0	88.1	0.1
Age at 2nd test				
Over 12 years 4 months	37	89.7	89.3	−0.4
Under 12 years 4 months	37	92.8	98.0	5.2

[8] Adapted from Freeman, Holzinger, and Mitchell (*27*).

these studies. The foster homes were appraised by means of a rating scale which took into account the neighborhood, the size and comfort of the building and the condition in which it was kept, the amount and nature of the reading matter there, and the education, congeniality, and kindliness of the foster parents. The children were tested shortly before being placed in the foster home and again about four years later. The average age at the first test was 8 years. The table shows that the children gained 5.3 IQ points in four years in good foster homes but practically none in poor foster homes. The table also indicates that the gains were made primarily by children under 12, or those younger than age 8 when placed. Other evidence indicated that even earlier placement, as in the preschool years, would probably have resulted in greater improvement. Where there were gains, a great variety of factors were apparently involved—not only better living conditions and a higher level of literacy but in particular a more friendly, encouraging, and stimulating social climate.

Education and Ability

The most systematic experimentation regarding effects of schooling on measured ability has been done in nursery schools. Substantial evidence indicates that children in orphanages or in drab and very inadequate homes may so benefit from the toys and the opportunities to do many things, and the stimulatingly friendly teachers in a good nursery school, that they make higher scores on tests of general ability. However, nursery-school children from very good homes showed little gain on such tests, wherefore it was hypothesized that the school added little to their already rich experience (47).

Unfortunately, there have been few experiments regarding the effects of elementary, high-school, and college programs on the general ability of the respective students. Extensive data from three well-known New York private schools showed no consistent gain in "intelligence" (47, pages 351–361). However, these pupils were as a group superior and came from superior homes. Perhaps children from poor homes and neighborhoods would gain in a good school, like the orphanage children in the nursery-school programs. Men inducted into the armed forces in the Second World War scored about two years higher in mental age than men in the First World War, and had had about two years more schooling (60). Furthermore, relationships of score to the adequacy of the young men's educational programs were found (5). For instance, in World War I, a correlation of .74 was found between tested ability and extent of schooling, and there was a correlation of .72 between the average score for men from each state and an index of the adequacy of the state's educational program (based on average length of school year, school expenditure per pupil, and so on). A follow-up twenty years later on a group of boys tested at age 14 showed that their scores on certain tests of general ability were roughly proportional to the amount of schooling they had since had (*41*). Those with more schooling tended to have more literate and often professional jobs; that they scored higher on tests involving reading and vocabulary and manipulation of verbal symbols is hardly surprising, and can mean little more than greater literacy. Furthermore, a greater proportion and presumably a greater number of the less able youngsters now go to high school, yet average intelligence test scores in high school seem not to have gone down. Hence it might be inferred that better previous schooling, and perhaps increased information gained from radio, movies, TV, and more travel, have kept the scores up (*26; 64*, page 173). Clearly more analytical evidence is needed.

Interplay of Influences Affecting Growth of Abilities

The preceding pages have attempted to differentiate the effects of this or that factor—such as home or education—on the development of abilities. The longitudinal studies are beginning to indicate how these factors operate—sometimes together, sometimes in conflict—to build up or retard the growth of abilities. Fig. 3.9 shows growth of general ability in three individuals from early childhood to 18, with notations as to special circumstances that apparently affected the ability of these youngsters. These three cases were selected from the others in the study as illustrating the effects of this or that influence in a child's life on his ability as measured. Most youngsters in the study showed no such marked changes in relative ability, or at least none so readily related to special circumstances in their life. That these changes did occur in these three youngsters, apparently in relation to the factors indicated, suggests that such factors may have a real effect upon mental growth. And it may be assumed that in other instances factors not thus clearly identified nevertheless had an effect.

The figure shows Jane dropping quite steadily in ability from an IQ of 133 to 77. She was an only child, born when the mother was 40 and the father 37; the mother's IQ ranged from 64 to 70 and the parents had gone to school only until the age of 14. Beginning in the preschool years Jane became increasingly obese until medical advice was obtained at 14; her weight finally returned to normal by the age of 17. However, it will be noted that this reducing and medi-

cal treatment seemed not to affect her ability. The girl was much overindulged
by the mother. Mediocre constitutional capacity, possibly glandular or nutri-
tional disturbance, overindulgence, and an unstimulating home may all be considered factors in this case.

In early childhood Ruth appeared to have been greatly handicapped by the
critical illness of her mother and brother, with the accompanying emotional and
financial strain, and by pneumonia at 6; but from 10 on "she had many sup-

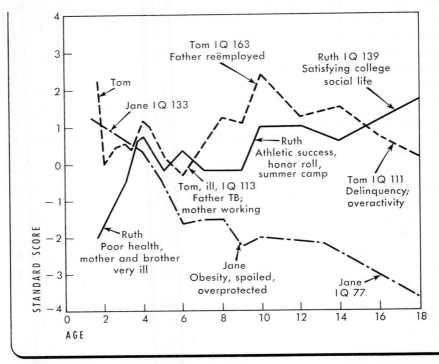

FIG. 3.9. Changes in general ability in three individuals from 2 to 18 years. (Adapted
from Honizik, MacFarlane, and Allen [35].)

ports in her life—music, athletic success, summer camps, the honor roll at
school." At 18 she went away from home to college where she found "her first
completely satisfying social life which resulted in great expansiveness." Ruth's
line shows rises in test ratings coincident with these favored conditions, her IQ
at 18 being 139. Both parents were college graduates.

Tom rated lowest on the Binet at 6 when he had chronic sinus trouble and
asthma and was in bed for twelve weeks; his father was suffering from tuberculosis and it was necessary for the mother to work. The school reported Tom
as being restless, sensitive, and shy at this time. The boy's highest rating was at
10 when the father was reëmployed; the school then reported Tom to be show-

ing "marvelous concentration"—everything seemed to be going well. Tom's drop in IQ to 111 at age 18 was coincident with compulsive delinquency, over-activity, and a preoccupation with emotional difficulties not understood.

The above cases show a variety of factors influencing ability. A careful analytical study of 140 children from age 3 to age 12 has yielded evidence not only that very young children from inadequate environments may show increases in ability, as evidenced by nursery-school experiments, but that older bright children from homes of comparatively good socioeconomic status may also gain in general ability. Case 1 in Fig. 3.10 shows quite consistent gains in IQ (except for an irregularity around age 6) from about 120 at age 3 to near 180 at age 12. Case 6 is somewhat similar. However, case 139 shows an even more consistent drop—from an IQ of almost 140 at age 3 to around 115 at age 12. Case 135 shows a slight drop, then a slight rise, and case 84's IQ continues to be about 90 throughout this age period.

The very extensive case material on these 140 children was carefully analyzed to see whether causes for these trends could be found. Physical growth factors and illness appeared not to be clearly related to changes in IQ. But certain attitudes in the home, and motivations in the young-ster, seemed important. During ages 3 to 6 "the child who is emotionally dependent upon his parents . . . would appear to be establishing a mode of behavior which is not conducive to 'learning to learn.' . . . However, if the child is learning to meet some of his needs through ap-propriate aggressive behavior, competitiveness, or individual problem-solving, it would appear that he is laying a groundwork for the kind of motivation characterized in need for achievement, which may operate as a motive in learning experiences. During the elementary school years it is therefore not surprising to see a high need for achievement being related to an accelerated growth rate. . . . The need for achievement appears to develop in a family situation in which the mother uses generally demo-cratic principles in disciplining the child and, at least in the case of boys, tends to stress independent achievement at an early age" (54, pages 138–139).

What influences seem to affect the development of special abilities? Unfortunately, no systematic data such as the above are available. But a good deal is known about the childhood and youth of individuals of notable special ability in some field. Many were remarkably precocious. Perhaps best known to the average American are instances of early su-periority in some form of athletics. For instance, Bobby Jones was state

golfing champion at 14 and won national championships at 18; Sonja
Henie was figure-skating champion of Norway at 10 and world champion
at 15; Maurine Connolly was woman's singles tennis champion at 16;
Bob Mathias won an Olympic gold medal in track and field events at

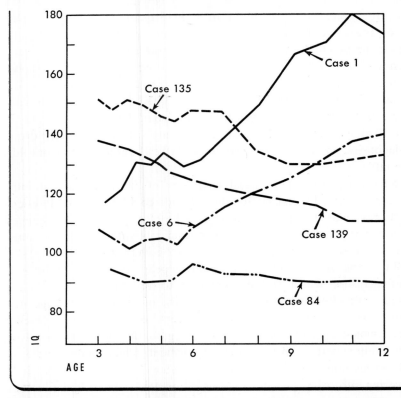

FIG. 3.10. Changes in IQ in four individuals from ages 3 to 12. (Adapted from Sontag,
Baker, and Nelson [54].)
   Careful analysis of the data led to the conclusion that practice effects were not important in the gains shown. Alternate forms of the Binet were used so that each form was
repeated only every other year. "Under the Fels testing program of administering different forms alternately, an identical item was presented an average of only slightly more
than three times to each individual" in the total period of the investigation. It was concluded that "the cumulative effects of serial testing are slight" under these circumstances;
"real changes in relative mental ability do occur in childhood" (54, pp. 43–44, 54).

17. Athletic champions in several fields seem to have had a handicap
which stimulated them to early special efforts and necessitated special
training. For instance, Nancy Merki at 10 was paralyzed because of
polio, but her intensive efforts to recover led to her becoming high-point

scorer in a national swimming meet when she was 13. Many famous musicians were precocious. Mozart played the harpsichord at 3, was composing at 4, and was on an international tour at 6. Handel was composing at 11. Chopin played in public at 8, Liszt at 9, Verdi at 10. Mendelssohn was playing in public and composing at 9, as were Debussy at 11, Dvořák at 12, and Berlioz at 14 (50).

Most of these cases seem to have been products of the following favoring circumstances. (1) There was early encouragement from family and friends. For example, Bobby Jones lived next to a golf course; while still a small boy he was given little clubs and followed his father around the links. Mozart's father was a musician, his older sister was his companion in music, family and friends admired and encouraged the boy. (2) There was early and continuing guidance and instruction aimed at excellence. Nancy Merki had an expert swimming coach. Mozart's musician father taught and guided his son, and managed his career practically from infancy. (3) There was frequent and continuing opportunity to practice and extend the special ability. From the age of 3 Mozart practiced with his older sister; he had an opportunity to play the violin, harpsichord, and organ, and to perform frequently in public. (4) There was great social facilitation because of close association with others in the field. Bobby Jones lived largely in a golfer's world throughout childhood and youth. Mozart's associations were almost wholly with musicians. (5) Finally, there was the stimulation of many and increasingly strong success experiences. Doubtless these individuals had very superior constitutional capacities. Both the athletes and the musicians obviously had superior motor coördination, and the musicians presumably had remarkable sensitivities to sound and rhythm. But it seems quite clear that such favoring influences as the above were also very important.[9]

Might a similar combination of favoring influences foster other abilities powerfully, including the more broadly intellectual? The biographies of many famous people present instances of the importance of early encouragement, special instruction, intensive experience, social facilitation, stimulating success. Extraordinary broad intellectual precocity may thus be fostered; this is illustrated in the extreme by John Stuart Mill. The issue will be discussed again shortly.[10]

[9] That Ellen, the mediocre artist mentioned near the beginning of this chapter, was not a better artist might be explained as due to a lack of sufficiently superior general or special potential capacities, or perhaps to a lack of sufficient association and competition with other and superior artists.

[10] There is some evidence that growing up in a varied and stimulating environment increases the readiness with which such animals as rats solve problems. See D. G. and

THE SCHOOL AND ABILITIES

The preceding discussion has indicated that children differ in the amount, make-up, and rate of development of their abilities, and also that potential abilities may be nurtured to a greater extent than has often been supposed. It will now be argued that a large part of the difficulties teachers have in their work is due to the gross failure of the usual school to adjust to or in fact take any account of the differences in abilities, and that the possibilities of effectively nurturing such abilities are so great that they can provide the most valuable rewards for effective teaching.

Organizational and Administrative Problems

The conventional school admits all children at the chronological age of 6, offers much the same program to all, and tries to promote all the pupils a grade each year so that all will graduate from high school around age 18. Illness or incompetence may prevent a few from being promoted at the end of a school year, and a few may be so handicapped physically or mentally as to need to be put in special classes. But the great mass of youngsters "lock-step" through practically the same program at the same rate.

However, as far as ability and general information and attitude are concerned, some children are "ready" for the first grade before they are six, and others are not ready till later. Numerous experiments (66) have shown that children of 5 or 5½, but who are mentally 6 or older and also superior to their age group in physique and personality, can wisely be admitted to the first grade before age 6. These experiments have shown such youngsters doing good school work and getting along well with other children. A six-year-old who is mentally superior may be started in the second grade, again with good results.

For example, six-year-old Susan was youngest in a family of five children in a highly literate home. Mentally she was over 8; physically she was big for her age, and her personality was such that she easily held her own with the older children in her family and with other youngsters in the neighborhood. Helped by her older sisters, she had begun to read before she was five. Even though she

J. W. Forgays, The nature of the effect of free environmental experience in the rat, *J. Comp. Psychol.*, 1952, *45*:322–328; D. O. Hebb, *The Organization of Behavior*, New York: Wiley, 1949.

started school in the second grade, she found herself somewhat ahead of the average second-grade child; she said that the other children in her class were sometimes "such babies." Quite clearly the second grade was more appropriate than the first for her to start school, for in every respect but chronological age she was 7 or 8 years old. But William, a slight and anxious only child, who has been overprotected and is really only average in ability, should not start in the second grade, even though his ambitious mother wants him to. Slow, clumsy Tom has passed his sixth birthday but is mentally not yet five; he may well remain in kindergarten or at home another year before starting first grade.

Wherever they start, children should not move forward at the same rate, because they develop at different rates. What can be done? The most common procedure has been to hold the dullard back occasionally to repeat a grade, and to skip the bright child a grade or half-grade. Big, alert, lively Bert, a disturber of the peace in the third grade, was promoted at the end of the year not to the fourth but to the fifth grade; here he found the work more challenging and the boys on the playground nearer his own size. But Jimmy did so poorly in the first grade that the teacher decided not to promote him but to have him repeat the work. This did not work out very well, for Jimmy felt the stigma of failure, applied himself only half-heartedly, and was little better at the end of his second year in the first grade. Special individualized help in reading or a "slow section" in the second grade might have been better for him.

Occasional double-promotion or holding back a pupil is a clumsy way of adjusting to differences in abilities. A better method in the primary grades is what is sometimes known as a "primary pool"; children of the first, second, and third grades are put together in one room, and advanced to the fourth grade whenever they are ready—some at the end of the second year, some the third, and some the fourth. A similar pool may be formed for Grades 4 to 6. Or a "fast" section may do the work of the first six grades in five years, and a slow section take seven. Special sections in junior or senior high school may do three years' work in two. Repeated experiments have shown that high-school students who thus progress rapidly not only do as well thereafter in school work, but also have as satisfactory status with their classmates, as other youngsters with the same ability and school record who took the regular three years of class work (49).

Another organizational device is a special enrichment class. Bright children are put in a special room where, instead of progressing extra rapidly, they take additional work—read more widely, undertake special projects, perhaps study a foreign language. Clearly this procedure does not allow for the more rapid intellectual development of the bright, but it does recognize their wider-reaching needs (*24*).

A method increasingly used at entrance to college, but desirable earlier, is credit by examination. For instance, students entering a college or university may be given an extensive set of tests in English or mathematics or chemistry, those who score very high being given credit for the first college course in that subject. Numerous investigations have shown that students thus credited do better in the next course in the subject than the students who took the regular beginning course. This method should be used also in secondary schools (*49*).

More and more high schools are offering advanced courses which lead to "advanced placement" in college if the student passes an examination in the subject. Experimentation here has shown that able high-school students can "skip" the senior or even the junior year of high school and still do outstandingly well in college (*19*).

Secondary schools should provide flexibility in grouping and in advancing in various subjects. A boy with a strong interest in science as a hobby might well enter a science class ahead of his classmates—perhaps on the basis of an examination or test showing his readiness for the work. A youngster whose family is planning a summer abroad may want to begin studying a foreign language before the trip, and on his return he may be ready for an advanced language class, though neither the beginning nor the advanced course is called for at these points in the regular schedule. Such subject flexibility is highly desirable, not only with reference to interest in a particular field, but also as a means of breaking up the usual association of grade and age. It seems better on almost all grounds for a pupil to think of himself as in high school rather than more precisely in the tenth grade.

It is obvious that different programs will be desirable for different children. Thus youngsters greatly handicapped in vision need the special equipment and methods available in a sight-saving class. Similarly, for a high-school boy who is mechanically apt but is slow and somewhat uncomprehending in a "college preparatory" curriculum, there should be available an industrial arts or other program suitable to his interests and capacities. All these various programs should have good status among students and faculty, and in the community itself. An industrial arts program may well have the prestige of a pre-engineering curriculum, as it may be for some pupils. An able student who is specially interested in science may go into an advanced class (*10*), and this in turn may lead to advanced standing in college.

May social maladjustments result from these various procedures that tend to put some bright children in mostly older groups, and some older children with younger classmates? Not if attention is given to physical and social maturity as well as to mental maturity. And if such flexibility becomes general and grade labels are minimized, the mingling of children of different ages in different groups for different purposes may be taken for granted. Now children of various ages are on an athletic team or in a band or orchestra, and a different combination is found on the neighborhood playground. Why not group and regroup similarly for English or chemistry or history, for differences in this or that ability or in general academic readiness?

Instructional Methods

The preceding paragraphs have dealt with problems of curriculum and guidance. But once pupils are in a class, how can the teacher's management of it, and her instructional procedures, best adjust to and foster their abilities? In any one class there are almost certain to be great individual differences in general and special abilities. A fifth-grade class, for example, may include pupils ranging in mental age from 8 to 14. Some of these children will need special help, but some of the bright youngsters will be bored by the class work. Moreover, such situations are often greatly complicated by socioeconomic differences.

Fourteen-year-old Sam (IQ 78) is one of a large family; the father is a factory worker and the family lives in a ramshackle house on the edge of town. Sam is unkempt, often plays truant, reads very slowly, wants to leave school and get a job as soon as possible. Raymond (IQ 128), also 14, is the only son of a lawyer; he finds school too easy and plans to enter his father's profession. Sam needs special help in reading (probably best provided in a small adjustment class), tactful advice about his appearance, and a prevocational program. Raymond needs a challenge, and experiences that will develop social responsibility. If two such boys are in a secondary-school English class, the teacher has an almost impossible problem.

Can a teacher "individualize" her program to meet diverse pupil needs to some degree? If she can get to know her pupils, she can draw each one out in terms of his experiences and interests and in proportion to his abilities. The bright students may help her in various ways, as in preparing and caring for certain class materials. They may follow up special interests in the school or public library. Those interested in science may be permitted to use certain laboratories after school or in a free period, if someone is available to help them (*10*).

Special arrangements extending beyond the classroom are especially valuable. Half-time work may meet many needs in an industrial or trade school. Junior Achievement groups give high-school youngsters an opportunity to work together in the evening on some business enterprise under the supervision of local businessmen; thus both groups get acquainted with each other, and the students may have community recognition of their undertaking in the local paper. Science fairs and Junior Academy programs provide similar opportunities in the sciences. The programs of the Future Farmers of America are notable for country youth. All these are coöperative programs, with tangible accomplishment and community recognition as their outcomes. The teacher who can relate her work to such projects will find her work much stimulated and better adjusted to different pupil abilities. A few pages earlier the point was made that very superior abilities of famous people in various fields seemed to have been especially nurtured by situations of these types, which gave special opportunity and encouragement and led to social facilitation and recognition. Increasingly, schools are becoming concerned about opportunities for the able. They may well hope, perhaps by such programs, to discover and develop persons of outstanding accomplishment. More broadly they may hope also that, partly as a result of Russian competition in science, accomplishment in school may have more status both in the community and among the pupils themselves, and that there may be a favoring social climate and an "achievement motive" which will increase functioning intelligence. But all this leads into problems of guidance, instruction, and adult attitudes which are discussed in later chapters.

SUMMARY

Concepts regarding abilities, and also our thinking concerning the best methods of dealing with children of various abilities, are now in process of revision.

The general notion of abilities in everyday life is fairly well understood. An individual's abilities are shown by the extent to which he can deal effectively with various types of situations in his daily life. Four general factors affecting abilities may be distinguished. A person is competent in dealing with a situation in proportion as he is informed about it, uses effective methods, is interested and not emotionally distracted, and has a constitutional aptitude for handling it. The last factor is obviously basic. Similar factors are involved in special abilities or disabilities. Thus the person with great artistic abilities usually has an acquaintance with art, artistic "know-how," great interest and confidence in the field, and also innate capacity possibly of a special nature.

Appraisal of a pupil's abilities may be made by a teacher on the basis of her total knowledge of him. However, much more broadly based, accurate, and useful information can be obtained with tests of general and special abilities. Certain of these, such as the Binet and the Wechsler, are given to one child at a time; the scores they yield are especially trustworthy, in view of the possibility of concurrent observation of each child. Group tests of general ability and also of special or primary abilities are also available; they are easy to use and have great comparative value. However, the results must always be judged in terms of the suitability of the test for the pupil and the desired purpose. Broad appraisals involving the use of various methods and taking cognizance of different types of ability are desirable.

Abilities grow; apparently they also change somewhat from one stage of development to another, somewhat as the physique does. Growth tends to be rapid during the growth years but to level off in the late teens or early twenties. Bright youngsters tend to increase in ability more rapidly than average children and to continue this growth longer, whereas dull children grow slowly and probably stop growing somewhat earlier.

People vary greatly in ability—from the idiot to the genius. In general, people of better socioeconomic status show better ability. Ability appears to run in families; but many able youngsters are found in families of lower socioeconomic status, and dull children in prosperous families.

In general, ability appears to be relatively unaffected by health, but an early debilitating illness may hamper mental growth, as may also a grossly inadequate home or school. That much can be done, especially for constitutionally superior youngsters, to nurture both general and special abilities is increasingly being realized.

The traditional school admits all children at the chronological age of 6, and puts them through much the same program until they graduate from high school at 18. However, almost all the evidence indicates that children are ready for school at different chronological ages, develop at different rates mentally as well as physically, and have different interests and aggregates of abilities. Flexibility in progress, and programs aimed at different types of interests and abilities, are needed. More and more it is becoming evident that when schools and communities are vitally interested in their children, able teachers can do much to nurture the potentials of these children.

BIBLIOGRAPHY

1. Abbott, Allan, and Trabue, M. R., A measure of ability to judge poetry, *Teach. Coll. Rec.,* 1921, *22*:101–126.
2. Anastasi, Anne, *Psychological Testing,* New York: Macmillan, 1954.
3. Anastasi, Anne, and Foley, J. P., *Differential Psychology,* New York: Macmillan, rev. ed., 1949.
4. Asher, E. J., The inadequacy of current intelligence tests for testing Kentucky mountain children, *Ped. Sem. and J. Genet. Psychol.,* 1935, *46*:480–486.
5. Bagley, W. C., Do good schools pay? *J. Nat. Educ. Assn.,* 1923, *12*:211–216.
6. Baldwin, A. L., *Behavior and Development in Childhood,* New York: Dryden, 1955.
7. Bayley, Nancy, Consistency and variability in the growth of intelligence from birth to 18 years, *Ped. Sem. and J. Genet. Psychol.,* 1949, *75*:165–196.
8. Bayley, Nancy, On the growth of intelligence, *Amer. Psychol.,* 1955, *10*:805–818.
9. Bayley, Nancy, A new look at the curve of intelligence, *Proc. 1956 Invitational Conf. Testing Problems,* Princeton, pp. 11–25.
10. Brandwein, P. F., *The Gifted Student as Future Scientist,* New York: Harcourt, Brace, 1955.
11. Brodbeck, A. J., and Irwin, O. C., The speech behavior of infants without families, *Child Devel.,* 1946, *17*:145–156.
12. Burt, Cyril, *The Backward Child,* New York: Appleton-Century-Crofts, rev. ed., 1950.
13. Burtt, H. E., An experimental study of early childhood memory: final report, *Ped. Sem. and J. Genet. Psychol.,* 1941, *58*:435–439.
14. Carmichael, L. (ed.), *Manual of Child Psychology,* New York: Wiley, rev. ed., 1954.
15. Cassidy, Viola M., and Phelps, H. R., *Post-School Adjustment of Slow-learning Children,* Ohio State University, Bureau of Special and Adult Education, 1955.
16. Charles, Don C., Ability and accomplishment of persons earlier judged to be mentally defective, *Genet. Psychol. Monog.,* 1953, *47*:3–71.
17. Combs, A. W., Intelligence from a perceptual point of view, *J. Abnorm. Soc. Psychol.,* 1952, *47*:662–673.
18. Conklin, A. M., Failures of highly intelligent pupils: a study of their behavior by means of a control group, *Teach. Coll. Contr. Educ.* No. 792, 1940.
19. Coombs, P. H., *They Went to College Early,* New York: Fund for the Advancement of Education, 1957.

20. Cornell, Ethel L., and Armstrong, C. M., Forms of mental growth patterns revealed by reanalysis of the Harvard growth data, *Child Devel.*, 1955, *26*: 169–204.

21. Cronbach, Lee J., *Essentials of Psychological Testing,* New York: Harper, 1949.

22. Cruickshank, William (ed.), *Psychology of Exceptional Children and Youth,* New York: Prentice-Hall, 1955.

23. Dearborn, W. F., and Rothney, J. W. M., *Predicting the Child's Development,* Cambridge: Sci-Art Publishers, 1941.

24. DeHaan, R. F., and Havighurst, R. J., *Educating Gifted Children,* Chicago: Univ. of Chicago Press, 1957.

25. Eells, K. W., *Intelligence and Cultural Differences,* Chicago: Univ. of Chicago Press, 1951.

26. Finch, F. H., Enrollment increases and changes in the mental level of the high school population, *Appl. Psychol. Monog.*, 1946, *10*:1–75.

27. Freeman, F. N., Holzinger, K. U., and Mitchell, B. C., The influence of environment on the intelligence, school achievement and conduct of foster children, *27th Yearb. Nat. Socy. Stud. Educ.*, 1928, Part 1, pp. 103–217.

28. Freeman, F. S., *Theory and Practice of Psychological Testing,* New York: Holt, 1950.

29. Gadson, E. J., Glutamic acid and mental deficiency—a review, *Amer. J. Ment. Def.*, 1951, *55*:521–528.

30. Garrett, H. E., A developmental theory of intelligence, *Amer. Psychol.*, *1*:372–378, 1946.

31. Greene, Edward B., *Measurement of Human Behavior,* New York: Odyssey, rev. ed., 1952.

32. Heck, A. O., *The Education of Exceptional Children,* New York: McGraw-Hill, 1953.

33. Hildreth, Gertrude, Three gifted children: a developmental study, *Ped. Sem. and J. Genet. Psychol.*, 1954, *85*:239–262.

34. Hollingshead, A. B., *Elmtown's Youth,* New York: Wiley, 1949.

35. Honizik, M. P., Macfarlane, J. W., and Allen, L., The stability of mental test performance between 2 and 18 years, *J. Exp. Educ.*, 1948, *17*:309–324.

36. Klineberg, Otto, *Race Differences,* New York: Harper, 1935.

37. Lamson, E. E., To what extent are I.Q.'s increased by children who participate in a rich vital school curriculum? *J. Educ. Psychol.*, 1938, *29*:67–70.

38. Lewinski, R. J., Vocabulary and mental measurement, *Ped. Sem. and J. Genet. Psychol.*, 1948, *72*:247–281.

39. Lewis, Claudia, *Children of the Cumberland,* New York: Columbia Univ. Press, 1946.

40. Loevinger, J., On the proportional contribution of differences in nature and nurture to differences in intelligence, *Psychol. Bull.*, 1943, *40*:725–756.

41. Lorge, I., Schooling makes a difference, *Teach. Coll. Rec.*, 1945, *46*:483–492.

42. McCandless, B., Environment and intelligence, *Amer. J. Ment. Def.*, 1952, *56*:674–691.

43. McGraw, M. B., *Growth: A Study of Jimmy and Johnny,* New York, Appleton-Century-Crofts, 1935.

44. McGraw, M. B., Later development of children especially trained during infancy; Johnny and Jimmy at school age, *Child Devel.*, 1939, *10*:1–19.

45. Musselman, J. W., Factors associated with the achievements of high school pupils of superior intelligence, *J. Exp. Educ.*, 1942, *11*:53–58.

46. Myklebust, Helmer R., and Burchard, E. M. L., A study of the effects of congenital and adventitious deafness on the intelligence, personality, and social maturity of school children, *J. Educ. Psychol.*, 1945, *25*:321–343.

47. National Society for the Study of Education, *Nature and Nurture,* 39th Yearbook, 1940, Part 1, Part 2.

48. Newman, H. H., *Multiple Human Births,* New York: Doubleday, 1940.

49. Pressey, S. L., *Educational Acceleration: Appraisals and Basic Problems,* Columbus: Ohio State Univ. Press, 1949.

50. Pressey, S. L., Concerning the nature and nurture of genius, *Sci. Mont.*, 1955, *81*:123–129.

51. Schlesser, G. E., Gains in scholastic aptitude under highly motivated conditions, *J. Educ. Psychol.*, 1950, *41*:237–242.

52. Skeels, H. M., and Fillmore, E. A., The mental development of children from underprivileged homes, *Ped. Sem. and J. Genet. Psychol.*, 1937, *50*:427–439.

53. Smith, M., University student intelligence and occupation of fathers, *Amer. Soc. Rev.*, December, 1942, 704–711.

54. Sontag, L. W., Baker, C. T., and Nelson, Virginia L., Mental growth and personality development: a longitudinal study, *Monog. Soc. Res. Child Devel.*, 1958, *23*:1–143.

55. Super, Donald E., *Appraising Vocational Fitness,* New York: Harper, 1949.

56. Terman, L. M., and Merrill, M. A., *Measuring Intelligence,* Boston: Houghton Mifflin, 1937.

57. Terman, L. M., and Oden, M. H., *The Gifted Child Grows Up,* Stanford: Stanford Univ. Press, 1947.

58. Thompson, N. Z., Education of the gifted in various countries, *J. Except. Child,* 1949, *15*:193–208, 239–254.

59. Thomson, G. H., *The Trend of Scottish Intelligence,* London: Univ. of London Press, 1949.

60. Tuddenham, R. D., Soldier intelligence in World Wars I and II, *Amer. Psychol.*, 1948, *3*:54–56.

61. Wechsler, D., Cognitive, conative and non-intellective intelligence, *Amer. Psychol.*, 1950, *5*:78–83.

62. Wheeler, L. R., A comparative study of the intelligence of East Tennessee mountain children, *J. Educ. Psychol.*, 1942, *33*:321–334.

63. Witty, P. (ed.), *The Gifted Child,* Boston: Heath, 1951.

64. Wolfle, D., *America's Resources of Specialized Talent,* New York: Harper, 1954.
65. Wood, Louise, and Kumin, Edythe, A new standardization of the Ferguson Form Boards, *J. Genet. Psychol.,* 1939, *54*:265–284.
66. Worcester, D. A., *The Education of Children of Above-Average Mentality,* Lincoln: Univ. of Nebraska Press, 1956.

Chapter **4**

Interests: Their Nature and Nurture

THE MATERIAL IN CHAPTER 2 SHOWED THAT THE school years are a time of extraordinary growth; from 6 to 18 the average youngster triples his weight, increases similarly in strength, is physiologically made over in his bodily proportions and tissues. Such a dynamically expanding and changing organism would be expected to have strong and changing wants and desires. The preceding two chapters stressed the extent and variety of individual differences between youngsters of a given age in physique and abilities, and also in rate of growth. Analogous differences might be expected in the variety of interests and the time at which they appear. Various conditions and circumstances of life were found to have important relationships with abilities and physique and perhaps to affect them; presumably this might be even more true of interests.

A teacher's success often depends primarily on the extent to which she can make what her pupils are expected to do in school appeal to their interests which are changing, diverse, and variously influenced. The present chapter is concerned with the basic and subtle problem of how interests grow and change and vary, and how they may be related to the school's program. Furthermore, it will maintain that most schools have not recognized their potentialities in the development of interests, and that conceivably new ways of meeting many of these problems may be found.

To discover their interests, children may be asked what they like to do. They may be watched to see how they spend their free time. Data may be gathered on what they read or watch on television. Apparatus is available that measures their pulse beat and can thus determine which movies stir them most. Children may be asked about their vocational ambitions.

This chapter will present various material and then attempt to draw conclusions of possible use in teaching.

LEISURE ACTIVITIES

If play is defined as what a person does because he likes to, surveys of play may be expected to indicate interests. On the basis of observations of babies and little children, observation or oral questioning of primary children, and written statements or the checking of lists of games and amusements by pupils from the third grade on, important factors in play have been determined.

Age and Play

Play evidently changes with age. Babies may play with their hands and feet (seriously contemplating them) at 4 months and around 6 months begin to whack the table with spoon or rattle; at about 1 year of age, they may begin to play some with blocks. By 3, a nursery youngster may dab paint on large sheets of paper, hammer at a nail in a piece of board, climb in a jungle gym, and earnestly ride nowhere around and around on a tricycle. But these are ages and activities prefatory to the concern of most schools—the play interests of elementary- and secondary-school youngsters.

Numerous observations and check lists have indicated the general trend, at least for American school children. Around 5 years, boys play with a ball or with blocks or a wagon, or they play house; girls may play with dolls, draw, or play house or school. At 10 years, boys may ride a bicycle, play baseball or basketball, or just play catch; girls of this age may roller-skate, play with dolls, play school. By 15, boys play football or baseball or basketball, and girls show an interest in social dancing, going to parties and picnics, watching sports events. At 20, dates and watching and partaking in sports are important for boys; and dates, dancing, and other social affairs for girls (28).

Major trends in interests are brought out well in Fig. 4.1. Students from the sixth grade through college were asked to go over a list of 90 amusements and recreations, checking those in which they were interested and double-checking those that interested them a great deal. The curves show total number of checks per 100 students, thus combining in one "score" the number of individuals interested and the extent of their interest. The active individual amusements of bicycling and roller-skating are popular

in the sixth grade but thereafter decrease in popularity. Dancing and social affairs are of relatively little interest to sixth-grade children, but have
increasing appeal in adolescence and young adulthood. And these last interests appeal to girls earlier and more strongly, as might be expected because girls mature earlier and sex-social relations and marriage are important in their lives.

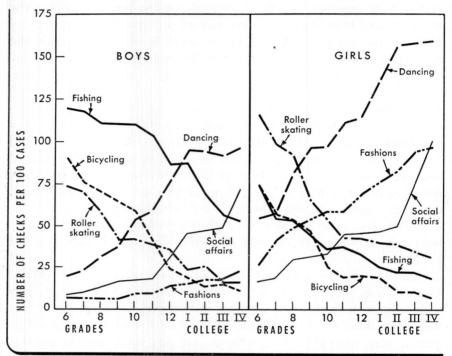

FIG. 4.1. Changes in certain interests with age as shown by number of checks for each
interest per 100 students at each grade from the sixth through college. The students were
directed to check items in which they were interested, and to double-check those in which
they were very much interested. (From unpublished data, 4187 cases, obtained with the
Pressey Interest-Attitude Tests.)

When the various data on play during the first twenty years are
viewed as a whole, two features are evident. (1) In the period of rapid
physical growth there is an increase in the vigor and complexity of play—
from the haphazard running about and shouting of the very small boy to
the team games of adolescence. (2) The social characteristics of play
change with age. Thus a very young child may play happily in a sandpile
by himself, a 10-year-old plays mostly with others of his own sex, a 16-

year-old wants amusements involving association with the other sex. As this last interest becomes of major importance and growth slows down, very vigorous recreation has less appeal; sports interests are more those of a spectator and less those of a participant. A third feature must also be mentioned. With increasing age, recreation becomes more and more influenced by the group, and conventionalized. Children 8 or 9 years old engage in a great variety of relatively simple activities. But gradually some games and amusements are dropped and others centered upon, until in the last years in high school the average youngster's leisure activities are largely restricted to a relatively few generally popular and socially almost necessary forms of recreation. These activities also become conventional topics of conversation and part of the American way of life. Today professional baseball and intercollegiate football games, and the fortunes of local high-school athletic teams, are almost universal topics of talk in the typical American community.

Thus far the discussion has been concerned primarily with the more active types of recreation—with what might broadly be called play. But all use of leisure should be included for an adequate consideration of interests. The information in Table 4.1 is of value here. Children in Grades 3 to 11 in Des Moines schools were asked what they usually did for fun both when they stayed home evenings and when they went out. The major features of the results are summarized in the table. The most frequently mentioned home leisure interest was listening to the radio (Des Moines did not have television at the time of the survey). The next most frequently mentioned was reading. The most mentioned interest away from home was movies. These three mass media of passive entertainment, and especially the first two, are outstanding—and their mention increases with age. Informal play at home decreased rapidly with age but playing games increased a little. Few children had hobbies.

By the eleventh grade, sports came next after movies as a leisure interest outside the home; that much of this was presumably watching sports is suggested by the 69 percent for the girls. Dancing was more frequently mentioned as the youngsters grew older. Visiting and just fooling around were common in the third grade but less common by the eleventh. As shown in the last line, the average third-grader was away from home more than one evening a week, the average eleventh-grader over three. Indeed, the complete report shows that by the fifth grade, 2 percent of the boys and 1 percent of the girls reported being out every night in the week, but 10 percent of the boys and 9 percent of the girls weren't out

TABLE 4.1. Evening Leisure-Time Activities of Boys and Girls[1]

	Boys—Grade						Girls—Grade				
3	5	7	9	11		3	5	7	9	11
					At home						
32	46	57	73	77	Radio	38	43	60	79	77
22	18	24	27	34	Reading	32	27	31	44	44
22	29	26	32	32	Playing cards and other games	23	29	28	35	33
51	14	11	2	2	Playing with friends and family	59	19	8	4	10
26	8	7	11	9	Hobbies	14	8	6	6	11
					Away from home						
26	35	51	72	67	Movies	25	48	56	77	83
38	21	16	26	26	Visiting friends and relatives	48	39	43	32	35
2	24	21	39	46	Sports	4	10	20	46	69
49	11	11	7	15	Riding around, fooling around	46	6	6	4	4
0	0	2	7	20	Dancing	4	4	6	22	27
0	0	7	9	8	Church activities	0	6	13	16	11
9	8	11	7	2	Scouting, YMCA, etc.	4	3	1	0	3
1.4	2.0	2.4	2.9	3.5	Average evenings away	1.7	2.1	2.1	2.6	3.2

Data obtained by a questionnaire. Activities ranked in average order of preference, all grades and both sexes combined. Figures show percentages mentioning each type of activity. Since more than one type of activity could be indicated, the percentages total more than 100. Only activities with an average over 3 were included.

at all. What are the most outstanding findings? The great importance of the mass media and passive recreation, increasing escape from the home, and wide individual differences.

Factors Influencing Leisure Activities

As already indicated, the stage of physical and intellectual development is a basic determiner of leisure activities. Obviously a boy at age 4 will have neither ability nor interest in football or chess but at 16 he may. At a given chronological age, the developmentally older youngsters are likely to be more mature in their interests. Bright youngsters are likely to be more interested in reading, and in consequence they are somewhat less active in social and very vigorous games; but they do not tend to be solitary or to have fewer interests (57). A special aptitude, as in music or athletics, usually causes a youngster to find satisfaction in related leisure activities. A handicap, such as a visual defect that makes a boy inept in sports, tends to make him turn to activities he can do better.

[1] Adapted from Lyness (31). Over 1300 cases.

As already mentioned, leisure activities are greatly influenced by conventions and cultural expectations. The writers are inclined to believe that the competitive character of much of our play should be regarded as a convention. After all, many recreational activities, such as fishing, canoeing, hiking, dancing, and singing, are not competitive. The tendency to identify recreation with competitive games and sports may be partly a product of our highly individualistic and competitive mode of life. However, it is probably more the result of the newspaper publicity given sports, the advertising by sporting goods manufacturers and bridge system authors, and the exploitation of sports by schools. The present emphasis on the competitive in recreation seems to be relatively recent[2] and, on the whole, unfortunate.

Play and leisure interests differ in various ways and for various reasons in country, small town, and city. For instance, in "Midwest," a little town with a population of 707, of whom 119 were children under 12 years of age, the smallness of the groups led to a much wider range of age contacts—far less "age segregation"—than would usually be found in a larger community. Thus in the "old settler's amateur program, contestants from four years to sixty-five appeared on the same stage." In one instance "a satisfactory ball game with nine boys ranging from seven to sixteen years of age was arranged by the fourteen-year-old and the sixteen-year-old 'standing' the seven younger boys with one 'out' per inning for the older boys and six for the younger. A good game ensued" (2, page 115). Because the town was so small, the youngsters there came in contact with a great variety of the goings-on, and in that respect their range of possible leisure interests and activities was great. But obviously, many diversions possible in a city were lacking. The facilities available in a given locality may markedly affect various characteristics of play. Thus a sandpile or a seesaw tends to bring young children together in more sociable play than a doll or picture book. Similarly leisure time is spent differently in various parts of the country; leisure activities will be different in the North, where there are winter sports, than in the South.

Social class influences leisure activities and interests in a variety of ways, as is shown succinctly in Table 4.2. Many upperclass girls in Elmtown bowled, but none in the lower class; bowling was a bit expensive, and of interest to upper- and middle-class adults. In contrast, many of the lower-class girls roller-skated; for a small fee they could enjoy a long

[2] One of the writers has some copies of *Our Young Folks,* a magazine for young people published in 1867, and also some diaries of that period. The absence of any mention of formalized sport or competitive amusements is striking. A charming story by Harriet Beecher Stowe about an adolescent girl who goes to the Academy describes bobsled rides, and a candy pull from which the young people did not return home "till almost nine o'clock." But a competitive game is never once mentioned.

session at a rink and meet town boys there. This fact in large part made
the rink a place where the upper-class girls rarely went, for the town boys
had a bad reputation and disorder at the rink was not unusual. Somewhat
the same situation held for the boys. Three-fourths of the lower-class boys
trapped, a diversion looked down upon by upper-class youngsters as
country and kid stuff. This amusement was also completely sex-weighted;

TABLE 4.2. Social Class Differences in Elmtown's Adolescent Recreational
Activities[3]

Social Class Group	Percentage of Girls Who		Percentage of Boys Who		
	Bowled	Skated	Bowled	Skated	Trapped
I and II (Upper)	64	14	52	9	0
III (Middle)	30	38	23	18	5
IV (Laborer)	20	48	17	23	20
V (Lower)	0	69	0	50	75

no girls went trapping (21). Differences in physique and vigor, but particularly differences in conventions, determined sex differences in leisure
interests.

INTEREST IN THE MASS MEDIA

The preceding discussion dealt primarily with active interests, but included figures indicative of the great appeal of radio and movies. These
mass media, and also reading and television, will now be further considered.

Reading

Table 4.1 listed reading as second to radio among home leisure interests of Des Moines school children. This same survey gathered data on
the type of books read; Table 4.3 summarizes these findings. Fifth-grade
boys and girls choose Westerns most often, for these ten-year-olds want
their reading lively and light. Sex differences are evident by the eleventh
grade, or around 16 years of age. The boys put sports first and adventure
second, the girls humor and comedy first and love and romance second;
the latter is hardly mentioned by the boys. For both sexes, Westerns and
mystery stories decrease in appeal with age. Neither for boys nor for girls,
at any age, was there much interest in biography, science and invention,

[3] Adapted from Hollingshead (21). Some 735 cases.

TABLE 4.3. Favorite Types of Books for Boys and Girls in Grades 5 to 11[4]

Boys—Grade					Girls—Grade			
5	7	9	11		5	7	9	11
13	15	19	18	Adventure	15	16	15	16
13	12	12	13	Humor and comedy	15	20	21	21
13	17	19	22	Sports	7	6	9	7
22	15	8	5	Westerns	17	8	4	2
10	10	9	8	Mystery: detective	10	14	13	6
1	1	2	1	Love and romance	9	14	16	18
11	12	8	11	War	1	1	1	2
6	4	5	6	History and historical fiction	1	2	4	9
4	6	8	7	Science and invention	3	3	2	2
3	1	1	2	Art or music	9	3	2	3
2	2	1	0	World of make-believe	6	5	3	2
0	1	1	2	Religious	2	3	4	3
1	1	2	1	Biography	3	1	2	4

Ranked in average order of preference, all grades and both sexes combined. Figures are percentages of weighted 1st, 2nd, 3rd, and 4th choices, as determined by questionnaires in a survey of school children in Des Moines, Iowa.

art or music, or history. Action fiction for the boys, romance and comedy for the girls—this seems to be about all the substantial reading interest developed by the eleventh grade.

However, not books but newspapers are the most universal form of reading matter for these same Iowa children. According to Table 4.4, the comics and sports are by far the most popular. With increasing age the children glance less at radio and movie items, read fewer continued stories, read more news items. But there is negligible interest, in any grade, in editorials or public affairs. In short, the book and newspaper reading of these Iowa children (and they seem largely typical of youngsters all over the country) shows the sex and age differences we would expect, the major preferences—and a universal consistent lack of interest in what might be considered the most worth-while topics.

As is well known, comic "books" are very popular among children. Surveys (66) indicate that children in Grades 4 to 6 habitually read about a dozen comic books, ninth-graders about 6, high-school seniors about 3. An extensive inquiry found that 93 percent of children aged 6 to 11 reported they regularly read comic books; this was true of 84 percent of youngsters 12 to 17—also of 35 percent of individuals 18 to 30 and 14 percent of adults 31 and over! Such material probably helps poor

[4] Adapted from Lyness (31). Over 1400 cases.

readers, for typically it contains an appreciable amount of reading with a vocabulary at the upper elementary or junior-high level. Moreover, pro-tests have largely eliminated undesirable topics, the comics now being given over to sports, adventure, and similar popular themes. But the pic-tures are usually poor, there is a complete lack of style, the topics are of little worth, and most important of all, better reading is probably crowded out.

Magazine reading follows the general trends already indicated—the younger set liking Westerns, the older girls turning to romantic fiction and

TABLE 4.4.   Favorite Newspaper Features of Boys and Girls in Grades 5 to 11[5]

Boys—Grade					Girls—Grade			
5	7	9	11		5	7	9	11
34	30	25	25	Comics	34	35	27	23
23	26	28	31	Sports	10	11	17	20
5	10	13	15	News	8	6	11	11
11	10	8	4	Movie or radio news	12	13	9	6
9	7	8	8	Pictures	12	10	8	6
6	7	8	6	Headlines	8	6	7	6
0	0	0	0	Society and women's features	2	3	6	12
5	3	1	1	Continued stories	5	4	1	0
1	0	1	1	Love and personal problems	3	5	6	5
1	1	2	3	Public affairs	1	1	2	3
1	1	1	1	Gossip columns	1	2	3	3
2	2	1	2	Advertisements	1	2	1	1
1	1	2	2	Editorials	1	1	1	2

Ranked in average order of preference, all grades and both sexes combined. Figures are percentages of weighted 1st, 2nd, 3rd, and 4th choices as determined by question-naires in a survey of school children in Des Moines, Iowa.

women's magazines, the older boys to science and science fiction, and news. As will be seen shortly, magazines seem to have suffered more than any other type of reading matter from competition with TV.

The above paragraphs indicate that our young people (and probably our adults also) read primarily material which is mediocre if not cheap. But that discussion dealt with averages. A survey in a large city showed that people in a good section read over twice as many magazines and books, and of far better quality, than the people in a relatively poor area. Gifted children read two or three times as much as the average youngster, especially informative material. A youngster with a hobby may read avidly along that line. Reading a biography of Pasteur led one boy to choose a scientific major in college and to go on to a professional career.

[5] Adapted from *ibid.*

What is read may not only support or stimulate an interest; it may indicate a frustrated desire. Success stories may bring brief specious thrills to commonplace underprivileged youngsters who in reality can anticipate only a drab future. A puny boy may obtain vicarious thrills and prestige feelings from a story about a football hero. The homely girl may find romantic satisfaction in reading "the pulps."

Moving Pictures

Certainly the movies are a major interest; attendance in childhood and youth is almost universal. What types of movies are preferred? As with reading, the chief interest in middle and later childhood is in active, swashbuckling tales. These youngsters also like comedy. The loss of interest in Westerns from grade to high school on the part of both boys and girls, and the girls' increased interest in romance, are the most marked changes with age. A lesser interest in adventure and a greater interest in romance are the most marked characteristics of girls as compared with boys.

The sequence is from the melodrama (in which the characters are readily classifiable as either good or bad, the plot is stereotyped, conversation unimportant, and action everything) to the romantic story that usually unfolds against a background of wealth (with characters and plot nearly as stereotyped as in melodramas, and conversation concerned mainly with lovemaking) to the adult story involving conversation and characterization. In childhood boys prefer actors, and girls actresses. In adolescence the girls shift their devotion to the current "great lover" of the screen, and the boys show a less striking interest in women stars. Interest in the movies, as in reading and daydreaming, brings vicarious desired experiences. By identifying themselves with the hero or heroine the audience tends to feel the satisfaction of being such a splendid person, having such exciting experiences, and receiving attention from such delightful individuals as the identified-with character on the screen.

An early analysis of 142 pictures showed 741 scenes of kissing and caressing, 522 involving the treatment of children by parents, 313 involving employees and subordinates. In scenes of the last two types, children, employees, "inferior" races, and persons of "inferior" social standing tended to be treated better in the movies than in the real world. In the movies girls are more aggressive in lovemaking than is generally approved in real life. If a major appeal of moving pictures is the fact that they provide vicarious satisfaction of desires not adequately met in real life, here is evidence as to what those unsatisfied desires are: the hunger of children and humble folk for status, sex hunger, and the hunger for activity, variety, excitement, and letting oneself go (11).

Now as to some research concerning the effects of movies on children. Records of pulse and breathing were obtained from certain children while they watched various types of movies. Melodramatic scenes were found to excite 9-year-old children strongly, but older persons sensed the unreality of these episodes and were little affected. Erotic scenes stirred a few children as early as 9 years, had the greatest effect (in heightened and irregular pulse and breathing) around 16 to 18, and stimulated older persons less, probably because of "adult discount" (12). A device under children's beds which recorded every movement showed that youngsters frequently slept more restlessly after seeing a moving picture—they were as restless as two cups of coffee made them (47).

Movies thus have demonstrable effects on a child's physical being. Other effects are also important. Movies affect play even more than reading does. The roles of hero and heroine are widely imitated in games. In most cases the victorious character assumed by the child in the play situation is a "good" character and the criminal is vanquished. Children seem largely to imitate situations in the movies that fit in with interests that are already established to some extent; the imitation does not include any or every scene but is highly selective in character.

The lively 10-year-old boy already fond of frontier stories starts a cowboy and Indian game that imitates an episode in a Western film—his father did much the same thing after reading a dime novel. A boy already headed toward a delinquent career may get further stimulus toward crime from a movie, but the average youngster is hardly affected in this way. A young burglar told how "when we came out of the show a couple of the boys suggested that we try to rob a store, the way we had seen in the picture. . . . We bought a crowbar and screw driver and went to a clothing store and sprung the lock" (5, pages 19, 51).

More important for the average youngster were suggestions regarding social behavior. Thus one girl "kept my hair just like" an admired actress did, imitated her mannerisms. Other girls reported learning from movies "what to do in a crowd . . . how to act with boys . . . to make love, to smoke, and to wear swell clothes." Desires were stirred: "When I see movies that show snappy clothes and wealth I want these things also." "Passionate love pictures . . . make me want to be loved" (5, pages 85 ff.). There seems little doubt that movies do exert influence.

Radio

The average American listens to the radio every day; it is a taken-for-granted part of his existence. Favorite programs may be regularly tuned in, and radio may be a background accompaniment of study, reading, or housework. On occasion, famous men are heard, and sports or political events are described on the spot. In the meantime there is available, literally around the clock, an extraordinary potpourri of music, comedy, drama, quiz show—almost everything. To what of all this do children pay most attention?

Table 4.5 is a sample of comparatively recent findings regarding childhood radio preferences. Trends are similar to those already noted in read-

TABLE 4.5.   Percentage of Boys and Girls in Grades 5 to 8 Who Listen to Certain Types of Radio Programs[6]

Boys—Grade					Girls—Grade			
5	6	7	8		5	6	7	8
93	87	93	91	Comedy-variety	94	96	96	95
82	82	89	81	Crime drama	75	85	84	79
65	64	72	70	Anticrime	46	59	55	47
23	37	41	48	Drama	37	48	64	72
38	39	48	48	Quiz	45	48	44	49
22	29	36	47	Modern music	39	47	61	75
69	52	44	37	Daily adventure	44	32	21	13
9	9	8	6	Soap opera	31	33	27	23
12	14	17	26	News	13	12	17	24
16	17	23	29	Sports	5	3	4	3
5	8	8	8	Education	19	16	12	11
1	1	1	2	Classical music	1	4	1	8
6	5	7	9	Miscellaneous	13	11	10	10

Ranked in average order of preference, all grades and both sexes combined, over 3000 cases in all. The children listed every program they listen to regularly, i.e., every time or almost every time it is on the air. Data obtained by questionnaire survey of school children in Waterbury, Connecticut.

ing and the movies. Both sexes and all the grades listened most often to comedy-variety and crime drama broadcasts. With increasing age, the youngsters liked daily adventure broadcasts less, and drama, modern music, and news more. Boys liked sports increasingly.

That movies may measurably stir a child's pulse or disturb his sleep was mentioned above. Studies made a few years ago, when radio was in its heyday, indicated that exciting broadcasts might also affect the sleep of some youngsters. But such values of radio programs as help with current events were also mentioned; the children learned songs, stories, jokes. Some entered radio contests, wrote letters to a radio star, had had

[6] Adapted from Riccinti (48).

their names broadcast. Clearly the radio played a considerable part in the lives of most children. But all this happened in the days before TV!

Television

"Judged by its rate of growth, the size of its audience, and the man-hours of attention devoted to it, television promises to become the nation's principal communications medium" (9). According to the same study, by mid-1955 two out of every three American homes had television sets, and these were in use nearly five hours a day, with watching per person running "upwards of two and three hours per day." Moreover, the time spent watching TV appears to increase with length of ownership of a set, not to decrease when the novelty wears off. Television is displacing other mass media, as is shown by Table 4.6; after getting a television set, radio

TABLE 4.6.   Changes in Time Spent Reading and Listening to Radio After Purchase of TV Set[7]

| | Minutes per Person "Yesterday" | | |
	Before TV	After TV	Percent Change
Magazines	17	10	−41
Newspapers	39	32	−18
Radio	122	52	−57
Television	12[a]	173	....
Total time	190	267	+41

[a] "Guest-viewing."

listening time in the average family was more than halved, and the time spent reading magazines decreased almost that much.

Television sets are commonly owned by families with children. What effect does TV have, besides reducing the time spent reading and listening to the radio? Movie attendance declines, and perhaps also interest in hobbies and extracurricular school activities. Children whose families have TV sets are home more; the family is together more, but in a passive rather than an interacting way. A majority of parents seem to think TV a good thing for their children—at least it makes them easier to take care of at home, but mealtime and bedtime may be irregular.

Though children may spend as much time watching television as they do in school, careful investigations—as by comparing children's grades before and after their family had a television set—have shown no definite

[7] After Coffin (9). Data from 2500 Fort Wayne homes.

effects of TV on school work; however, children whose parents controlled their TV viewing did a little better in school. Teachers are more likely than either parents or pupils to feel that school work has been affected. Whether exciting TV shows tend to increase children's pulse rate and make their sleep restless, as exciting movies do, is not clear. Perhaps watching TV in familiar home surroundings where tension-relieving comments can readily be made—and the frequent interruptions for commercials—may lessen such emotional involvement.

The Mass Media and Child Development

Probably only a person who can remember life before there were movies, radio, and television can have any adequate appreciation of the extent to which these means of communication have widened the world and made it more immediate. And now there is such a profusion of offerings of these media. Even more than is true of the movies, one effect must be the quick spread of fashions and fads of dress, speech, amusements, ideas. It seems a fair guess that the increase in average intelligence over the past forty years is in part a product of the great increase in the number and range of ideas reaching the average youngster by these media. The increased sophistication and liberalization of attitudes over the same period that will be mentioned later presumably in part stem from the same cause. Certainly interests have been changed and extended through these means. That such effects have not been brought out more fully by research is probably attributable to the gradualness and the massive nature of these changes and the inadequacy of tests adequately to appraise them. It is almost inconceivable that the effects have not been more substantial than investigations thus far have indicated.

A recent investigation compared youngsters' lists of most admired individuals with similar choices made by children fifty years earlier (1). Fifty years ago such persons as Washington topped the list, but recent lists were newly featured by such people as Bing Crosby and the current baseball "great."

It seems clear that in view of the profusion and variety of such programs, the schools should teach discrimination in listening and viewing and understanding these media. The small boy who was not worried about the plight of the hero of a TV serial because he knew "the sponsor would want him back tomorrow night" had a healthy juvenile sophistication. Interest in good documentaries should be fostered. We said earlier that although the average level of leisure reading might be rather low, the youngster with a special interest or superior ability can easily find material of interest to him. But such a youngster cannot as easily find radio or television programs that appeal to him—unless perhaps his interest is in music. However, as greater varieties of recordings and films and similar materials become generally available, it is to be hoped that they will be used increasingly in such special ways, so that if three or four secondary-school youngsters wish to study a film strip or a movie on plant growth, they will be able to do so.

LARGER INTERESTS AND DESIRES

Since this chapter thus far has dealt primarily with what children do "for fun" or diversion, the superficial and perhaps cheap nature of many of these interests should not be criticized too heavily. But what about their more serious interests—in school, in careers, plans for the future?

Interest in School Work

Table 4.7 summarizes replies of over 2000 children in Grades 1 to 12 in a small midwestern city, when asked what they liked best in school.

TABLE 4.7. Things Liked Best in School by Pupils of Various Grade Levels[8]

Boys—Grades					Girls—Grades			
1–3	4–6	7–9	10–12		1–3	4–6	7–9	10–12
11	13	31	35	Sports, gym	8	9	33	34
28	24	24	14	Arithmetic, mathematics	21	26	19	8
32	19	10	11	English usage, reading, etc.	36	28	20	28
0	3	7	21	Nature study, science	1	4	9	9
1	9	7	8	Local and world affairs	1	11	10	6
13	11	10	16	Art, music, dramatics, etc.	17	15	16	14
0	0	0	5	Self-improvement, vocations	0	0	0	15
363	309	282	159	Number of cases	331	343	290	171

When asked about "one of the happiest days of my life," no subject-matter areas were mentioned by as many as 1 percent of any group. The figures are in percentages.

Both sexes became increasingly interested in sports as they grew older. Boys became steadily more interested in science, and both high-school boys and girls showed a sudden interest in self-improvement and vocations. Social studies and current affairs were far from popular. In general, interest in school work seemed to wane as the children grew older and

[8] Adapted from Jersild and Tasch (23).

had been in school longer. The investigators made the following summarizing statement:

"The typical first or second grader is interested in school and what the school represents. More likely than not he likes his teacher, too. The life of a scholar appeals to him. He is challenged by what there is to learn. He may say, as one child in this study said, that one of the happiest days in his life was the day he learned 'to take away.' When he tells what he likes about school he mentions things that distinctly belong to school much more frequently than he mentions things that school shares with life outside, such as games and outdoor play.

"The young child's friendly feeling about school appears not only when he talks about school as such but also when he happens to mention school in describing his likes and wishes. When describing what he dislikes most in life outside school, the young child is likely to make very few unfavorable references to any burdens or discomforts which the school had placed on his out-of-school life.

"As the average child moves up through the grades he seems to become less eager about things that distinctly belong to school and scholarliness, more inclined to complain, more interested in the things that go along with school rather than with work in the classroom. He becomes relatively more interested in recess periods than in class periods. He mentions play and sports more often. There is a greater hiatus between his wishes and what the school offers" (*23,* pages 41–42).

Why this decrease in most school work, though interest in sports was growing? Failure to relate school topics to the needs of each age was probably a factor. For instance, an analysis showed interest in such health topics as digestion decreasing with age, but concern about the cause of pimples, grooming, and sex hygiene increasing. The boys' increased interest in science in Grades 10–12 and the girls' interest in vocations suggest types of school work which might be stressed. But an inquiry that reaches beyond the school is needed.

Wishes

An investigation with a somewhat wider reach concerns the wishes of children and adolescents in two other small midwestern cities. Table 4.8 presents in condensed form, in percentages, the answers of nearly 2000 children to the question of what their strongest wish was. The answers were grouped under certain main heads such as "personal achievement," which included more specific items such as "professional career." The table includes only items mentioned by 4 percent or more of all pupils of either sex.

The wishes most frequently mentioned by the high-school boys came under the "personal achievement" head; under this head the desire for a successful life was mentioned most often and desire for a professional career next, but interest in farming was mentioned almost as often. The high-school girls were likewise much interested in personal achievement, a professional career (presumably teaching or nursing) being the specific type of occupation mentioned most frequently. But these adolescent girls were as interested in personal-social relations, with marriage the first item mentioned under this general head, followed by the wish to be more

TABLE 4.8.   Children's Completion of the Statement "I wish more than *anything* that . . ."[9]

Strongest Wish	Boys—Grade			Girls—Grade		
	4–6	7–8	9–12	4–6	7–8	9–12
Personal achievement	15	24	30	8	15	24
Successful life		3	10		2	7
Professional career	2	2	2	3	4	4
Personal-social relations	12	9	17	14	18	24
More popular, liked	1	3	1	5	5	5
Marriage	2	1	6	1	2	11
Family (health, security, etc.)	10	11	4	21	20	12
Possessions	23	20	12	14	9	2
Motor vehicle	1	10	7	1	1	1
School	8	10	13	5	14	15
Living situations	14	10	7	13	12	3
Live on farm	5	6	2	4	2	
Social welfare	8	5	13	10	4	11
Peace	6	4	11	6	3	9
No. of cases	248	376	250	284	419	350

popular and liked. Not to be overlooked is the fact that 6 percent of the high-school boys also listed marriage as their strongest wish—three times as many as mentioned a professional career.

Third in frequency of mention (both sexes and all grades combined) were wishes having to do with the family, solicitude regarding a parent and the wish that the family not be broken being the most frequent specific desires. Wishes for possessions were most common in elementary-school pupils (as for a bicycle or a pet). Complete data showed that the high-school students' most frequent wish regarding schooling was to go to college (6 percent of the boys and 3 percent of the girls), but their next

[9] Adapted from Cobb (8).

most frequent desire was to be out of school or to have completed it. The increasing concern with social welfare suggests a growing maturity of viewpoint.

Such material suggests that these schools should have been concerned with vocational choice and preparation. Material on marriage and the family, now often included in home economics courses, seems both desirable and desired. A practical course in psychology aimed at self-understanding might be suggested by much of the material. Many of the items suggest need for counseling and guidance. Clearly these youngsters have more serious interests than reading newspaper comics and listening to radio crooners.

Vocational Interests

Another part of the investigation on which Table 4.8 is based asked the youngsters to complete the statement, "I wish I were . . ." Their completion of the statement named the occupation most frequently desired.[10] Table 4.9 summarizes these statements, in percentages.

TABLE 4.9.   Completion of the Statement "I wish I were . . ." by 1809 Pupils to Indicate Vocation[11]

Career	Boys—Grade			Girls—Grade		
	4–7	7–8	9–12	4–6	7–8	9–12
Professional	5	3	8	16	8	5
Action—daring	14	11	7	2	2	2
Farm	3	3	5	0	0	0
Athletic	2	3	3	0	1	0
Business	1	1	3	0	0	0
Artisan	3	4	1	2	2	5
Theatrical	1	1	1	4	1	3
Artist	2	1	0	2	2	2
Religious	0	0	0	1	1	0

Elementary-school boys most often wanted such active and daring occupations as being cowboys or policemen, and girls of these ages most often wanted to be teachers or nurses. These are childhood notions, indicative of a stage of development, and not to be taken too seriously. But

[10] A great variety of scattered statements were also made, however. For instance, 7 percent of the high-school boys and 8 percent of the girls wished they were smarter; 4 percent of these same boys and 8 percent of the girls wished they were more popular; 3 percent of the boys wished they were bigger and the same percentage of girls wanted to be smaller.

[11] Adapted from Cobb (8).

how realistic is it for 3 percent of these South Dakota high-school girls, who should be thinking seriously about their occupational plans, to want a theatrical career, or for 8 percent of the boys—that is, one-fourth of all who named an occupation—to hope for a career in medicine or engineering or some other profession? That such wishes are often grossly out of accord with reality was shown by an investigation (*51*) regarding plans of 4700 high-school seniors in Philadelphia and New Haven in 1952. Of these seniors, 91 percent believed that they had reached a decision regarding a career. And 4 out of 10 of both sexes had chosen a profession, though in those cities only 19 percent of employed people 25 years of age or older, with a four-year high-school education or more, were doing professional or semiprofessional work. Six out of 10 boys sought a profession. A 1948 inquiry into vocational plans of the seniors in a large Indiana high school found no girl planning or expecting to do such work as waitressing, maid service, or cleaning; but a follow-up one year later showed that 20 percent were actually doing such work (*22, page 83*).

Such outcomes further emphasize the need for educational programs which give accurate information about vocational realities, and for counseling which guides wisely. Actual experience working during vacations or in secondary school may be highly educative and interest-stimulating or redirecting (*22*), and many values may result from it.

Many parents of high-school youngsters in a small city became disturbed because of their children's aimless idleness, sometimes mischievous and occasionally delinquent, during the long summer vacation. As a result a group of parents was formed to canvass businessmen in the community as to possible summer jobs. Some jobs were found, others created by putting through repairs or redecorations ahead of time; many openings were made available. Most of the youngsters were delighted to have something to do and to earn a little money. There was a sharp decrease in idleness, time spent in questionable amusements, and delinquency, and business that summer was given a bit of a lift. Though this was not primarily the original intent, many of these boys and girls became interested in the work they were doing and found out about other jobs from friends who worked in them. Vocational interests and plans became more realistic and broader. And instead of going to a nearby big city after finishing school, more youngsters found jobs in town than had previously been the case.

CONCRETE REALITY: THE LIFE HISTORY OF INTERESTS

Although the preceding discussion has indicated the general characteristics of interests as shown in play, in reading and movies and TV, in wishes, in vocational choice, it was general, and in that respect false. Interests are always the interests of a particular person and hence extremely personal; they are relatively specific, often highly so. Ruth likes chemistry, hiking, and John; Madge loves dramatics, dancing, and Tom. Furthermore, interests are the product of very specific influences in the life of each individual. A given interest may be the manifestation of an underlying urge or circumstance which is not apparent in the interest as an outsider sees it. John's great interest in chemistry may in reality be a major factor in Ruth's interest in that subject. Harry's interest in travel books may stem from his desire to get away from a restrictive and unhappy home. Homely Helen's absorption in romantic movies and the lack of any romance in her own life have an obvious possible relationship.

Sample Interest Biographies

To bring out the concrete reality regarding interests, an interest biography is very useful; in many ways it remakes the whole picture and gives insights otherwise unthought of. The following two interest biographies are samples of such an approach. The first is that of a young man, a graduate student in psychology.

Earliest play recollections are of ringing a handbell which his mother had hung up so it would ring when he pulled a string, and of digging in the back yard with a toy shovel. A little later (around 5 years of age), much interest in playing train following a train trip and in playing horse after a trip to his grandfather's farm.

When the boy was 6 his family moved to a more northern state. The novelty of a long winter led to great interest in coasting and such activities as building snow forts. In summer, he frequently played soldier, this play being led by a neighbor boy whose father's war record was a matter of much pride to his sons. A frequent indoor winter amusement was gathering at some boy's home to compare stamp collections and trade stamps; how this interest began he does not now remember. The gift of *Swiss Family Robinson* led to fascinated reading of this story and then of *Robinson Crusoe* and various other stories of adventure. A Christmas present of an air rifle and trips with his father hunting squirrels developed a boyish interest in "hunting." However, because of undetected near-sightedness he was a poor shot and was also poor in baseball; in consequence his interest in these sports was slight.

In his ninth winter the boy was frequently ill, went to school irregularly, seemed to have no energy for or interest in active play. His mother bought him some water color paints to use at home and he greatly enjoyed painting and drawing. His teacher came to see him and encouraged him; some of his work was displayed at an exhibit of pupils' work. Much set up by all this, he thought of being a designer or illustrator. But with spring his health returned, and sedentary interests were forgotten in his renewed zest for vigorous outdoor play.

Beginning when the boy was about 10 years old it became the father's regular practice to give his son certain carpenter's tools for Christmas. The boy's interest in making things had been fostered by his father's stories about a little mill he himself had made when he was a boy, like the real sawmill the grandfather owned. A workbench was built for him in the basement. At about this time a new bridge was built near by; all the boys watched the steam shovel and derrick, and then began making model steam shovels and derricks. With a little help from the father the boy made a better derrick than the other boys. He also looked up bridges in his father's encyclopedia, and as a result made a different and better bridge than the other boys made. He thus received admiring and even jealous attention from his friends and a great access of self-esteem. He read widely on mechanical topics and became much interested in being either a skilled mechanic or an engineer.

When he entered high school his father urged him to take a college preparatory program, but the boy insisted on including a course in manual training. The first two weeks of this course disgusted him. He had been making complicated objects, but the manual training instructor insisted that everyone make a whisk-broom holder. The youngster abandoned the course and became so busy with his other high-school work that the mechanical interest faded.

For a while in high school he had no definite vocational objective. He took it for granted that he was going to college and that a vocational choice could be made later. He became greatly interested in a girl. However, in his senior year was greatly influenced by his history teacher, one of the few men teachers in the school. As a result he decided to major in history in college. He had joined the high-school debating society and was greatly interested in the governmental problems there discussed.

He went to a small college but found it rather difficult to adjust to students of a different type from those he had associated with before. He also became increasingly dissatisfied with his history major; he was now taking both chemistry and biology, and science with its experimentation and its progressive advance to new understandings seemed to have greater potentialities. Furthermore, historical events apparently could be explained only in terms of the ideas and emotions of the human beings involved. And his history professor was stodgy! The combination of concern over personal problems of adjustment, impatience with history and his history teacher, and the thrilling potentialities of the scientific method all seemed to merge in a new interest, a vigorous course in social psychology. His major was changed to this subject, and he is now taking graduate work in this field.

This biography begins with very simple play activities. There follow progressive changes due partly to underlying slow processes of intellectual growth and physique, and partly to such circumstances as moving to a colder climate and being given tools. Ill health changed the nature of the boy's interests for a time. The influence of his parents and teachers was frequently important, as were also success and recognition, and social maladjustment. Both good and poor teachers had an effect on him. The final outcome was highly individual and personal, but also very understandable once all the main factors are known.

The second biography is that of a young woman, a college student majoring in home economics.

As a small child her sole companions were boys. She enjoyed their games and pranks, did not like girls' more sedate amusements.

As she advanced in the primary grades she slowly fell away from male companions and took to dolls. She enjoyed treating them for sickness, bandaging their wounds; she came to think that it would be wonderful to be a nurse and help the sick. At about this time an illness took her to the hospital where she remained over a month, becoming even more interested in and acquainted with a nurse's life and duties. After finishing her sophomore year in high school she declared this ambition to her parents. They objected and refused to give their consent to her entering nursing training. She acquiesced in their decision.

In grammar school and the freshman year of high school her teachers had told her that she was talented in painting and drawing. When she gave up the idea of nursing she turned with vigorous reaction to painting as a possible career. She visited galleries and museums, went sketching, and dreamed of a trip abroad for training. This she felt was certainly her vocation. But she gradually came to realize that to be famous would take years of toil and hardship. She therefore put aside this ambition as impractical. However, she liked to cook. And she said frankly that the old adage, "The way to a man's heart is through his stomach," was also a factor in this thinking, as one of her ambitions was to marry. She therefore decided to major in home economics, still keeping in the back of her mind the thought that perhaps sometime she might return to her interest in painting (15, page 377).

The above biography shows this girl's playmates initially affecting her interests, a period in a hospital influencing a vocational choice especially strongly because of her already present interest in nursing, the influence of her parents, and the hope of marriage as a factor in her vocational thinking.[12]

You should find it illuminating to write similarly about your own interests and to compare your account with those of other students. As already brought out earlier in this chapter, interests show certain very general trends from the younger to the older ages. Generalizations may be made about the influences that affect interests—physical environment, socioeconomic status, conventions—but such generalizations are very inade-

[12] Note that neither of these young people had any information about probable opportunities in the field they finally chose, or any evidence of their aptitude for such work. Both would have been helped by knowledge of vocational opportunities and by counseling to help their choice.

quate for understanding a particular individual's interests at a certain time. His interests are a complex result of his entire history. They cannot be understood from generalities but must be seen in the perspective of his total life experience.

Interests and Feelings

The first impression obtained from an interest biography is the extent to which each person's total interest pattern is an individual matter. But consideration of such biographies—especially one's own biography, with all the vividness that one's own life has for oneself—emphasizes a further point. A generalized treatment of interests makes the topic objective and cold. To the person concerned, however, an interest is dynamic and feelingful. Surely a high-school boy's interest in a certain girl was stirring, and rich in feeling tone. And those October afternoons—what with the tangy weather and abounding health, his whole body seemed to hunger for activity; to run and jump and shout was a highly desirable and delightful thing to do, whereas being still made him restless and miserable. To be mentally active was also natural and interesting for his healthy nervous system, and there was a restless urge to talk, ask questions, solve puzzles, make things.

The vicarious experiences gained from reading, movies, and TV similarly involve feelings. As was said earlier, objective physiological evidence shows that melodramatic or romantic moving pictures get right down into a youngster's vitals, stirring his pulse and undoubtedly his impulses and emotions. To have an interest is to feel a hunger, an urge, a craving, a restlessness. And when he is in the grip of an interest, he feels excitement, thrill, satisfaction, and a sense of expanding well-being—or letdown, discouragement, frustration, depending on whether the interest is satisfied or not. Obviously his interests and their gratification or denial are matters to which he is acutely sensitive. Since different people have different interests and those of adults differ from those of children and adolescents, it is easy for a teacher to fail to comprehend a pupil's interests or to treat them lightly or even with impatience or scorn. She is surprised or angered at the strength of his reaction to this slight. She should keep always in mind that interests and feelings are part and parcel one of the other, and treat her pupils' interests with considered tact.

Interests and Success

A few sentences back we mentioned the feelings of expanding well-being which come with satisfaction of an interest, and the letdown and discouragement if the interest is frustrated. In this connection a second major point emerges from the above biographies: an interest grows and flourishes if it is satisfied and if it is approved and brings recognition, but it tends to weaken if such results are not obtained. The boy's craftsmanship and the girl's painting were recognized as good, hence these interests became strong. Baseball had slight interest for the boy because he was poor at it, and the girl's interest in nursing decreased when her parents disapproved. Interests feed on success and on the approval which is social success; they starve to death if success and approval are lacking, or else manifest themselves in desperate or morbid fashion (this is treated in a later chapter).

THEORY AND APPLICATION

Understanding of interests has been sought by a study of play, of such mass media as reading and television, of school likes, of wishes and vocational choice, and of development of interests in the individual. Does this overview permit the basic elements of interests to be inferred, the important influences that shape them to be noted, and suggestions for their direction and nurture to be derived? The writers suggest that the total situation may be interpreted with reasonable adequacy as follows.

Basic Urges

Back of particular interests, and the source of their energy, are certain physiological tensions or pressures or urges. Broadest and greatest in importance is the urge toward activity that is normal in every healthy organism. That dogs run about and bark and children run and jump and shout requires no special explanation; this "going off" of a healthy organism is simply the normal and inevitable product of structure and organic constitution. (Failure to be active *would* call for explanation.) Such activity is not limited to mere physical exuberance but includes mental activity, i.e., curiosity, playing with ideas, imagining.[13] This basic urge or pressure to be active is strongest during the growth years; restless energy is recognized as characteristic of childhood and youth. In adolescence the powerful urge of sex appears. This raises the individual's total energy and gives it a sex-social direction. This redirection is the basic background phenomenon

[13] "The needs to know and to understand are seen in late infancy and childhood, perhaps even more strongly than in adulthood. Furthermore, this seems to be a spontaneous product of maturation rather than of learning, however defined. Children do not have to be taught to be curious. But they *may* be taught, as by institutionalization, *not* to be curious" (*34*, p. 96).

during adolescence. These two physiological urges—the pressure for both physical and mental activity and the pressure of sex—are, in the writers' belief, the two major drives behind the doing and thinking of human beings. There are other physiological pressures or tensions in the background, however, such as the urge of hunger and appetite. The discomforts of heat or cold make the individual seek more pleasant conditions. The total of all these physiological stirrings, restlessnesses, and urges is the force behind any interest or activity.

Into the complex urges and tensions of the normal person may come the peculiar tensions and discomforts of physiological malfunctioning, pain, or illness. If these discomforts are strong and the individual is weak, he may be preoccupied with them largely to the exclusion of other urges. Thus the sick child has little attention (or vitality) for other interests.

These are the background physiological pressures that constitute the driving power behind human interests and activities. To these must be added a major derivative. The one most evident, most useful fact learned in helpless infancy and dependent childhood is the importance of favorable attitudes on the part of other people. The competition of middle childhood and the sex interests of adolescence enforce this social sensitivity. Little wonder, then, that hunger for attention and for approval of others appears very early and, enforced by the sex urge, grows until, once the most elementary physiological demands are satisfied to some extent, it is the most powerful of all drives. It is not easily satisfied, because the various groups whose acceptance the growing child wishes to obtain— family, classmates, gang, and community—tend to set up still higher goals as he attains initial status.

The strength of these basic drives differs greatly in different people. Thus some children have an almost feverish urge for physical activity, whereas others are listless; some are mentally very lively, others lumpish. Sex is much stronger in some persons than in others. Some people have a hysterical craving for the approval of others, but a few people seem indifferent. This, very briefly, is the concept regarding the basic urges underlying the interests of children and young people. What inferences and implications valuable for education follow from this concept?

In the first place, any educational program which tries to block one of these basic urges or drives is sure to give rise to conflicts and disciplinary problems and to lack vitality and interest for the pupils. The old-fashioned school which asked children to sit still and be quiet was contrary to nature. The conservative secondary school or college which separates adolescent boys and girls just when they are most interested in each other and might be going through processes of healthy acquaintanceship, is contrary to nature. Any school which rules it wrong for pupils to talk together and work together is going against the most established and pervasive of all human tendencies, and one of the most desirable.

In the second place, if vigor and liveliness of interests originate in physiological pressures and urges, the first step in stimulating a pupil's interests is to see that he is vigorously healthy. Undernourished sick children usually have sluggish inert interests. They may be docile in the sedentary program of a conventional school. But genuine and effective interest in play or in the activities of a modern school must stem from the energy of a sound physique—the neuromuscular system in good tonus and quick to respond, the ductless glands all making their proper and balanced contributions to the internal chemistry, reasonably adequate nourishment, sleep that is sound and long enough, and a system not burdened by injury or disease.

Up to now Harry had been interested in his school work and active in play. But this September he was listless in school, seemed bored with his work, participated little in the activities of his neighborhood gang, did little with his stamp collection. Investigation showed that the family had just returned from a trailer trip in which the sleeping quarters had been cramped, the hours of rest irregular, the diet poor; constipation had alternated with diarrhea, and Harry had a chronic cold. His teacher's efforts to interest him in his school work proved futile, but with gradually improving health his interests slowly returned.

Limiting and Stimulating Conditions

Taken for granted, but its pervasive importance often missed, is the fact that interests are highly adaptable and responsive to the conditions and circumstances of each youngster's life. His playthings and play places, the family's resources as regards a car and money for amusements and clothes, the community's resources as regards recreation and vocation—for the average person these factors are largely definitive as to what his interests will be.

Mr. Thompson grew up on a farm forty years ago. As a boy he hunted and fished, enjoyed helping his father look after the farm machinery but did not like farm work, was fascinated by the trains on the railway which ran along one side of the farm. There was little reading matter in the home except a farm journal and the newspaper from the small city up the line, no school or village library, no radio or moving pictures or automobile, no organized team games because there were so few boys of the same age who could conveniently get together. Social contacts were restricted to the immediate neighborhood and to social affairs centered around the church; there was no dancing or card playing, and little money or time for vacation trips, parties, shows. Mr. Thompson left school at 14 to help on the farm, married a neighbor girl at 19, and moved to the nearby small city to work for the railroad which had so fascinated him as a boy.

His son Tom, growing up in a comfortable suburban home, had no farm chores or other work to do, and little occasion to tinker with machinery. Instead, sports that were fostered by both the schools and the city playgrounds absorbed his energies, and he had been a Boy Scout. He spent a part of two summers in a camp. In fairly comfortable circumstances, the family had such modern conveniences as an automobile and a radio; movies were commonplace, also week-end trips which would have been an event in his father's boyhood. Tom was on the high-school football team; dances and dates were a taken-for-granted part of an active social life. He rather looked down on his father's rough heartiness of manner and also felt a little apologetic about his father's job. After two years in college, Tom obtained a business position in a big midwestern city. Although constitutionally he and his father are much alike, the different circumstances of their lives led to the development of very different interests.

Conditions which limit or stimulate interests may be found in the individual as well as in his environment. Obviously a deaf child is likely to have little interest in music, or a crippled child in active sports. Such factors are frequently much more important than these two extremes suggest. A big strong boy has the energy and strength to initiate and foster an interest in athletics for which the puny lad has neither vigor nor capacity; however, the latter's inadequacy may find compensation in stories and novels about athletes. It would be strange indeed if the girl with the lovely voice did not like to sing. The dull boy will hardly enjoy chess or debating or mathematics, but the bright youngster may. In general, interests and capacities go together.

Tom (in the above anecdote) was a husky active lad for whom athletics was as natural as the frisking of puppies; the admiring regard his athletic powers brought from his associates accentuated that interest. The total pattern and development of his interests was very different from that of his classmate William, who was short, slight, and bright. William had a great longing for physical strength and status and tried to make the track team, but did not. His urge to achieve some sort of recognition thus frustrated, he threw himself vigorously into debating, and he tried extra hard to be agreeable since he could not muscle his way into popularity.

The practical applications of the above facts are so obvious that there is danger of their being neglected. A playground creates different play interests from those which develop in slum alleys. Having the schoolyard open after school and in the summer and the school industrial arts laboratory open evenings for both boys and their fathers will affect the interests found in the neighborhood. Playthings deserve discussion by teachers and parents as interest-making materials. A community hall or church may foster games, socials, dances, and dramatics, and be a major influence in shaping the interests of the community.

One high school the writers know had no athletics except for its interschool teams and no music except its much-featured band with its much-photographed drum majorettes. Another big school had football teams for boys of different weights, fostered such simple and inexpensive games as paddle tennis, and aimed at an overall athletic program broad enough to include something for everyone. It had not only a band but orchestras and glee clubs and informal sings. Obviously this school stimulated a wider variety of athletic and musical interests in a far greater number of pupils than the first one did.

The high school in one small city had only a conventional academic program. But a nearby school of about the same size offered practical industrial arts, secretarial, commercial, and home economics courses; and it had a vocational counselor who kept in touch with the community's business and industrial life. Various feasible vocational interests were thus stimulated and furthered, and led to jobs after graduation. Moreover, this school's evening programs reached many adults; the courses ranged from "great books" and chorus singing to making decoy ducks. One high school was widely known for its winning football teams, another for the number of students who won scholarships in a national "science talent search."

The Anthropology and Sociology of Interests

The preceding section stressed how a person's interests are shaped and limited by the physical conditions and circumstances of his life, and by his physique and capacities. Often even more important are customs and conventions, fashions and fads which make certain things accepted or admired as *the* things to do, whereas other interests are considered inappropriate or even taboo. Thus hunting and fishing were interests every country boy of Mr. Thompson's generation was expected to have, whereas football and basketball were the interests expected in his son's group. Dancing was expected of the son but taboo when his father was a boy. Railroading had glamour and status among Mr. Thompson's boyhood group but was looked down on by his son's more sophisticated society. As has been stressed, social class is very important (*29, 38, 45*).

But the total way of life in which Mr. Thompson grew up was more different from the interest-molding culture of his son's boyhood than the above anecdotes indicate. The competitive urge to beat someone—to beat a classmate for a place on the team, to help the team beat the rival school —is pervasive in the life of the present-day high-school boy but was largely absent in Mr. Thompson's rural boyhood. Similarly an investigation by one of the writers showed that girls in a midwestern community are distinctly less interested in cooking and sewing now than was the case thirty years ago; they are more interested in athletic team games. As will be pointed out in a later chapter, high-school social life is different today from social life of an earlier day. The dominant desire now is to be among those who "belong," but there was little social striving and climbing among Mr. Thompson's boyhood associates. Sex-stimulating association with girls is also more frequent today.

An interest inventory for the sixth grade through college in a certain Ohio community in 1923, 1933, 1943, and 1953 yielded data evidencing such changes. Over the thirty years, the number of interests increased, especially for the girls and especially in the college years. A "wrongs" test given at the same time showed liberalization of attitude. For example, at the later date, smoking was less often thought wrong for girls and was more often liked. Some of the changes were marked (46).

If the differences in one midwestern family over one generation can be as great as in the case of Mr. Thompson and his son, how much greater will differences be over longer periods of time, or from one nation or race to another. Organized team games were an Anglo-Saxon development, not very popular on the European continent until relatively recently. For a boy to have mechanical interests is part of the American tradition, but such interests are less approved and fostered for boys in Europe. Vocational interests are different here than there. And if non-European cultures are examined—the development of interests, for example, among young people in India or China or Samoa—then indeed are striking differences found (38).

In sum, the total society in which the individual grows up has an enormous influence upon his interests. Within the limits set by his capacities and the gross circumstances of his life, a person's interests are primarily the product of the culture and the society in which he lives. However, it is possible, by persistent shrewdness, to modify and even somewhat redirect these influences. A school can easily stimulate interest in its basketball team, but it can also arouse interest in its science club, its Junior Achievement group, its Future Farmers chapter. Their activities can involve much pleasant work and informal association, and also receive publicity not only in the school but in the local paper—perhaps with pictures. Local industrialists may be interested in the science club; local businessmen will support and work with the miniature-business enterprisers of the Junior Achievement group; adults in agricultural communities may be as much interested as the youngsters in the accomplishments of the Future Farmers, and one of them may gain state or even national recognition for his prize pig or his selection as the "Star Farmer of America." A popular teacher can make it the thing to belong to the glee club or the home economics club or the science club. Apparently the mounting prestige of science in this country following the launching of satellites—both our own and the Russian—is leading to a general increase in intellectual interests in this country.

The Nurture of Interests

In short, a vigorous interest must have its roots in the basic urges. It should involve liveliness—mental if not physical—and companionship. It should be appropriate to the stage of development and abilities, to the physical and socioeconomic setting.

For an interest to grow, there needs to be room, time, and a place for it to do so, and usually some cultivating. Thus a high school well known for its stimulation of interest in science keeps its laboratories open at the noon hour and in other free periods for students who wish to use them; a teacher is there to give help if desired (6).

If an interest is to grow, it should have the warm sun of success and approval. If it is to grow strong, there should be rich rewards for various drives and purposes, with continuously opening possibilities for yet further satisfactions. Interests, wishes, larger purposes become coördinated, other diversions subordinated. Teachers and counselors can do much to further these processes.

A certain small boy in grade school loved to sing. One day the singing teacher was testing the voices of various pupils. This youngster, too eager, sang with uninhibited boyish vigor. With an annoyed look which the child did not miss, the music supervisor said, "At least he has volume." The other children snickered and the boy never showed any interest in music again.

Contrast this episode with the way in which interest in drawing was stimulated in the case described on page 105. Both the boy's teacher and his mother helped him so that he made great progress in it. They approved and admired his work. The exhibiting of some of his sketches at school gave him status with the other pupils, and as a result his interest was stimulated even more.

Many if not most men of great achievement—in science, invention, literature, music, art—showed their interests early. For instance, over a third of a group of mathematicians reported that they were much interested in that field before they were 10. The age at which a group of famous physicians decided to study medicine averaged 14. Edison at the age of 9 read a book on science and began to experiment. Sir Isaac Newton as a boy made and played with mechanical toys. Mozart was fascinated with music from infancy. When he was 15, Milton was writing notable poetry (27, 44). Obviously if a teacher can discover and encourage the interests of a very able youngster, a notable career may result. Recently a young science teacher in a small high school received national mention because of the number of students he had inspired and helped to enter advanced university work.[14] The principal of a well-known school for gifted children told one of the writers that she had seen special interest and aptitude in science in children even as early as age 6.

Typically, biographical and autobiographical accounts of famous people show early strong and increasingly powerful interests, encouraged by parents, nourished by reading, hobby activities, trips, creating friendships with other similarly-minded youngsters, gradually gaining friendly attention and support in the community. And an encouraging and helpful teacher is often a central figure (6, 27, 34, 44). The present mounting effort to improve education in this country offers opportunities to enthusiastic teachers as never before. And one last point. Whether or not there are very able pupils in her class, the teacher may herself find zestful interest in developing the interests, abilities, and personality of each youngster in accordance with his potentialities.

SUMMARY

By means of surveys of leisure-time activities, preferences as to reading and television and vocation, and wishes, an attempt is made to determine the nature of interests and the factors which shape them.

In step with the individual's growth, play develops from simple and solitary to more vigorous, complex, and social activities; in adolescence it is dominated by sex-social interests. Great individual differences are found in the nature and variety of leisure-time activities. Physical and mental ability, circumstances, and especially the attitudes and customs of

[14] F. V. Rummell and C. M. Johnson, Bill Lane's students win the prizes, *Reader's Digest,* January, 1955, p. 29.

the group are important in differences in interests from age to age and within any age group.

Data on reading, movies, radio, and television also show the progression from simple and active interests in childhood to the sex-social interests of adolescence. These mass media, a major feature of modern life, may strongly stimulate or modify certain interests. Their ready-made vicarious satisfactions may take the place of real consummation, when major interests are blocked. A primary duty of schools is to create some discrimination in youngsters as to the merits of the extraordinary abundance of material offered by these media, and exploit their educational usefulness.

From the primary grades through high school, educational programs seem to satisfy pupil interests less and less adequately. By broadening their programs, schools could maintain interests better. Occupational interests that are often impractical could be made more practical by appropriate instruction and counseling.

Interest biographies emphasize the fact that interests are perhaps the most modifiable of all human traits. They are vivid with feeling. They change, grow, or wither according as they achieve success and approval or are blighted by frustration and loss of status, and as they further or interfere with the individual's predisposition and purposes. Schools should be able substantially to direct and control the development of interests.

Interests draw their energies especially from three sources: the urge to both physical and mental activity, the sex urge, and the desire for companionship, attention, and approval. They develop within the limitations of the individual's physical and socioeconomic environment and his physical and mental capabilities, and in accordance with the patterns set by his culture. Their development within these limits depends especially upon the extent to which they reach success. Teachers find perhaps their greatest opportunities in nurturing desirable interests in their pupils. A friendly helpful teacher has been a major factor in stimulating and guiding the early careers of many famous men.

BIBLIOGRAPHY

1. Averill, L. A., The impact of a changing culture upon pubescent ideals, *Sch. & Socy.*, 1950, *72*:49–53.
2. Barker, R. G., and Wright, H. F., *Midwest and Its Children,* Evanston: Row, Peterson, 1954.
3. Berlin, H., The community occupational survey and studies of occupation choice, *Personnel and Guidance J.*, 1953, *31*:455–457.

4. Biber, B., Murphy, L., Woodcock, L., and Black, I., *Child Life in School,* New York: Dutton, 1942.
5. Blumer, H., *Movies and Conduct,* New York: Macmillan, 1933.
6. Brandwein, P. F., *The Gifted Student as Future Scientist,* New York: Harcourt, Brace, 1955.
7. Butterworth, R. F., and Thompson, G. G., Factors related to age-grade trends and sex differences in children's preferences for comic books, *J. Genet. Psychol.,* 1951, *78*:71–96.
8. Cobb, H. V., Role-wishes and general wishes, *Child Devel.,* 1954, *25*:161–171.
9. Coffin, T. E., Television's impact on society, *Amer. Psychol.,* 1955, *10*: 630–641.
10. Cunningham and Walsh, Inc., *Videotown. Annual Census of TV and Its Effects on Family Life in a Typical American City,* New York: Cunningham and Walsh, Inc., 1948–1954 incl.
11. Dale, E., *The Content of Motion Pictures,* New York: Macmillan, 1935.
12. Dysinger, W. S., and Ruckmick, C. A., *Emotional Responses of Children to the Motion Picture Situation,* New York: Macmillan, 1933.
13. Erikson, E. H., Sex differences in the play configuration of preadolescents, *Amer. J. Orthopsychiat.,* 1951, *21*:667–692.
14. Fleege, V. H., and Malone, H. J., Motivation in occupational choice among high school students, *J. Educ. Psychol.,* 1946, *37*:77–86.
15. Fryer, D., *The Measurement of Interests,* New York: Holt, 1931.
16. Hall, W. E., and Robinson, F. P., The role of reading as a life activity in a rural community, *J. Appl. Psychol.,* 1942, *26*:530–542.
17. Harrison, E. C., One year later: vocational choices and reality, *Personnel and Guidance J.,* 1953, *32*:144–146.
18. Havighurst, R. J., *Human Development and Education,* New York: Longmans, Green, 1953.
19. Heisler, Florence, Comparison between those elementary school children who attend moving pictures, read comics, and listen to serial radio programs to excess, with those who indulge in these activities seldom or not at all, *J. Educ. Res.,* 1948, *42*:182–190.
20. Heisler, Florence, Comparison of the movie and non-movie goers of the elementary school, *J. Educ. Res.,* 1948, *41*:541–46.
21. Hollingshead, A. B., *Elmtown's Youth,* New York: Wiley, 1949.
22. Ivins, W. H., and Runge, W. B., *Work Experience in High School,* New York: Ronald Press, 1953.
23. Jersild, A. T., and Tasch, Ruth, *Children's Interests and What They Suggest for Education,* New York: Teachers College Bureau of Publications, 1949.
24. Latham, A. J., Job appropriateness: A one-year follow-up of high school graduates, *J. Soc. Psychol.,* 1951, *34*:55–68.
25. Lazarsfeld, P. F., and Kendall, P. L., *Radio Listening in America,* New York: Prentice-Hall, 1948.

26. Leach, K. W., Intelligence levels and corresponding interest area choices of ninth grade pupils in thirteen Michigan schools, *J. Exp. Educ.*, 1953–1954, *22*:369–383.

27. Lehman, H. C., *Age and Achievement*, Princeton: Princeton Univ. Press, 1953.

28. Lehman, H. C., and Witty, P. A., *The Psychology of Play Activities*, New York: Barnes, 1927.

29. Lewis, Claudia, *Children of the Cumberland*, New York: Columbia Univ. Press, 1946.

30. Lyness, P. I., Patterns in the mass communications tastes of the young audience, *J. Educ. Psychol.*, 1951, *42*:449–467.

31. Lyness, P. I., The place of the mass media in the lives of boys and girls, *Journ. Quart.*, 1952, *29*:43–54.

32. Macoby, E. E., Television: its impact on school children, *Publ. Opin. Quart.*, 1951, *15*:421–444.

33. Mallinson, G. G., and Crumrine, W. M., An investigation of the stability of interests of high school students, *J. Educ. Res.*, 1952, *45*:369–383.

34. Maslow, A. H., *Motivation and Personality*, New York: Harper, 1954.

35. McClelland, D. C. (ed.), *Studies in Motivation*, New York: Appleton-Century-Crofts, 1955.

36. McKellar, P., and Harris, R., Radio preferences of adolescents and children, *Brit. J. Educ. Psychol.*, 1952, *22*:101–113.

37. Miller, D. C., and Form, W. H., *Industrial Sociology*, New York: Harper, 1951.

38. Murphy, G., *In the Minds of Men*, New York: Basic Books, 1953.

39. Olsen, E. G., *School and Community Programs*, New York: Prentice-Hall, 1949.

40. Passow, A. H., and others, *Planning for Talented Youth*, New York: Teachers Coll. Publications, 1955.

41. Porter, Richard J., Predicting vocational plans of high school senior boys, *Personnel and Guidance J.*, 1954, *33*:215–18.

42. Pressey, S. L., *Educational Acceleration: Appraisals and Basic Problems*, Columbus: Ohio State Univ. Press, 1949.

43. Pressey, S. L., Outcomes of a special "honors" program 20 years later, *Sch. & Socy.*, 1955, *82*:58–59.

44. Pressey, S. L., Concerning the nature and nurture of genius, *Sci. Mon.*, 1955, *81*:123–129.

45. Pressey, S. L., and Crates, W. E., Sports and the public mind, *Sch. & Socy.*, 1950, *72*:373–374.

46. Pressey, S. L., and Jones, A. W., Age changes in moral codes, anxieties, and interests, as shown by the "X-O Tests," *J. Psychol.*, 1955, *39*:485–502.

47. Renshaw, S., Miller, V. L., and Marquis, D. P., *Children's Sleep*, New York: Macmillan, 1933.

48. Riccinti, E. A., Children and radio: a study of listeners and non-listeners to various types of radio programs in terms of selected ability, attitude and behavior measures, *Genet. Psychol. Monog.*, 1951, *44*:69–143.

49. Schramm, W., and White, D. M., Age, education, economic status: factors in newspaper reading, *Journ. Quart.*, 1949, *26*:149–159.
50. Sears, Pauline S., Doll play aggression in normal young children: Influence of sex, age, sibling status, father's absence, *Psychol. Monog.*, 1951, *65*, No. 6.
51. Shosteck, R., How well are we putting across occupational information? *Personnel and Guidance J.*, 1955, *33*:265–269.
52. Stone, C. P., and Barker, R. G., The attitudes and interests of pre-menarcheal and post-menarcheal girls, *J. Genet. Psychol.*, 1939, *54*:27–71.
53. Stone, L. J., and Church, J., *Childhood and Adolescence*, New York: Random House, 1957.
54. Strang, Ruth, Why children read comics, *Elem. Sch. J.*, 1942–1943, *43*:336–342.
55. Sullenger, T. E., Parke, L. H., and Wallin, W. K., The leisure time activities of elementary school children, *J. Educ. Res.*, 1953, *46*:551–554.
56. Terman, L. M., The discovery and encouragement of exceptional talent, *Amer. Psychol.*, 1954, *9*:221–230.
57. Terman, L. M., and Oden, Melita, *The Gifted Child Grows Up*, Stanford: Stanford Univ. Press, 1947.
58. Tyler, L. E., The relationship of interests to abilities and reputations among first grade children, *Educ. and Psychol. Meas.*, 1951, *11*:255–264.
59. Wall, W. D., and Semson, W. A., The emotional response of adolescent groups to certain films, *Brit. J. Educ. Psychol.*, 1950, *20*:153–163.
60. Williams, H. F., Jr., The town tells teens about jobs, *Personnel and Guidance J.*, 1954, *32*:266–269.
61. Wilson, Mary D., The vocational preferences of secondary modern school children, *Brit. J. Educ. Psychol.*, 1953, *23*:97–113, 163–179.
62. Witty, Paul A., *The Gifted Child*, Boston: Heath, 1951.
63. Witty, Paul A., Children's interests in comics, radio, motion pictures and TV, *Educ. Adm. Superv.*, 1952, *38*:138–147.
64. Witty, Paul A., Comparative studies of interest in TV, *Educ. Adm. Superv.*, 1954, *40*:321–335.
65. Witty, Paul A., and Bricker, H., *Your Child and Radio, TV, Comics and Movies*, Chicago: Science Research Associates, 1952.
66. Witty, Paul A., and Sizemore, R. A., Reading the comics: a summary of studies and an evaluation I, *Elem. Engl.*, 1954, *31*:501–506.
67. Witty, Paul A., Coomer, A., and McBean, D., Children's choices of favorite books: a study conducted in ten elementary schools, *J. Educ. Psychol.*, 1946, *37*:266–278.
68. Worcester, D. A., *The Education of Children of Above-average Ability*, Lincoln: Univ. of Nebraska, 1956.
69. Wylie, J. A., Survey of 504 families to determine the relationships between certain factors and the nature of the family recreation program, *Res. Quart.*, 1953, *24*:229–243.

Chapter 5

The Development of the Emotional Life

CHAPTER 4 PICTURED CHILDREN AND ADOLESCENTS AS having a variety of interests and as being eager for their fulfillment, for recognized accomplishment and companionship and approval. It stressed that the development of an interest depended upon the extent and nature of the fulfillment; an interest might flourish if it led to success experiences, or wither if it met only failure. Such outcomes must now be given more detailed consideration, with special reference to the cumulative effects of repeated experiences of one type or the other. What are the effects of continued failure and frustration of interests, of chronic neglect or disapproval from teachers or associates, of continuing uncertainty and insecurity? How much difference does it make if a youngster generally enjoys reasonable fulfillment of his interests, is usually approved, and feels that his world can be depended upon to be consistent in these respects? He *should* enjoy school—find zest in his work, pleasure in his companionships there, enjoyment in his relations with his teachers. Here is a problem of outstanding and pervasive importance on which considerable work has been done. For teachers, the problem is central as regards their relations with their pupils and their own success, for they *should* find great satisfaction in their work and in their contacts with pupils and the community.

Shy, shabbily dressed Jim had been "carried along" into the fifth grade but obviously could not do the work there. He was clumsy and inept at games. He was frequently scolded by an impatient teacher, and was either disregarded or teased by the other children. He was criticized and bullied in his overcrowded shabby home by a father who was often out of work and by an overworked mother. The boy was in a chronic state of bewilderment and fear because he did not know what to do in most of the situations he had to meet, and was in constant dread of failure or rebuff. Somewhat similar as far as the nature of his difficulty was concerned, but not in most other respects, was an intelligent college freshman who did night work to pay his way. Because he had no leisure and his hours of work were inconvenient he had made no friends; irregular and inadequate meals had disturbed his digestion. Finally, fatigue and loneliness and poor health so upset him that he failed a course. He was bewildered and on the verge of panic because he did not know how to meet the manifold problems presented by his first year in college.

In contrast, plump Polly found her high-school lessons easy. A youngest child whose large family was well known in the little town, she was popular with both students and teachers. Confident, active, smiling, the picture of health, she well illustrates how consistent success experiences—including satisfactory social adjustment—foster effectiveness, pleasant emotional tone, and physical well-being.

A FUNCTIONAL CONCEPT OF EMOTION

The basic concept holds that the nature of a person's emotional experiences depends primarily on the extent to which his interests and drives are satisfied. If they are frustrated, he will be unhappy and either timid and withdrawing or angry and aggressive. The results of frustration may be varied indeed; the withdrawing person may be angry too, and the aggressor timid but desperate. They depend upon a great variety of factors, such as the individual's stage of development, health, previous experiences, present status, and the way the immediate situation is handled. But it often seems forgotten that habitual success experiences also have important and largely opposite effects upon the personality; there is not frustration but furtherance. These various features and types of emotion are now considered in more detail.

Physiological Effects of Emotion

Certain physiological aspects of strong emotion are well recognized. A person may tremble from either rage or fear. Fear or embarrassment, as when before an audience, may make the mouth dry because of constriction of peripheral blood vessels and lessened salivation. Excitement increases heart rate and blood pressure, and affects such ductless glands as the adrenals. It is common to hear a person say, after some emotional experience, that he was "too excited to eat." Experiments have demonstrated that emotion reduces the normal digestive movements of the stomach and small intestine and the secretion of digestive juices. There may be either constipation or diarrhea; some students have "examination diarrhea."

These are effects of strong emotional episodes. Chronic emotional distress may cause these same types of condition to become chronic. The timid, often rebuffed youngster may not actually tremble, but he is likely to be hesitant and awkward in his actions and to stammer when he talks. His appetite and digestion may be poor, and he may be underweight. Sleep disturbances may be frequent—restlessness, trouble in going to sleep, frequent waking. There is chronic fatigue. In contrast, a child who secures reasonable satisfaction of his interests, including the social satisfactions of companionship and status, is likely to be sure in movement and speech, have a good appetite, and sleep soundly.

That children with emotional problems often show various symptoms like those mentioned above is illustrated by the following list of difficulties found in children who were brought to a clinic because of fearfulness. Sleep was disturbed in 65 percent of these children, etc. (23, page 599).

Sleep disturbances	65%
Feeding problems	45%
Temper tantrums	34%
Nail biting	33%
Enuresis	29%
Crying and whining	18%
Masturbation	8%
Stuttering	6%

You yourself may possibly have had this experience: The imminence of an important examination or interview or other similar occasion so worried you that you dropped things, stumbled on stairs, started and stammered when spoken to, found food less interesting, were constipated. If the crisis was passed successfully, you found yourself perhaps a little too active, talking a little too readily, eating very heartily.

Emotion and Intellectual Efficiency

As was said in Chapter 3, emotional distresses and frustrations interfere with intellectual efficiency. The unhappy individual seems abstracted, has difficulty keeping his mind on a task, and may become stalled by emotional blocking. However, as we saw in connection with special abilities, interests which bring approval and status make abilities grow.

One student, who was supposed to be taking a final examination, spent most of the time staring at her paper or out the window. Occasionally she wrote a few sentences, then relapsed into inactivity again. Up to this time the girl had done fairly satisfactory work. On investigation it was discovered that her parents had decided to obtain a divorce on particularly unpleasant grounds, and that for about a month both of them had been pouring out their difficulties to her.

All her feelings and affections for them were thrown into confusion. She was fearful of what people would say. Gradually she became more and more unable to concentrate and more fatigued, until finally she reached the distracted and blocked condition described above.

In contrast, a music student had not been doing outstandingly well, but to her delight she was chosen for a solo at a recital. She practiced as never before under the stimulus of this recognition, did excellently, applied herself even harder, became one of the best musicians in the school, and chose the teaching of music as a career—all this largely because of the stimulus of the satisfaction of her desire to achieve status.

That even mild frustrations are likely to interfere to some extent with intellectual efficiency, and mild success to increase effectiveness, is shown by a somewhat unusual experiment with 24 high-school seniors. Each boy was first asked to wait a few moments in a comfortable reception room where he thought himself alone; in reality, however, he was being secretly observed as to whether he played with some games that were in the room, looked at pictures and other objects, or sat and daydreamed. Then the experimenter came in and had the boy sort a pack of cards fifteen times. Toward half the boys he was bored and contemptuous of their work; he faked a record that showed them to have done far below the "norms." Toward the other lads he was congratulatory and enthusiastic; the record he faked for them showed very superior work. Then each boy was left alone again, and the concealed observer watched what he did. On the second day the procedure was the same for each boy, with concealed observation again following the card sorting. But after that, both groups were given a somewhat different task, and all the boys were praised and "made to feel as phenomenally successful as possible"; then they were secretly observed once more. Table 5.1 shows some of the things these boys did after these experiences of "success" and "failure."

The first line shows changes from the initial observation, in number of 5-second intervals spent daydreaming or just sitting. The second line shows similar intervals spent looking at the norm sheet and record sheets. The third shows the total number of times that a boy, when alone, started sorting the cards again of his own volition, but never finished the job. Clearly failure caused these boys to daydream even more than in the preliminary period, to look only little at their records, and to fumble in discouraged and inefficient fashion with their task—often starting but not finishing. In contrast, the boys who were successful daydreamed less than in the initial period, often examined their records, and never once sorted the cards without finishing. If such effects on ways of working can be obtained in only two days of brief experimentation, clearly months or years of continued failure may establish very serious habits of turning away from work or fumbling with a task inefficiently and in discouragement (49). Continuing success might increase one's ability to be businesslike.

TABLE 5.1. Effects of "Success" and "Failure" on Behavior[1]

| | "Failure" Group | | | "Success" Group | | |
	First Day	Second Day	Final Success	First Day	Second Day	Final Success
Daydreaming	3	8	1	−6	−2	1
Looking at record	2	1	0	9	5	4
Unfinished sortings	26	11	5	0	0	0

The "failure" group spent an average of three more 5-second intervals daydreaming in the supposedly unobserved time after the first day's card sorting than in the time before, but the praised group six intervals less (−6). The failed group thereafter looked at their record twice but the praised group 9 times, etc.

Frustration or success may affect the quality of work. A group of children who took a drawing test, solved a puzzle and obtained a reward for it, then took the test again, did better on the second test. A similar group who were tested twice but did not have the intervening success experience did not do so well the second time. Nor was the reward without the success so effective (44). A group of high-school students was given a test for recall of words, had a success experience, then was tested again. This group improved. But another group, for whom a frustration experience was interpolated, did poorer on their second test (56). Some 9-year-old boys were given certain Binet tests, solved a puzzle successfully, then were given equivalent tests. They did better on the second test than another group who failed to solve the puzzle; moreover, the successful boys became more coöperative, alert, friendly, persisting (26). College students who were anxious learned less than others who were not (30), and students who were made anxious did poorer on a digit-span test than others who were not made anxious (34). In short, a variety of investigations have indicated that frustration lessens intellectual effectiveness, and that success increases competence (29). Moreover, it has been found that, by being encouraged in persistence and helped toward success, frustrated children can be rehabilitated (24).

[1] Adapted from R. R. Sears, Success and failure, a study in motility, in *17*, pp. 235–258.

Emotional Conditions and General Attitude

Emotional strain and frustration may cause attitudes of timidity and withdrawing or of irritability and aggressiveness. Such attitudes may appear only in certain situations or in the presence of certain people. Thus a high-school freshman was surly toward his Latin teacher, whose sarcastic criticisms of him in class had affronted his pride. But he was shy and apologetic in an after-class discussion with his algebra teacher, who had been more tactful. An attitude may be more general, appear elsewhere than at its source, or be shown only where it is safe. Thus a child may be aggressive at school because of conditions at home, or a father irritable at home because his foreman is domineering. A sensitive child who has been criticized and humiliated for failing a recitation may come to dread first reciting, then teachers, then school; he may play truant, have trouble at home, and finally run away from all authority. Moodiness due to distress at home may become the habitual emotional tone.

It has been shown experimentally that frustration makes attitudes in general less favorable to other things and persons. Thus, boys at a summer camp were prevented by a tedious examination from going to see a much desired program at a local movie theater. Before and after this frustration, they indicated on a rating scale their attitude toward Mexicans and Japanese (half rated Mexicans before the frustration, and half afterward, so that initial attitudes would be balanced). The attitude toward either group was less favorable after the frustration (*10,* page 43). Rural districts are likely to vote officeholders out after a season of poor rainfall, though obviously they were not responsible for the weather.[2]

The person whose interests have found fulfillment is friendly toward the people and circumstances about him, for they are fostering pleasant experiences. If he is experiencing the satisfaction of recognition and acknowledged accomplishment in school, he participates readily (perhaps sometimes too readily) in class discussions, likes his teachers and the school, and may develop a general attitude of friendly confidence in his relations to those in authority. His morale is likely to be good.

It must not be inferred from this emphasis on the desirability of success experiences that an individual should have *all* his paths smoothed and *all* his

---

[2] An amusing illustration of shifts in broad attitudes after frustration was provided by a student who had recently had a falling-out with his girl (*37*). Asked for an estimate of the state of the world, he wrote: "I believe the world is going socially and morally to destruction. Society is on the downgrade now, even as that of Rome." If the two had made up, doubtless his judgment of the world's future would have been bright.

efforts made successful. He should experience frustration in activities that are undesirable. He should experience difficulties—if he learns from them. Although frustrations may cause fruitless anger, they sometimes, as is seen in the lives of many famous individuals, give rise to a drive that accomplishes more than would otherwise be expected. But if this is to occur, there must be no collapse of morale. The individual must find ways in which he can succeed, and into which he throws himself with increased satisfaction and vigor because he is frustrated elsewhere. A challenging thus accepted may be fun, and success is then great fun.

Changes in Emotion with Age

Being a function of his interests and their frustration or fulfillment, and of his growth and experience, the individual's emotional reactions develop in congruence with all these facts. The evidence in Fig. 5.1 is illustrative of this. It indicates the reports of some 5000 students from Grade 6

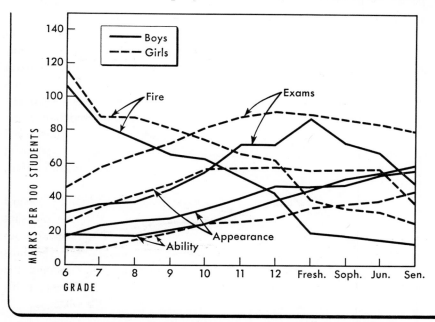

FIG. 5.1. Changes with age in tendency to worry about certain topics, from Grade 6 through college. The "worries" test with which these data were obtained consisted of a list of 90 topics such as fire, examinations, money, morals, appearance. The student was to put one cross or check before each item about which he had felt worried or anxious, and two marks before any items he had worried about a great deal. The figure shows number of marks per 100 students of each sex in each grade; for example, "fire" was checked 115 times per 100 sixth-grade girls, indicating that some of these girls worried much about fires. (From unpublished data of S. L. Pressey.)

through college regarding their worry about certain topics. The figure shows number of checks per 100 people in each grade. Most obvious is the marked anxiety about physical dangers, such as fire, in the younger years, and the way these fears are largely replaced by what might be called social and career worries by the end of college. The girls are apparently more worried by physical dangers such as fire. Until the last two years of college, they show greater concern about appearance, as might be expected from their earlier sex-social maturing. The boys worry more about ability. Clearly, emotional development is a complex phenomenon that involves rate of physical growth and sex differences therein, and also social expectations.

Moreover, youngsters of the same chronological age but differing in physiological maturity usually show emotional traits characteristic of the latter. For example, a group of postmenarcheal girls reacted as more mature emotionally on the Rorschach inkblot test than another group who were the same age but had not reached puberty (9).

Fig. 5.1 was concerned with the unpleasant frustration-produced emotion of worry. But it must not be forgotten that there are also positive

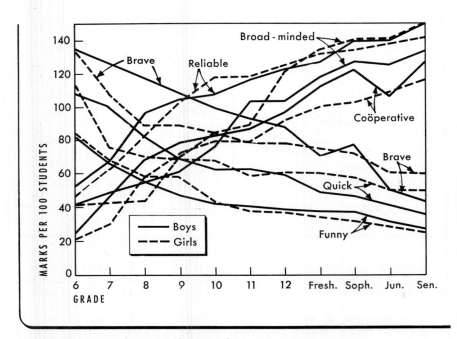

FIG. 5.2. Changes with age in admiration for certain traits.

emotions. Fig. 5.2, from the same investigation, indicates changes with age on certain items of an "admirations" test. Thus the preadolescents in Grade 6 especially esteemed certain lively extrovert traits such as bravery and quickness, and also the superficial ability to be amusing or funny. But these traits were admired less with increasing age; such traits as broad-mindedness and reliability and coöperativeness, all of them involving ability to live and work with other people, are favored instead.

When a youngster recognizes an admired trait in others, he tends to have a positive and favorable feeling toward them; and if others recognize such a trait in him, he has the satisfaction of being socially approved. Again there is a maturing with age which is the product partly of physiological maturing but perhaps even more of social expectations and furtherings; here the school can have a part. Further, it should be noted that the admiration curves in Fig. 5.2 rise higher than the curves for worries in Fig. 5.1. That 100 college senior girls put 149 checks beside "broad-minded" means that about half of them admire this trait very much. In general, with increasing age, there seems to be less emphasis on the frustration-induced emotions of anxiety and fear, and more emphasis on positive feelings of liking and admiration.

A Positive Program for Desirable Emotional Development

This last trend—toward positive pleasant emotions that result from developing desirable interests and finding satisfactions for them—is especially to be sought. It is sometimes said that a child or adolescent is not emotionally mature. Too often what is referred to are his temper tantrums or other displays of frustration-induced emotions. Maturity seems to be thought of as simply the control or elimination of these emotional trends. But healthy emotional maturity is much more than that; there is a pleasant emotional tone that results from the furtherance of desirable interests and attitudes which are increasingly integrated in a personality with desirable positive goals. The concept will be returned to; but certain problems of the frustration type of emotions must first be considered.

COMMON CAUSES OF EMOTIONAL STRESS

Almost any situation may cause emotional distress if it is so unfamiliar to an individual or so difficult that he does not know how to deal with it. Certain confusing or frustrating situations occur so frequently during the school years that they deserve brief mention. As will be stressed shortly, in dealing with an emotional problem the first step is to find its cause.

Adjustment to a New School or Neighborhood

Every nursery-school, kindergarten, and first-grade teacher knows that the first day or two of school is a time of great perturbation for many children because they do not know how to behave in their strange new surroundings. A somewhat similar difficulty arises when the youngster enters secondary school or goes away from home to college. On every such occasion he may feel distressingly uncertain as to what to do, and hence insecure in status. Moving to a new neighborhood, especially if it is distinctly different from the old, may be similarly upsetting.

Because of the itinerant nature of his father's work, an unhappy boy over a period of eight years went to 22 different grade schools and never had a chum or felt secure in any neighborhood or school. His most vivid boyhood memory was of a teacher who understood his problem and, in the five months he was in her class, helped him really to participate in school life.

Social Problems

Adolescents are subject to more varied and often more conflicting social pressures than most adults. Desires stimulated in adolescent groups may be disapproved by church or home, and school-fostered interests derided by companions.

Thus in Elmtown "a youngster who is known as 'a reader' is looked down upon by non-readers, and in a sense pitied, for he is left out of the group activities which form such an important part of 'life' in their age group" (*19*, page 307). The girl who wants to make a high-school social group may find herself snubbed because of her father's occupation or her mother's social ineptitude. A girl of a working-class family in Elmtown made this statement:

"Frankly, for a lot of us there is nothing here, but just going to classes, listening to the teacher, reciting, studying, and going home again. We are pushed out of things. . . . A group of girls here look down on us. . . . They are a group of girls from the higher families. They have a club that is supposed to be outside of school, but it's really in the school. They hog all of the offices. They're in all of the activities. They talk about what they're going to do, and they won't pay any attention to us. They snub us and they won't talk to us" (*19*, page 202).

Such blocking or conflict of desires may cause a lifelong warping of personality; often the real cause of the emotional attitude is concealed because of hurt pride.

Vocational Problems

The preceding chapter presented evidence that many youngsters fail to enter the occupation they want to when they grow up. Many of the high-school girls who planned to be teachers or secretaries were undoubtedly upset when they ended as waitresses. The youngster's vocational desires, and those of his family for him, may conflict. The emotional strain of attempting an impossible vocation, then giving up and, dissatisfied, doing some other work, may be preferable to the longer strain of allowing family influence to make him strive on to a goal he doesn't desire, obtain a job he doesn't want, and do uninteresting tasks for his whole lifetime. A realistic vocational plan that takes sensible account of the individual's abilities, resources, and probable opportunities is a major contribution to emotional well-being.

An acquaintance of one of the writers wanted to be a physician but could not meet medical-school entrance requirements. Even after his marriage and the birth of his first child, he returned to college for one more trial; again his record was too low for entrance to medical school. Only then was he finally convinced of the impossibility of his goal. And in spite of this experience, he wants his oldest boy to study medicine, although the boy does not want to and does not have sufficient ability.

School Failure as a Cause of Emotional Problems

Failure in school is another common and potent cause of emotional disturbance. Adults often fail to realize the extent to which frustration of a youngster's desire for success and status in class and consequent regard at home may distress him. The number of youngsters who avoid this distress by becoming truants or who leave school at the first opportunity is large.

THE PATHOLOGY OF EMOTION

When an individual undergoes continuing strong emotional stress and frustration, the results may vary, depending on his vitality and ability, his previous habits, and the total situation. The results of continued emotional stress are sufficiently common, may have such serious effects, have such a large part in such classroom problems as discipline, and yet are so often misunderstood, that they will now be carefully considered.

The seriousness of some emotional stresses in childhood may not be evident unless there is knowledge of their later consequences. Accordingly, some of the following discussion follows cases of emotional stress into adult life.

Emotional Exhaustion

When an individual remains face to face with a difficulty for a long time he may be worn out by it. He becomes abstracted, inefficient in work, unable to concentrate, irritable; he sleeps poorly, is restless, has indigestion, and shows marked and chronic fatigue. This condition is sometimes called neurasthenia; and if a general collapse follows, the individual is usually said to have a "nervous breakdown." Such people have tolerated an emotional maladjustment until it has exhausted them.

An only child, whose mother died when the girl was born, was "brought up" by her father, of whom she was very fond. She was physically not vigorous and had a quiet and retiring disposition. During her first year in high school her father married a woman whose daughter was also in the first year of high school. The stepsister was a bright, vivacious, attractive youngster who soon overshadowed the other girl both socially and academically. The girl's father did not sense his daughter's difficulty, and she felt that she had lost her previous close companionship with him. She lost appetite, slept irregularly, and began to complain of headache, indigestion, eyestrain, and attacks of dizziness and faintness. There was no evidence of physical disease, although her physical condition was not good. But the emotional invalidism had these two advantages for her. It kept her away from situations where she could not successfully compete, and it brought her, as an ill person, more attention from the family than she could otherwise obtain. Her condition might be described as involving both emotional exhaustion and a hysteroid pseudoillness.

The neurasthenic is finally worn out because he neither solves his emotional problem nor finds any emotional relief. Although other individuals fail to solve their difficulties, they nevertheless manage to avoid them in some degree by what might be called pseudosolutions.

Escapes and Pseudosolutions

Perhaps the most obvious thing a person can do when faced by an unpleasant situation is to run away from it. Sometimes the escape is actual—the youth leaves school, the man resigns his job, the wife leaves her husband, the mother abandons her illegitimate child.

Some individuals cannot or will not run away, in the sense of actual flight to a new locality. However, they can still escape almost as completely by other devices. Perhaps the most common is daydreaming. Everyone daydreams a bit; if not so habitual that they interfere with the youngster's real work and play, such imaginings give some emotional relief and no harm is done. The trouble comes when a child settles into habitual daydreaming instead of trying to make good in his work or play.

This may happen when a youngster who is not very aggressive or sure of himself is faced day after day with a total situation that seems unsolvable. He cannot run away, although he may try to; and since he is not vigorous or assertive, no outbursts of resentment are likely. However, a retreat from the whole unbearable situation is both possible and comfortable—he can simply not notice what is going on around him but substitute daydreams in which he plays with imaginary companions, is liked by them, and can do as he wishes.

If such "escapes" are indulged in long enough, the individual may finally even become mentally ill, develop schizophrenia. The essential characteristic of this disease is a withdrawal from reality to a world of fantasy. The condition may often be traced back to persistent odd behavior in adolescence and even childhood. In its early stages, parents rarely appreciate the danger; unless the teacher does, no preventive steps are likely to be taken.

The unhappy, socially isolated youngster who finds relief in reverie is often overlooked because he is so quiet and well behaved. For instance, one girl moved from the country and went to a large city high school, where her somewhat boisterous, unsophisticated efforts at friendliness were rebuffed. She was hurt and bewildered at first, then irritable and defiant; her class work slumped badly. But gradually she seemed to become reconciled to the situation; she would sit for long periods of time apparently deep in thought, occasionally smiling to herself. A little later she dropped out of school. She tried to get a job but was too abstracted and absent-minded to be employable. Gradually she lost contact with the real world; she sat still, apparently in a daze and smiling oddly, developed queer mannerisms which were apparently related to her imaginary experiences, suddenly became excited or exhausted occasionally, apparently without reason. Finally she had to be sent to a hospital for the mentally ill.

These extreme cases are not common; but their possibility should make the teacher carefully consider any pupils who show such symptoms. Although the final collapse rarely occurs while the youngster is in school, the teacher should realize that the disease has its start in the frustration and withdrawal into an imaginary world just described. She may be able to help bring the withdrawn child back into friendly association with other children and into active interests. But if the difficulties increase, she may refer the youngster to a counselor or school psychologist if available, or talk over the case with the principal. Sometimes a psychiatrist may be needed.

Reading too many sentimental stories or watching television or movies or listening to the radio may be an escape from and a substitute for an unhappy situation. The physically weak boy may not only dream of being a star in athletics but read stories about athletes. The homely shy girl may dream of being popular and find a wistful pleasure in romance and in stories of girls who are happy in home and school.

"Rationalization," "projection," and "sour grapes" are common types of response. A boy who wants to belong to a neighborhood gang but is rejected may rationalize his exclusion by saying that his parents object to his playing with these undesirable boys. Or he may project the blame on some boy in the gang, saying that this boy has always disliked him for no reason at all. Projection is, in essence, merely a particular form of rationalizing in which the individual shifts the burden of his own maladjustment to someone else. Again, he may tell anyone who will listen that the gang is not really worth belonging to—just like the fox in the fable who could not reach the grapes he wanted and so said they were sour and not worth getting.

Overcompensation

Feelings of inferiority may cause an individual to pretend to be self-confident and desperately make himself look adequate when he really is not. He pushes into everything, brags about his achievements, is generally obnoxious, usually resists discipline, and constantly tries to "show off." But a little close observation usually shows that a bewildered and unhappy youngster is frantically trying to conceal his inadequacies and to bluff through situations that are difficult for him. Some of these extroverts succeed, emerging with a real adjustment and a truly self-confident personality. But other people, their bluff called, collapse, with courage gone and spirit broken.

A teacher should understand these conditions for what they are and help the youngster to a real adjustment, instead of adding to his burden by disciplinary measures which, at best, can serve only to eliminate certain symptoms.

Hysteroid Reactions to Emotional Distress

Children who are frustrated and in emotional distress may hit upon a peculiar, inadequate response which they use because it seems to work—at least it gives some release to the stress.

A dull third-grade boy was failing in school, chronically scolded by his teacher, and looked down upon by the other children. One afternoon he vomited his lunch—partly because of indigestion and partly because of emotional distress from a scolding. To his astonishment, his illness aroused sympathy in both teacher and children, and for the first time in his life he was the center of attention. Thereafter, whenever he was scolded or his desires were blocked he vomited.

A little girl had been told some smutty stories that had greatly disturbed her, especially because she was assured, on what she considered undebatable authority, that her adored mother and father indulged in the practice so lewdly described to her. She could not reconcile what she heard with her previous estimate of her parents' moral infallibility. The conflict continued to disturb her, causing general restlessness, careless school work, and sexual fantasies. Finally she struck out at the problem and her discomfort by stealing money from the cash register in her father's store. By some obscure reasoning, this act seemed to bring relief. Several thefts followed directly after she received more sex information from an older child, thus precipitating the fundamental problem once again.

These special devices for gaining attention or getting one's own way range all the way from the small child's simple tantrums to almost unbelievably bizarre hysterical episodes. But they all have this in common —they originate in frustration and emotional distress and are aimed at relieving that distress and achieving the frustrated desire in some form. In handling such cases, therefore, it is exceedingly important that the teacher seek the cause and not merely the symptoms. Obviously, exposing the girl for her unconscious subterfuge or punishing the boy for his gastric gymnastics might or might not suppress the particular symptoms in question, but it would increase the emotional distress, and almost inevitably other similar devices would appear.

In both cases, the hysteroid symptoms disappeared after their cause was dealt with. For the boy, treatment consisted in transferring him to a special class for slow learners where he could do the work and was acceptable like the other children. During the period of his readjustment, his vomiting was disregarded as far as possible. When he could gain normal attention and satisfactions in other ways, it ceased. The girl was talked to quietly until her deep conviction regarding the nastiness of sex relations was replaced by an attitude of understanding. Her stealing has stopped. At the moment both children are free of their earlier troubles, but this freedom may not last. The dull boy will undoubtedly meet failure again, and the girl may find heterosexual adjustment and marriage difficult.

Stammering and Other Incoördinations

Prolonged emotional stress may be manifested by stammering. For a few unfortunate children thus afflicted, actual anatomical defects or dysfunctioning is at the base of their difficulty. Most stammerers, however, have no physical handicaps; that the major cause is emotional distress is shown by the fact that when the person feels relaxed and comfortable he speaks normally, but when he is embarrassed or excited he stammers. School obviously offers the stammerer numerous opportunities for embarrassment. Most cases clear up early in adulthood, after the stresses of adolescence and schooling are past; but residues of shyness and reticence unfortunately remain.

Instead of stammering or in addition to it there may be other inco-ordinations such as tics, peculiarities of movement or posture, or clumsiness. Again these may have a physical basis; thus the tic or the clumsiness may be a residual of chorea. More often, however, the cause is emotional.

Belligerence

A person who is too vigorous to admit defeat, too pugnacious to run away, and too clear-headed to fool himself by pseudosolutions, may fight back at a world that is so uncomfortable. Naturally, this type of behavior leads to acute and stubborn problems of discipline in school and at home.

The father of a high-school boy was in the penitentiary—unjustly, according to the boy. For a time after the commitment the boy was somewhat dazed, was humiliated by comments about the matter, was ignored when invitations for social gatherings were issued. Presently, however, he began fighting back. He struck anyone who mentioned his father; when a little girl ignored him, he twisted her arm until he had forced her to kneel and apologize; his bellicose attitude extended to adults. On one occasion, he tinkered with the brakes on a teacher's car so that they would not hold; the teacher was nearly killed. Twice he set fire to valuable property. This striking back at society was his method of responding to intolerable humiliation.

Aggression may manifest itself in various ways. Most obvious is aggression against the cause of the frustration—the adolescent is angry at the parent who objects to his late hours and to his other efforts to escape from childhood restraints. But there may be displacement. Thus a brilliant college girl had been dominated all her life by her brilliant and very dominating mother. She admired her parent too much to rebel but became a great advocate of causes to aid the oppressed; her latest episode was leading a student strike against a faculty rule.

Especially important here is an early calm understanding of the real situation and alleviation of the frustrations, or the provision of substitute responses which enable the individual to make good.

Efforts were made to help the belligerent boy just described. The other pupils were asked to be considerate of him and to accept him. He was helped to make good in athletics. His escapades were disposed of out of court, and one teacher who understood him had many friendly talks with him. Unfortunately, however, things had gone too far; most of the other students and teachers, and the boy himself, were too bitter to permit reconciliations. He was given just enough help to keep him out of trouble and to let him get by, and he began to take pride in his ability to get along in this way. After leaving school he became notorious as a man who engaged in shady business practices but with whom the law never quite caught up.

The girl who led the strike was talked to in a considerate way by a teacher who knew her very well; and when she had calmed down a bit she was asked if her difficulties with her mother might not have something to do with her crusading zeal. After a moment of spluttering protest she laughed and admitted that this might be so. The strike was soon over. But the girl is a chronic agitator and leader of causes. And in all fairness it should be said that often the cause is good and she renders a real service. As was said earlier, many famous people seem to have obtained their drive from psychological backgrounds like those described above. In his autobiography Benjamin Franklin said that his lifelong desire for liberty may have had its origin in his boyhood resentment at an older brother's domination.

Factors Determining Mode of Response to Emotional Strain

Why one person reacts to persistent emotional strain in one way, another person reacts in very different fashion, and a third seems hardly affected, is often not clear. It is generally recognized that individuals who are suffering from illness, fatigue, or lack of sleep are especially subject to emotional upset. Differences in physical vigor may affect the mode of response, the physically strong people tending more toward belligerence and the physically weaker to escape or exhaustion. The stage of physical development is probably a factor. Thus one investigator found a high correlation between aggressiveness in boys and evidence of the onset of puberty (10, page 103).

Social and cultural factors are important. Aggression is a more approved reaction for boys than for girls. A repressed New Englander seems more likely to become neurasthenic than a Southerner. A person from a lower social class is perhaps more likely to overcompensate. The family "culture pattern" is undoubtedly influential. We probably all know some families in which the children rarely cry when hurt, and others in which crying or hysterical outbursts are the expected form of response to any difficulty. But within each family there may be differences in reaction to emotional strain.

Frequency of Emotional Distress

It remains to emphasize that a considerable degree of emotional distress is by no means rare. A careful and intensive study of the emotional life of a group of college students, selected more or less at random, showed that 68 percent had either a past or a present inferiority feeling. One-third had experienced rejection in childhood. One-third had had a marked guilt reaction. According to a concluding paragraph of the study:

"Most of our subjects were carrying . . . a heavy load of crippling anxiety, inferiority feelings, guilt feelings or dejection. Many of them, of course, were troubled by thoughts of financial insecurity, but the majority were more concerned about their general social status. They doubted that they could live up to their own standards or to the expectations of their parents. Frequently, they suffered from memories of stinging humiliations, and when they went to their books in the evening, overriding apprehensive thoughts of future failure or depressing feelings of separateness and forsakenness prevented concentration. A basic sense of insupport aggravated by dissensions with one or both parents was a frequent finding. This was commonly accompanied by moral conflict" (37, page 730).

Most people, knowing little about the emotional distresses of other people, overestimate their own and underestimate others' troubles. Increased considerateness toward others and an increase in one's own comparative self-confidence may well follow recognition of the double fact. The need for much more helpful consideration of these so frequent and so distressing problems is also emphasized.

"The patterns of affective behavior shown by children are certainly as important as their number knowledge, eye-movement habits, and language skills; yet they are widely ignored by school people. Tantrums, daydreaming, fighting, shyness, teasing and bullying, bidding for the attention and approbation of the teacher, masturbation, impertinence, and a host of other ways of behaving are the patterns by which pupils try to relieve tensions or work out their personality needs. To recognize these behavior patterns for what they are, to understand their causes, to know the manner in which they were learned, to find more mature ways of behaving appropriate to the particular child and to evoke that mature behavior—these are not easy tasks for school people" (42, page 202).

THE DIAGNOSIS OF DISCIPLINARY PROBLEMS

Chronic or severe emotional strain has been emphasized thus far because in a young person's development this condition is far more important than occasional outbursts of talking back, laughing uncontrollably, fighting, swearing, or crying, and because, being more extreme and persistent, it shows more clearly the important phenomena involved. Furthermore, the discussion was not restricted to emotional problems in the school, because it is vital that emotional distress be understood as a whole, in relation to the child's total existence. The question now arises as to what understanding may be obtained concerning episodes of conflict in the school. Since disciplinary problems are usually the most difficult ones the young teacher has to handle, insight into them should be of great value.

Chronic Emotional Distress and Disciplinary Problems

First to be considered are situations in which the chronic emotional conditions discussed in the preceding section cause disciplinary crises. Belligerence and overcompensation are almost bound to create episodes of classroom conflict. The rationalizing pupils who are always blaming someone or something else are usually irritating to the other pupils and the teacher. Hysteroid behavior is likely to be both disturbing and puzzling. The daydreamer and the neurasthenic usually present no classroom police problems, except as the daydreamer may resent the teacher's efforts to break in upon his reverie, or an unsympathetic teacher may push a neurasthenic so far beyond his strength that he becomes desperate (that they are particularly in need of her help has already been stressed). In view of what was said in the preceding two sections, it should not be necessary to elaborate further on the extent to which children who are suffering from persistent emotional distress may present persistent problems of classroom management. If a teacher will locate and carefully study such children, she will be on the way to a solution of her most baffling disciplinary problems. However, even though a pupil is not emotionally "sick," he may nevertheless present disciplinary difficulties.

Disciplinary Problems Arising from an Unsuitable School Program

Difficulties may result from the reaction of healthy children against an unsuitable school routine or work program. Healthy children are active and restless; being still for any length of time is almost intolerable for them. And they are highly social. But the conventional school routine is inactive and tends to repress sociability.

The curricula of the average school are all too often out of contact with the pupils' interests. Girls who would enjoy good modern literature and who should be helped to a discriminating acquaintance with it may be required to read Shakespeare. Modern-minded youngsters who would read avidly about current events must consider instead the state of the Roman Empire under Augustus or study the weary details of the Hundred Years' War. Many children still plod wearily and resentfully through the intricacies of Latin grammar. Little wonder that an alert and questioning younger generation, hungry for knowledge about the manifold problems of the modern world, should be chronically rebellious against the inanities still found in many high-school courses of study. And the teacher who must force such a program on her pupils must expect to have continuing disciplinary difficulties in holding them to such tasks.

Finally, in the average school there are numerous instances of maladjustment between work and ability. The boy in the algebra class who cannot learn algebra is a frustrated, unhappy, resentful youngster who is almost certain to cause the teacher trouble. The daughter of a factory worker who is being forced to wade through *Hamlet,* though she has no understanding of it, is more than likely to pass notes or whisper to her neighbor. The highly intelligent girl in the first-year French class who can read better than the average third-year pupil is almost certain to lapse into periods of inattention which are irritating to her teacher.

In some schools, then, many of the conflicts between pupil and teacher are the fault of the school, not the pupil. It may almost be said that the healthier and more intelligent the pupil, the more frequent such conflicts. Therefore, if minor disciplinary problems are frequent, a teacher should consider whether such factors may be the real cause. To be sure, she is largely helpless to remedy certain of the above faults, as in the course of study. But if she understands the situation she will at least be more tolerant; and perhaps, when she is on some curriculum committee, she can do a little to make things better. In numerous little ways she can bring the work into more vital contact with the needs and interests of her class.

The Teacher's Attitude as a Cause of Emotional Stress

Often a teacher's attitude toward her pupils arouses in them feelings that engender disciplinary problems. Significant here is Table 5.2. Clearly the teacher who loses her temper, has favorites, and is overbearing is likely to stir up resentful emotions in her students and to have disciplinary problems.

TABLE 5.2. Four Best- and Least-Liked Teacher Characteristics Mentioned
by 3725 High-School Seniors[3]

Best-Liked Teacher	Mentions
Helpful with school work, explains lessons clearly	1950
Cheerful, jolly, can take a joke	1429
Human, friendly, companionable, "one of us"	1024
Interested in and understands pupils	1024
Least-Liked Teacher	
Cross, crabby, nagging, sarcastic, loses temper	1708
Not helpful with school work, work not planned	1025
Has favored students and "picks" on others	859
Haughty, overbearing, does not know you out of class	775

HANDLING PROBLEMS OF EMOTIONAL DEVELOPMENT

It remains to bring together the implications in this chapter regarding the handling of emotional frustration and fulfillment. The following points seem most important.

Going Back of Symptoms to the Underlying Situation

It is first of all fundamental to recognize the inadequacy of treating symptoms without considering the underlying situation. The pupil who is belligerent, morose, a daydreamer, or a truant is not adequately dealt with by being punished for his aggression, berated for his moodiness, rudely interrupted in his "woolgathering," or pursued by the attendance officer; such treatment may instead aggravate the basic difficulty in each case. The important questions are: What frustration or confusion is causing the aggressiveness or moodiness or the imaginary or real flight from the schoolroom? How can that situation be cleared up? These problems, not the symptoms, require attention.

Even where there is not frustration but furtherance, the background situation must be considered. Mabel seems particularly interested in history and is doing notably well, but a crush on the history teacher proves to be the key factor in the situation. Ruth writes so well that her delighted English teacher hints at a possible career as an author; but Ruth is a shy little girl whose interest in literature is almost as unhealthy a substitute for real experience as daydreaming. Bill's long hours and beautiful work in the industrial arts shop are in part an escape from and a compensation for the poor work he does in his other subjects. Mary's

[3] From Prescott, *42*, pp. 273–274.

interest in preparing to teach is found to be due primarily to her mother's interest in having her do so; Mary's good work in normal school is motivated by her loyalty to her parent, not eagerness for her prospective profession. John's good work in algebra is partly a drive to beat Algernon, son of the community's haughty social leader. Whatever the nature of the emotional experience, unless the teacher considers the background situation she may make sad and even ridiculous mistakes.

The puzzled mathematics teacher found that when Algernon dropped out of the class John's work slumped. Ruth's interest in literature evaporated after she acquired a boy friend. When Mabel's crush came to its inevitable disillusionment, she "hated" history.

Possible Emotional Involvement of the Teacher

In the second place, it is of prime importance that the teacher keep her own emotions from becoming so involved in her relations with her pupils that she acts to satisfy her own feelings rather than her pupils' needs. A youngster's inattention, stubbornness, or insolence naturally arouses irritation and aggressive responses in the teacher, and giving vent to her own feelings by sarcastic remarks is a release and satisfaction to her. But usually it only increases the tension. Instead of reacting subjectively in terms of her own feelings, the teacher should remain objective; her attitude should be a calm, friendly open-mindedness and a desire to understand what the trouble really is. Often nothing more is needed to handle a disciplinary situation than easy good nature and a refusal to take a little excitement seriously.

"Objectivity" means further that the teacher is not shocked or upset by the various types of distressing information which come to her. For instance, a desperate youngster may blurt out a story of a sex episode which to her seems disgusting. But she must not show that feeling, any more than a physician does when he sees a patient. Nor should she go into a dither of sympathy for the unhappy youngster, any more than a physician does in connection with a patient. An important attribute of a good physician is his relaxed, confident cheerfulness in the sickroom— the feeling he gives that things aren't as bad as the patient thinks, that many people have been ill before and recovered, that there is no need for worry, that if the patient will only keep calm and follow the doctor's directions he will be better before long. Similarly, the distraught youngster needs reassurance, an understanding of his problem, and common-sense suggestions as to what he should do. The well-informed teacher knows that, among children, various episodes and habits are not so ab-normal as was once supposed. She will not be prudish or moralistic; she may give, either directly or in suggested reading material, information which will be of aid; she will make helpful suggestions or suggest where they can be obtained—perhaps from the physician, nurse, or psychologist.

A teacher should be objective and on guard against any possible in-volvement of her own emotions in connection with her pupils' likes and accomplishments as well as their antagonisms and wrongdoings. Thus Mabel's interest in history, mentioned above, was at first encouraged by her teacher in large part because this teacher greatly enjoyed the girl's admiring attentions. The English teacher encouraged Ruth in her idea of becoming an author and helped her get a story published in the local paper, because it added to the teacher's own self-feeling and reputation as the one who had discovered and developed this girl's "unusual talents." The mathematics teacher did not like Algernon much better than John did, and partly for that reason encouraged John. In fact, the aver-age teacher, being human, probably deals with her pupils' emotional problems most of the time on the basis of her own feelings rather than theirs.

Deep-seated and long-established attitudes present especially difficult prob-lems here. Two teachers in the same school—we shall call them Miss Wright and Miss Frank—had both come from very strict homes. Miss Wright was a repressed sensitive woman who was so shocked and upset by student delin-quency that she was worse than useless in dealing with it. But she did a great deal to encourage and help shy sensitive girls such as she had been. Miss Frank was a big hearty rebel who was impatient with sensitive people but rather admired pupils with "spunk" even when they got into trouble. Youngsters who liked one of these teachers usually disliked the other. As faculty advisers, each was good—in fact, sometimes too sympathetic—in dealing with the emo-tional problems of some pupils but only stirred up trouble in contacts with others. In assigning students to advisers the shrewd principal kept these facts in mind, and the two teachers nicely supplemented each other, each handling especially well the youngsters the other disliked.

The teacher's as well as the pupil's emotions are thus involved in most emotional problems that arise in school—and to keep thinking straight is indeed a task for all concerned. Perhaps the greatest single help in this—beyond understanding it—is a sense of humor. If in considering these problems a teacher can laugh at herself—and with but not at her pupils—tensions are released and perspectives gained.

Inadequacy of a Police Point of View

All too often administrators (and visiting parents) consider a teacher capable in proportion as she keeps order. And the teacher approves the pupils who never upset the order in her room, but exerts herself especially to restrain the lively youngsters who "disturb the peace." This is a police point of view.

However, if the vigorous outgoing development of each child is considered the main objective of education, criteria for judging both teacher and pupil will be very different indeed. The quiet repressed child will be regarded as a problem, as will also the repressive teacher who tends to make the children repressed. The good teacher will be recognized as the one whose pupils feel so secure and unrepressed that legitimate activities can be undertaken without hesitation. She will try to free them of frustrations, fears, and resentments, and resolve any impasse that creates unpleasant emotion. There is evidence that teachers understand such matters now far better than they did formerly (*51*).

Fostering Desirable Emotional Experiences

Again it must be emphasized that a teacher should do more than prevent frustrations; she should foster desirable emotional experiences. It was suggested at the beginning of this chapter that pleasant emotions result from the satisfaction of interests—in contrast to emotional distress, which is caused by their frustration. We saw in the preceding chapter, however, that interests are the complex product of many factors, and that they have their roots in biological urges. But specific interests are largely determined by the total socioeconomic and cultural environment in which the individual develops. Therefore the school can make an initial contribution to a youngster's happiness by directing his interests sensibly so that they are in keeping with his abilities and hence feasible for him.

In the second place, the school can help the youngster realize his interests and aspirations at a given time, assuming that they are good. As was emphasized earlier in this chapter and also in the discussion of special abilities, the satisfying of interests can be as pleasant and as upbuilding as their frustration is distressing and destructive. It is to these constructive tasks that the teacher should direct her chief efforts, and it is in them that she will find her own greatest satisfactions. Her work should be a deeply satisfying experience for her.

Clearly this point of view calls for both school and teacher to recognize a wider variety of interests—as in activity, social interaction—than used to be acceptable, and for freer and more lively emotional satisfactions. But psychologists are increasingly recognizing that intellectual interests are part of human nature and that "insight is usually a bright, happy, emotional spot in any person's life, perhaps even a high spot in the life span." This is well brought out by the grade-school child, mentioned in the preceding chapter, who reported being thrilled when he learned to "take away" in arithmetic. "Thinking in the healthiest people—if they are also intelligent—is not only . . . stimulated by some disequilibrating problem or nuisance, and disappearing when the problem is solved. It is also spontaneous, sportive and pleasurable, and is often emitted or produced without effort, automatically, as the liver secretes bile. Such men *enjoy* being thinking animals, they do not have to be harassed into it" (*31*, pages 96, 369). In school, gifted pupils who are taking programs that are suitable for them often show such feelings. They "get a joy (one called it a 'thrill of the brain') when they get an 'idea' or make an 'original discovery.' . . . These youngsters give the impression that they enjoy thinking. Their 'I've got it' lights up their faces." And to work with them is a joy to their teachers, who "often came to school long before their first class to meet with students or prepare for special work with them" (*3*, pages 58–59, 67).

The preceding paragraph stressed the emotional satisfactions that are to be found in school work, for these are often not recognized. Efforts to heighten them may well be made. "Mild excitement is sought by most people. . . . Its effects are physically desirable rather than undesirable. . . . Educators may find justification here for making vivid experiences an integral part of many phases of the educative process" (*42*, page 21). For this reason and because of their inherent value, sundry experiences which may occur in connection with school must also be emphasized. In school, youngsters may form pleasant and often long-continuing friendships. A teen-ager may find all that goes on in a good secondary school richly satisfying. And a capable and popular teacher, as the person who in various respects is at the center of all this and is most important, may find satisfaction as she could in few other occupations. Certain of these points will be taken up again in the next chapter; others, toward the end of the book.

There is reason to hope that, as more and more courses in psychology and mental hygiene are given in the public schools, these courses will increasingly help pupils understand their emotions and plan their interests and the emotional satisfactions they seek wisely (*12, 39*). Indeed, children as well as adults may find emotional understanding in reading, or "bibliotherapy" (*18*). But most of these materials place too little emphasis on the pleasant and desirable emotions mentioned above.

SUMMARY

The chapter has stressed what has been called a functional concept of emotion. Emotion was defined as a condition of heightened feeling which may be pleasant or unpleasant according to whether the interest involved is satisfied or frustrated. If frustrated, the individual may draw back, or he may become aggressive and drive ahead with increased and angry effort. When there is success, there is usually furtherance of the activity —a tendency to continue it with heightened vigor. The total individual responds to this total biological situation. With frustration there is interference with normal physiological activities; with success, a heightening of them. The person who is failing tends to give up what he is doing, but one who is succeeding applies himself more. With frustration there is irritability or fear; success brings confidence and agreeableness. Emotional experiences naturally are affected by age and by socioeconomic circumstances. Growth should lead toward an increasingly positive happy emotional life.

Some frustration and emotional distress are likely whenever a particularly difficult problem arises. A child or adolescent is especially likely to have difficulty when he enters a new school or neighborhood; when his development, as in adolescence, provides him with new interests; when he has trouble with his school work, social ambitions, or vocational plans. When such crises are apparently at hand, a wise teacher will make a special effort to help.

If frustration becomes acute or chronic, abnormal psychological conditions may result. The unhappy person may be exhausted by his struggle. He may try to run away or escape from his problem, or deceive himself about it, or adopt a pseudosolution. He may become angry and aggressive. Such conditions are symptoms of emotional illness and call for careful study and treatment.

Emotional problems are particularly difficult to handle because pupils often dissimulate, and the teacher's own feelings are frequently involved. It is therefore very important to get back of symptoms to the underlying causes, and to be objective. Most important of all, the teacher should try to foster success and desirable emotional experiences, rather than simply to prevent emotional distress. She herself may find rich emotional satisfaction in her work.

BIBLIOGRAPHY

1. Anastasi, A., Cohen, N., and Spatz, D., A study of fear and anger in college students through the controlled diary method, *J. Genet. Psychol.*, 1948, *73*:243–249.
2. Barker, R., Frustration as an experimental problem. The effect of frustration upon cognitive ability, *Character and Pers.*, 1938, *7*:145–150.
3. Brandwein, P. F., *The Gifted Student as Future Scientist*, New York: Harcourt, Brace, 1955.
4. Brown, C. H., and Von Selder, D., Emotional reactions before examinations, *J. Psychol.*, 1938, *5*:1–9, 11–26, 27–31.
5. Buswell, Margaret M., The relationship between the social structure of the classroom and the academic success of the pupils, *J. Exper. Educ.*, 1953–1954, *22*:37–52.
6. Cole, Charles C., Jr., *Encouraging Scientific Talent*, Princeton: College Entrance Examination Board, 1956.
7. Cruikshank, W. M., and Dolphin, J. E., A study of the emotional needs of crippled children, *J. Educ. Psychol.*, 1949, *40*:295–305.
8. Cummings, Jean D., The incidence of emotional symptoms in school children, *Brit. J. Educ. Psychol.*, 1944, *14*:151–161.
9. Davidson, H. H., and Gottlieb, L. S., The emotional maturity of pre- and post-menarcheal girls, *J. Genet. Psychol.*, 1955, *86*:261–266.
10. Dollard, J., and others, *Frustration and Aggression*, New Haven: Yale Univ. Press, 1939.
11. Ellis, A., and Beechley, R. M., Emotional disturbance in children with peculiar given names, *J. Genet. Psychol.*, 1954, *85*:337–339.
12. Engle, T. L., and Bunch, M. E., The teaching of psychology in high school, *Amer. Psychol.*, 1956, *11*:188–193.
13. Filer, R. J., Frustration, satisfaction, and other factors affecting the attractiveness of goal objects, *J. Abnorm. Soc. Psychol.*, 1952, *47*:203–212.
14. Fite, M. D., Aggressive behavior in young children and children's attitudes toward aggression, *Genet. Psychol. Monog.*, 1940, *22*:151–319.
15. French, T. M., An analysis of the goal concept based upon study of reactions to frustration, *Psychoanal. Rev.*, 1941, *28*:61–71.
16. Gebbard, Mildred E., Effect of success and failure upon the attractiveness of activities as a function of experience, expectation, and need, *J. Exper. Psychol.*, 1948, *38*:371–387.
17. Goodenough, F. L., and others, *Studies in Personality*, New York: McGraw-Hill, 1942.
18. Gottschalk, L. A., Bibliotherapy as an adjuvant in psychotherapy, *Amer. J. Psychiat.*, 1948, *104*:32–37.
19. Hollingshead, A. B., *Elmtown's Youth*, New York: Wiley, 1949.

20. Holmes, F. B., An experimental investigation of a method of overcoming children's fears, *Child Devel.,* 1936, *7*:6–30.
21. Jersild, A. T., Emotional development, chap. 14 in Carmichael, L. (ed.), *Manual of Child Psychology,* New York: Wiley, 1954.
22. Kahn, Jacob P., Treatment of a withdrawn girl, *Amer. J. Orthopsychiat.,* 1953, *23*:3, 629–643.
23. Kanner, L., *Child Psychiatry,* Springfield: Thomas, rev. ed., 1948.
24. Keister, M. D., and Updegraff, R. A., Study of children's reactions to failure and an experimental attempt to modify them, *Child Devel.,* 1937, *8*:241–248.
25. Kimball, Barbara, Case studies in educational failure during adolescence, *Amer. J. Orthopsychiat.,* 1953, *23*:2, 406–415.
26. Lantz, B., Some dynamic aspects of success and failure, *Psychol. Monog.,* 1945, *59,* No. 1.
27. Lewin, K., Lippitt, R., and White, R. K., Patterns of aggressive behavior in experimentally created "social climates," *J. Soc. Psychol.,* 1939, *10*:271–308.
28. Lewis, Nan A., and Taylor, Janet A., Anxiety and extreme response preference, *Educ. and Psychol. Meas.,* 1955, *15*:111–116.
29. Lowenstein, P., and Svendsen, M., Experimental modification of the behavior of a selected group of shy and withdrawn children, *Amer. J. Orthopsychiat.,* 1938, *8*:639–653.
30. Mandler, G., and Sarason, S. B., A study of anxiety and learning, *J. Abnorm. Soc. Psychol.,* 1952, *47*:166–173.
31. Maslow, A. H., *Motivation and Personality,* New York: Harper, 1954.
32. McKinney, F., Hines, R. R., Strother, G. B., and Allee, R. A., Experimental frustration in a group test situation, *J. Abnorm. Soc. Psychol.,* 1951, *46*:316–323.
33. Mensh, I. N., and Mason, E. P., Relationship of school atmosphere to reactions in frustrating situations, *J. Educ. Res.,* 1951–1952, *45*:275–286.
34. Moldawsky, S., and Moldawsky, P. C., Digit span as an anxiety indicator, *J. Consult. Psychol.,* 1952, *16*:115–118.
35. Moncur, J. P., Symptoms of maladjustment differentiating young stutterers from non-stutterers, *Child Devel.,* 1955, *26*:91–96.
36. Murphy, Lois B., and Ladd, H., *Emotional Factors in Learning,* New York: Columbia Univ. Press, 1944.
37. Murray, H. A., and others, *Explorations in Personality,* New York: Oxford Univ. Press, 1938.
38. Muste, Myra J., and Sharpe, Doris F., Some influential factors in the determination of aggressive behavior in preschool children, *Child Devel.,* 1947, *18*:11–28.
39. Patti, J. B., Elementary psychology for eighth graders, *Amer. Psychol.,* 1956, *11*:194–196.
40. Podolsky, E., The father's occupation and the child's emotions, *Understanding the Child,* 1954, *23*:22–24.

41. Postman, L., and Brown, J. R., The perceptual consequence of success and failure, *J. Abnorm. Soc. Psychol.*, 1952, *47*:213–221.

42. Prescott, D. A., *Emotion and Educative Process*, Washington: American Council on Education, 1938.

43. Redl, Fritz, and Wineman, David, *Children Who Hate*, Glencoe: Free Press, 1951.

44. Reichenberg-Hackett, Wally, Changes in Goodenough drawing after a gratifying experience, *Amer. J. Orthopsychiat.*, 1953, *23*:501–516.

45. Remits, E. L., *The Feeling of Superiority and Anxiety-Superior: The Ottawa Pilot Study*, Ottawa: Runge Press, 1953.

46. Remmers, H. H., and Bauerfeind, R. H., Children worry too, *Natl. Elem. Principal*, 1952, *32*:27–29.

47. Reymert, M. L. (ed.), *Feelings and Emotions: the Mooseheart Symposium*, New York: McGraw-Hill, 1950.

48. Rogers, C. R., *The Clinical Treatment of the Problem Child*, Boston: Houghton Mifflin, 1939.

49. Sandin, A. A., Social and emotional adjustments of regularly promoted and non-promoted pupils, *Teach. Coll. Child Devel. Monog.*, 1944, No. 32.

50. Schoeppe, A., Haggard, E. A., and Havighurst, R. J., Some factors affecting 16-year-olds' success in five developmental tasks, *J. Abnorm. Soc. Psychol.*, 1953, *48*:42–52.

51. Schrupp, Manford H., and Gjerde, Clayton M., Teacher growth in attitudes toward behavior problems of children, *J. Educ. Psychol.*, 1953, *44*:4, 203–214.

52. Sears, Pauline S., Doll play aggression in normal young children: influence of sex, sibling status, father's absence, *Psychol. Monog.*, 1951, *65*, No. 323.

53. Sears, R. R., Hoyland, J., and Miller, N. E., Minor studies of aggression: I, Measurement of aggressive behavior, *J. Psychol.*, 1940, *9*:275–294.

54. Sears, R. R., Whiting, J., Nowlis, V., and Sears, P., Some child rearing antecedents of aggression and dependency in young children, *Genet. Psychol. Monog.*, 1953, *47*:135–234.

55. Seyle, Hans, *The Stress of Life*, New York: McGraw-Hill, 1956.

56. Sherman, M., and Bell, E., The measurement of frustration: an experiment in group frustration, *Personality*, 1951, *1*:44–53.

57. Shirley, M. M., and Poyntz, L., Children's emotional response to health examinations, *Child Devel.*, 1945, *16*:89–95.

58. Skubic, Elvera, Emotional responses of boys to little league and middle league competitive baseball, *Res. Quart.*, 1955, *26*:342–352.

59. Smock, C. D., The influence of psychological stress on the "intolerance of ambiguity," *J. Abnorm. Soc. Psychol.*, 1955, *50*:177–182.

60. Thompson, G. G., and Hunnicutt, C. W., The effect of repeated praise or blame on the work achievement of "introverts" and "extroverts," *J. Educ. Psychol.*, 1944, *35*:257–266.

61. Thompson, G. G., and Kepler, M. O., A study of the production of

pleasant and unpleasant items as related to adolescent development, *J. Educ. Psychol.,* 1945, *36*:535–542.

62. Waterhouse, I. K., and Child, I. L., Frustration and the quality of performance, *J. Pers.,* 1952–1953, *21*:298–311.

63. Zachry, C. B., and Lighty, M., *Emotion and Conduct in Adolescence,* New York: Appleton-Century-Crofts, 1940.

Chapter 6

Social Development in Childhood and Youth

CHAPTER 4 INDICATED THAT INTERESTS ARE LARGELY determined by social influences. But even more than that—interests increasingly *are* social until in adolescence they are predominantly so; the drive for social recognition and status becomes the most pervasively important of all. Emotional stress was found to be largely the product of social conflict or maladjustment, and various types of mental abnormality to be the result of such distress when long continued. Disciplinary problems in school usually have such backgrounds. Hence the pupil's social development provides the key for understanding many of the most difficult problems with which a teacher has to deal. Guiding this development along healthy and desirable lines might well be considered the first concern of modern education. Therefore an adequate treatment of the social psychology of the first twenty years should be essential in educational psychology.

Social development is continuous and cumulative; how a child gets along with other people at 10 or even at 5 may be of great importance in understanding his social difficulties at 15 or 20. Nevertheless, it must be stressed that changes in a child's nature plus changes in the circumstances of life combine to make the social psychology of the various age periods very different. Three age periods can be profitably differentiated here—the preschool years, up to 6; the elementary-school or middle-childhood period, from 6 through about 12; and the adolescent period, from puberty to about 18. A concrete description of a typical boy and a typical girl at each stage will make the differentiation clearer.

First, Jimmy at 5. Much of the time he plays happily by himself, often talking to himself. Even when with other children he may pay little attention to them. Play groups are small at most—not over five other children—and play is usually largely running about at random, riding a tricycle, working with building blocks, or digging in the sandpile. He is still very much a home body. His parents are the all-important people in his social world. He plays with children of either sex and even in a group consisting entirely of girls; he fights physically with girls and is not embarrassed by physical contact with them. Betty at the same age is socially quite similar.

Jim at 10 is a different boy. He is very insistent on the fact that he is no longer a baby; the neighborhood rather than the home is his social habitat. A chum of his own age and sex is now at the center of his social interest and he spends much time in the company of seven or eight other boys of his own age. Jim's mother is afraid the group may take on the character of a gang, but the association is too casual and the composition of the group too variable to be called a gang in any unfavorable sense. Games are social and loosely organized, like marbles or cops-and-robbers; Jim plays only little by himself. He pays little attention to girls, will not take part in a game or join a group in which he is the only boy. He is sufficiently conscious of sex to be modest around girls and to avoid touching them. And for her part, Betty, now 10, has pulled into her own sex group, sits with other girls, whispers and giggles with them, plays with them. She is more conscious of her sex than Jim is, partly because she is a bit older physiologically and emotionally, partly because society emphasizes sex to her more, by stressing modesty and the proprieties and restraints of conduct which parents and teachers think appropriate for a girl.

At 15 James is socially a still different person. Now he likes organized team games. He begins to participate in such social activities as dancing with girls, and is interested in them. Whereas previously the chum of his own age and sex was socially central and the gang of seven or eight other boys his social group, now a member of the other sex is more the center of social interest and his social group includes both sexes. Further, his parents are still more out of his social world and he often is impatient with them because of their "old-fashioned" notions about hours and behavior. He will not tolerate any form of physical attention from adults or from members of his own sex. Elizabeth is very much interested in boys, likes to dance with them, sit next to them, have their attention; she spends much time primping when she is to be with them. In contrast to James, she is demonstrative in showing physical affection for other girls of her own age.

In short, it is clear that there are marked changes in the social life of children at different ages. These will be now looked at in somewhat greater detail.

THE PRESCHOOL YEARS

At first thought the preschool years might seem of no concern to the school or teacher. But investigation often shows major personality trends already clearly evident in these first six years; habits of social adjustment or maladjustment that are formed at this time may determine the course of the individual's social relationships for the remainder of his life. Indeed, so important are these years that the nursery-school movement, designed to guide children's development better than is usually the case in the average home, has become one of the most distinctive and scientifically productive movements in modern education.

By the age of 3 or 4 some childhood personalities are already clearly recognizable—some fretful, others gleeful, some placid or quiet, others restless or assertive. By these ages some youngsters have learned so well to use temper tantrums to get their way that years later they use similar techniques in managing their mates. Spoiled 4-year-olds grow up into willful adults. A child who has lived in a quarrelsome home or been constantly shouted at and yanked around for the first six years of his life is likely to have formed attitudes of cringing timidity or callous, noisy self-assertion which continue for years thereafter. In almost all such cases, wise handling during the preschool years could have largely avoided such unfortunate results.

Social Trends During the First Six Years

The newborn infant is a squalling little animal, but response to social stimulation appears surprisingly early. Around 2 months a baby may begin to smile in response to a human voice even though he does not smile at other stimuli. By 7 or 8 months he will stretch out his hands toward an adult, pull at an adult's clothes, cry when an adult stops talking to him. If another infant is placed near him, the baby may touch him, coo, and smile; otherwise his behavior may be described as socially blind—the other baby is treated about the same as play materials are. But around 18 months the interest gradually shifts to include the partner. A nursery-school investigation (46) showed that in free-play situations 2-year-old children spent 41 percent of their time in social contacts, 3-year-olds 64 percent, and 4-year-olds 77 percent. Further, social play for 2-year-olds is likely to be some relatively asocial act with one other child like mutual admiration of mud pies, whereas 4-year-olds coöperate in making sand pies. Older nursery-school children respond to social contacts by laughing and smiling more often than younger children do. With increasing age, other children are referred to more frequently by name. That the social world of young children is still greatly home-centered is evidenced by the finding that of the total number of word concepts used by children aged 2 to 5, one-third referred to mother, father, sibling, or home (67).

Of interest are the following percentages of American children who exhibited competition at each age from 2 to 7 (26):

Age group	2–3	3–4	4–5	5–6	6–7
Number of cases	8	15	11	20	11
Percentage showing competition	0	43	69	75	86

A growing social understanding of sorts is shown in a summary of behavior, presumably involving anger, that was kept for a month by certain mothers. The following figures show the percentage of outbursts at each age involving undirected energy and retaliative behavior:

Age	Under 1 yr.	1–2 yrs.	2–3 yrs.	3–4 yrs.	Over 4 yrs.
Undirected energy	89	78	75	60	36
Retaliative behavior	1	6	11	26	28

Presumably the competition and retaliation were in large part culturally determined. Thus Margaret Mead reports that Arapesh children play no games "that encourage aggressiveness or competition. There are no races, no games with two sides" (51, page 141).

Intensive observations of 20 infants from birth showed that "personality" differences—in irritability, in tone and timbre of the cry, in tonicity of the muscles, as well as in quality of reaction to the test situations— were present in some from birth but appeared in all within the first three months (66). A follow-up fifteen years later showed that some of the personalities manifested in the first two years still clearly persisted (54). One child in a nursery-school group played alone only 1 percent of the time, but four others played alone 33 percent of the time (58). Some children in a kindergarten made twice as many social contacts as others did (76). Even in nursery school some children seem to be "born leaders," whereas others are passive and easily led. Certain sex differences in social behavior are evident even in these early years—boys quarrel more, girls talk more.

Continuing study of the group of 20 infants from birth into early childhood brought out strikingly the differences in total personality and especially in social reactions and attitudes which children may exhibit. The children were seen at home, at play, at the nursery school, and in neighborhood play; the investigators became well acquainted with these children and their families and were accepted by the children and their families as a friend. Even in the earliest weeks these children showed differences. A boy and a girl who were twins were in many respects oddly contrasting. The boy was active, expansive, smiling, constantly seeking the attention of other people; but the girl was more quiet, serious, thoughtful. Yet even in nursery school this little girl took a some-what protective and slightly condescending air toward her twin brother. A boy in another family was exceptionally strong and adept in movement from his earliest weeks; he was something of a problem on the playground because his great vigor and skill made him dominate all too easily, and literally run over other children. But in social relationships he was relatively silent and shy. In all these respects—physique, strength, skill, and reticence—he was very like his father. Another girl was wiry, tomboyish and very active, like her mother in physique and behavior when she was a child. This little girl preferred to play with boys, was more competitive than the average girl, more assertive. Another girl was described, even in diapers, as petite and as having a certain air which some people never attain. She had a way with her; clearly the social personality showed early (66).

The Child's Social Nature and His Home

The preceding discussion indicated that constitutional factors are im-portant in determining a child's relations with others, his social person-ality. Constitutionally, almost from birth some children are energetic, quick, attractive in appearance or manner, responsive to the presence and behavior of other human beings; other children are passive, unap-pealing, shy. But almost from birth, the baby's responses begin to be modified by other people's responses to him, and more broadly by the total circumstances of his babyhood.

Quite obviously the child of a half-sick harassed mother in a crowded noisy slum home develops different reactions to others than does the only child of doting parents in a quiet suburb. Many other factors are at work. The youngest in a large family may be babied and the oldest be neglected early in life for the next child, with important consequences as regards the social personality in each instance. Personalities in the home may interact in many ways. Thus the father of an exceptionally strong and vigorous boy was strong and active and delighted to play with his son; he also enjoyed having the youngster in his basement workshop. Socially, however, the father was shy, and there were few visitors in the home. Shyness on the part of the boy, and development of mechanical and athletic interests, were natural outcomes. A little girl was high-strung and tended to have temper tantrums. The mother was also high-strung and indulged in emotional outbursts. The father was reserved, dreaded such outbursts, and almost invariably gave in to whatever was wanted. Presumably the child was constitutionally more excitable than the average child. More im-portant, however, is the further fact that she was frequently excited by her excitable mother and found she could get her own way by such means.

Numerous investigations have shown that homes of different types tend to develop distinctive social characteristics in young children. Children whose families are overattentive tend to be too dependent on adults, avoid aggressive play with other children, dawdle and leave tasks incomplete, cry easily and lack emotional control. Children whose mothers are irresponsible or negligent tend to seek attention by showing off, telling fanciful stories, crying easily. Children whose parents share work and play experiences with them have a better understanding of property rights, are more coöperative, get along better with other children (31). Nursery-school children from homes where there are tension and conflict between the parents are more likely to show problems of social adjustment than youngsters from reasonably harmonious homes (4).

Discipline is a matter of obvious concern to both parents and children, and different types of discipline affect the child's social adjustment. Child specialists also agree that consistency of discipline is exceedingly important. Demoralizing to anyone would be inconsistent discipline such as the following: An 18-month-old baby refused to take his nap; after he kicked and screamed for five minutes his mother gave in and the nap was omitted. That night when he was put to bed he repeated his tantrum, but this time he was spanked. A day or so later he refused to take his nap without being rocked, and after five minutes of screaming he was rocked. Next day he demanded rocking but was spanked.

Perhaps it need hardly be added that consistency does not mean unreasonable rigidity. Reasonable compromises between parent and child often avert clashes. Thus a small child wanted to carry a pan of potatoes, but his mother would not let him because it was too heavy; however, he was quite satisfied when she gave him two of the potatoes to carry. Sometimes a tantrum may be largely justifiable. Thus a 2-year-old repeatedly made a reasonable request for help in getting up on a davenport, but was completely ignored. Finally, she began to kick and scream in desperation and was then lifted up.

As intimated by various of the above illustrations, not only what is done, but the "home atmosphere" where everything occurs, is exceedingly important. Calmness, tolerance, humor, an unexcited voice and an unhurried manner, a perspective such that the parent is not unduly disturbed when a nap is not taken or when one child pinches another, calm and prompt application of corrective methods when called for but without nagging afterward—such a home atmosphere prevents many problems from arising and facilitates the handling of those that do arise.

Nursery Schools

The little everyday happenings in the life of a 3-year-old may seem very unimportant indeed, yet they may determine the direction of his whole social development. Adults who complain or are petulant or irresponsible or subject to emotional outbursts may act in this way because of habits formed in this preschool period. These problems of social adjustment in infancy are subtle and difficult; few parents understand them. And though most mothers won't admit it, a small child in the home is not always an unmitigated joy; he is sometimes a burden or even an exasperation. Furthermore, many homes today provide no contact with adults other than the parents; aunts and grandparents and family friends visit less often than used to be the case. The modern small family may have only one child. How splendid it would be if a spoiled pet might spend part of each day some place where he would in the care of adults who *do* know about small children, and would be with other babies who might themselves teach him a thing or two. The nursery school may well seem the answer.

The nursery school sees as its most important and explicitly recognized task guiding a child's relationships with other people, especially through two critical phases of such relationships—achieving the first independence of parents and the friendly acceptance of adults outside the family, and entering the society of other children of the same age outside the home. In these new contacts the small child must learn appropriate manners as well as ways of holding his own and getting along with all these new associates—indeed a task for both child and school.

The personnel in a good nursery school know much about the child and his home before the school year begins. His parents have been interviewed, and he has visited the school with his mother. Perhaps arrangements were made for several mothers and their children to visit the school at the same time. For half an hour, while the children played and the mothers chatted in comfortable chairs at the edge of the playground, the teachers could observe and make some contact with both the youngsters and their mothers.

If a child is timid or not used to being away from home, his mother may be asked to stay at school the first day or so. But she must stay at one side, knitting or reading, and not urge the child to stay with her. Attractive play materials are placed at a little distance away from her, and a teacher encourages him to play with them. Usually after a day or so the child pays little attention to his mother.[1] Then she tells him casually that she is going on an errand but will return shortly. If her absence has not

[1] Sometimes much to her distress she discovers that she is not so essential to the happiness of her offspring as she would like to believe. The mother may be more of a problem than the child, staying morning after morning when she should go home. Parent education is an important phase of an adequate nursery-school program.

disturbed him, she can thereafter leave as soon as he has become interested in some activity. Thus an event of tremendous importance to him has been brought about dexterously and without his awareness—he has left his home and his family and ventured out into the wide world by himself.

Usually he finds this new world delightful. Very possibly the teacher's calm, imperturbable know-how with children is something of a relief from a home not always imperturbable. There are many things to do: blocks to pile, easels to paint at, an aquarium with fish to watch, picture books to look at, a piano which the teacher plays. No less interesting are the other children; to an only child they are the greatest novelty. Watching them is an important aid in social development. The shy child is not hurried into participation. The teacher finds play which interests him; and as he becomes accustomed to the school, she soon has him playing near other children, perhaps in the sandbox. She may have him and another child help move the teeter-totter and then suggest that the two of them play on it; or she may show him how to do something special which he then shows another child, thus acquiring importance and self-confidence.

If two children are too much together she arranges activities that involve their joining different groups. If in social difficulties a child regresses to merely crying, the teacher may say, "Tommy doesn't understand what you want when you cry. Talk to him." And both talking and social cooperation are furthered. Friendly acts are publicly commended. A tease or a bully is kept busy at activities which bring him legitimate satisfaction. A contagious good humor eases the way through social crises that might otherwise cause conflict. The able nursery-school teacher regards guidance of each child's social development as her major function, and her outstanding trait is tact; she is not so much a teacher as a hostess.

It is clear that nursery schools foster social contacts between children. However, more happens than a simple increase in sociability; a positive personality develops. A nursery school is a lively place; one study has reported that the average nursery-school child gets into conflict with another child twelve times an hour (conflicts of brief duration, of course, and far outnumbered by contacts friendly in nature).[2] That independence grows is shown by a count of the number of times a child refuses, by word

[2] It may be some comfort to the parent of a lively youngster to know that within bounds all this is healthy. The more a child "gets around" the more he is likely to bump into others. As one investigator has stated it epigrammatically, "Mutual friends are more quarrelsome, and mutual quarrelers more friendly than the average," and "Quarreling is part of friendly social intercourse at these ages" (25).

or deed, to give ground when others demand that he do so. Children who had been in nursery school six months were rated higher in sympathy, independence, and self-reliance than youngsters new to the school (75). Careful comparison of over 100 children who had been in nursery school only six weeks with others who had been there nine months showed the latter group less likely to grab toys or attack others. Various ways of developing desired traits are tried. Thus several children who were shy and unassertive were helped until they could do especially well certain things of interest to the other children—such things as fitting together a picture puzzle, making designs with blocks, telling an interesting story. When these formerly shy children were paired with other youngsters while the latter were dealing with these materials, they showed a much greater tendency to lead and assert themselves (57).

THE ELEMENTARY SCHOOL YEARS

The nursery school has bountiful possibilities for constructive social education. Unfortunately, however, few children go to nursery school. During the first five or six years most youngsters have little contact with adults other than their parents, and few associations with other children, except if there are brothers or sisters, or neighbor boys or girls of about the same age. Social life is very simple. The parents are the all-important center of regard and prestige; and they, with any other members of the home group plus a few neighbor children and perhaps a pet or two, make up a single compact primary social group, as the sociologists would call it.

When the child enters school a new adult, Teacher, takes a place of great importance in his life and he becomes a member of a new child group, his class. As he goes about more, he may become a member of other groups—Sunday school, club, gang. Initiation into each, even the most hospitable, presents the new member with certain problems of adjustment. Between these groups there are certain disjunctions and incoördinations; there may be acute conflict, as between home or school and a delinquent gang. In each group the child is faced with certain questions as to his status in it. The problems which confront him soon become bewilderingly complex. And truly marvelous is the extent to which most youngsters in the few short years from 6 to 12 do find their place in these various groups and get themselves more than reasonably well coördinated. Around age 12 many persons are better adjusted than at any other time in their entire life. This is the period of happy confident childhood to which adults look back with longing.

The Class as a Little Society—And Teacher

Most children start to school at 6. Suddenly—usually there are no first visits and gradual contacts such as the good nursery school uses to ease the child into his new experience—on a bright September morning the small child finds himself facing not only a strange new adult in a strange new place but also a roomful of strange children. For a timid or sheltered only child the situation may be bewildering indeed.

It will be difficult for you, who after at least twelve years of being in school take the routines and the manners and customs of education for granted, to have any conception of that bewilderment. A college freshman from the country is a sophisticate by comparison! The little first-grader must learn the comings and goings, and when things are done, and being on time. There are numerous details concerning manners and customs: when it is appropriate to speak to another child and when not; when it is commendable to help a friend and when it is considered wrong to do so (a most puzzling matter); when and how the teacher may be addressed. Sundry crises may occur. Thus when a physiological need becomes insistent in the presence of this strange adult and in this great crowd of children, there may be embarrassing episodes, as every primary teacher well knows.

The teacher is far more important in this little society than you might assume, after a dozen years of habituation to the breed. To the small child her size, adulthood, strangeness, authority, similarity yet difference in status as compared with his parents, all combine to endow her with an influence far greater than she usually realizes. The children watch her closely, and they are often far more sensitive and more keen in understanding her attitude toward them than she knows. A smile and a word of praise may make a little girl exquisitely happy. Sarcasm, public ridicule, and especially unfair criticism or punishment may produce an attitude that remains for years.

Strikingly illustrative of this fact is the true story of Grace, as told by herself and also by her teachers. A sensitive only child, she entered the first grade with great anticipation of the joys of school. But the first-grade teacher humiliated her by saying that she was behind the other pupils in her reading; furthermore, she had difficulty in getting used to the other children. The second-grade teacher was young and pretty, but never recognized the children on the street. The next teacher was ill and irritable and jerked the children about. In notable contrast the fifth-grade teacher was friendly and her room quiet and restful. But the seventh-grade teacher was one of those big ones who shouted.

Meantime the teachers were reporting that Grace was anxious to please but was shy and nervous. Brief success as a leader in a student activity in junior high school built up her confidence greatly, but things went back again to the old level. In college, a short note of encouragement from an English teacher thrilled her so much that she could hardly keep back the tears, but she lost confidence again when criticized. She was very pleased when a teacher put her on a committee, and she worked very hard; as she said, it was the first time she had had a chance to take part in social activities as a leader. These teachers reported the girl as "shy, almost like a frightened animal, very responsive to kindness."

Grace is now teaching in a one-room country school, beloved by her pupils and their parents perhaps because she knows how to give the encouragement and kindness she desired so much. It might well be said that her life had been formed by the inconsiderateness and obtuseness of her teachers, especially those in elementary school (73).[3]

Thus an exceedingly important, rather obvious, but nevertheless often overlooked characteristic of a successful teacher is the elementary social virtue of considerateness—more generally, the "psychological atmosphere" of her classroom. If she is friendly, fair, and encouraging—not impatient, impulsive in discipline, or critical and sarcastic—she will have met the first requisite of successful social leadership. The social atmosphere thus created may largely determine the personalities the children exhibit there. Miss Brown is a calm, friendly young woman; an unhurried composure is typical of her room, and Johnny is friendly and coöperative in it. Miss Thompson is anxious and suspicious; in *her* room there always seems to be an undercurrent of restlessness and resentment, and there John is irritable and full of mischief. But much more may and should be involved than the teacher's temperament and good will; basically more important is the nature of the social structure and the procedure in the group. What is meant here can be best made clear by a famous investigation that both illustrated and evaluated such factors.[4]

Three groups or "clubs," each composed of five 10-year-old children, undertook painting murals, making masks, building model airplanes, and other

---

[3] This case may be considered extreme. But time and again college students report incidents from their childhood that show how for many years they vividly remember similar episodes; often their feelings about them are still so strong that they cannot bring themselves to tell the class about them. You will do well to go back in your own memories and see whether you don't have poignant recollections of some kindness or a slight from a teacher when you were a small child.

[4] The following description takes the liberty of combining the results of two of Lewin's experiments to give a more adequate picture of the outcome of democratic versus autocratic procedures (43).

similar activities calling for planning and working together. A graduate student took charge of one group and in autocratic fashion told each pupil one step at a time just what to do, how to do it, and with whom to work; he bestowed praise or blame in a personal way, but remained aloof and did not participate in the work of the group. In short, he behaved very much like an old-fashioned teacher. A second graduate student handled the second group along laissez-faire lines. He let it do as it pleased, did not take part in discussion or work, and made only infrequent comments. The graduate student associated with the third group used a democratic technique. He discussed the total project with the pupils and gave them suggestions when requested, but let them decide among themselves who would do the various portions of the complete project, with whom each one would work, and which method of working would probably be best. He tried to help them to plan and to clarify their thinking, was "objective" in criticizing and praising, and worked with them. Each group met twice a week for 50 minutes, and observers kept a careful record of what went on at each meeting. After six weeks leaders and methods were changed about; that is, the leader of the autocratic group moved to another group with whom he used democratic procedures; the democratic group was handled by another leader in an autocratic fashion, and so on. Thus it could not be charged that the findings concerning a given method were due to peculiarities of a particular group or leader.

Two differences between these groups, particularly between the autocratic and democratic, should be stressed. First, the pressure exerted by the frequent directions and demands of the autocratic leader produced a state of *tension* in his group. He made about six times as many "directing approaches" as the democratic leader. And second, since he determined the goals, methods, work companions, and tools, the children's *range of free movement* was much less than it was under the democratic leader. This tended to cause trouble in much the same way that there was trouble when a group worked in too small a room. Under laissez-faire methods there was also little range of free movement because the children got in one another's way.

The detailed record of what each group said and did showed that there were about thirty times as many episodes of hostility in the autocratic as in the democratic groups. Sometimes the children handled dictatorially were apathetic; but if their leader left the room, their work fell off quickly and there were marked displays of irritable aggressiveness toward others in the group. In the other autocratic groups the youngsters were markedly aggressive toward one another even when the leader was present, though they were subservient to him. In the democratic group work went forward much as before if the leader left. The laissez-faire group "ran wild" whether the leader was present or not. A child worked by himself instead of coöperatively with one or more others twice as frequently under the autocratic regime. Twice children in an autocratic group ganged up on a scapegoat and forced him out of the group; their repressed feelings apparently were relieved in this way. Toward the end of the experiment the democratic group voted that they would like to continue the work, but the autocratic group did not wish to do so. Informal talks with the children showed that they liked the democratic leaders best. At the end, the democratic group either kept the results of their work themselves or gave them to the leader, but some of the children in the autocratic group threw their work on the floor and jumped on it.

In summary, then, if a teacher is to meet the sociopsychological problems of her classroom successfully, she should maintain a "psychological atmosphere" and an attitude of considerateness, fairness, and friendliness. She should appreciate the importance of the total situation in her class and have some ability to construct situations which guide without putting such pressure on the children as to cause undue tension or restrict their free movement. A teacher who is at all sensitive to the happenings in her little classroom society (many teachers are not) is aware that a great deal is happening "off-stage." In certain respects the children live in a society of their own; when they are not in school, this society becomes increasingly important for them. Since much that happens in the classroom has its origins in child society, this topic will next be considered.

Child Society: Problems of Belonging and Status

Going to school is the distinctive social experience that for the average child distinguishes the years after 6 from those before. But the outstanding social change from the age of 6 to puberty is the escape from the family into the society of other children, primarily of the same sex. The great questions for each child in relation to child society are: Does he "belong"? What is his status? These are the central problems of these years.

What is the nature of child society? For the average child entering elementary school it hardly exists. He probably knows two or three neighborhood children, and he comes to know others in the neighborhood from going to and from school with them—these are times when socialization goes forward more rapidly than in the conventional classroom. Spontaneously formed child groups are small; they rarely consist of more than five youngsters, and even these small groups do not stay together. First-grade children have no sense of belonging to the whole class, and they are unable to designate those they like or dislike outside their little circle of acquaintance. Moreover, they are little aware of any code of social behavior, though they soon learn such elementary requirements as waiting one's turn, not tattling on other children, and playing simple games according to rules.

By middle childhood (roughly 7 or 8 to 11 or 12 years of age) the groups have grown in size; they now include from six to ten children and they tend to be unisexual. But these groups are still flexible as to membership; and though group undertakings are fairly frequent by now, they are often not completed because the group does not hold together long enough. And the group's codes of conduct expand increasingly—one must play fair, do one's share in any group undertaking, divide the spoils evenly, and so on.

In later childhood or preadolescence (11 or 12 to 13 or 14) the social coalescing goes even further. The group is likely to contain ten or fifteen youngsters and to be much more explicit as to membership and activities. It may call itself a club or gang, and as such have a definite membership with a badge or other sign by which a member is known; it may have an element of secrecy, specified times and places of meeting, special activities, and leaders or officers.

However, the observer who notices only the gross fact that there are groups is socially almost as blind as the individual who can distinguish the outlines of large objects but cannot see the details of their structure. Perhaps first to be noticed is the fact that there are some individuals who do not belong to groups. They are isolates. To the wise teacher they present more serious problems than the child who fails his arithmetic or throws spitballs. They are bewildered and miserably unhappy over their unpopularity, and are establishing habits of timidity or resentment toward others which may continue throughout life.

Sometimes the causes of the isolation are fairly obvious. Thus Harry is slightly deaf and James very near-sighted; the sensory handicap in each case hampers their play with the other boys. But sometimes these problems are more subtle. For example, one record of playground activity begins with 7-year-old Ralph wandering aimlessly along the edge of the playground looking bored and ill at ease. Two other boys run up to him and grab him—apparently the game is "cops and robbers." Ralph pulls away. He goes over and watches some children swinging, but they don't speak to him and he wanders off dejectedly. He sits down at one side of the playground and watches the other children. Ralph's whole recess is taken up with withdrawings, attempted approaches, and failures to participate. The situation is explained in part by the fact that Ralph is an only child of strict parents and has no social resources or initiative in child society.

At the other extreme is the leader. What characterizes him? Several studies have been made of him. The leader has interests common to the group and is very much of the group, not apart from it or too markedly superior to it. He is above average in certain traits the group regards highly; thus the leader of boys is more active and successful in games, the girl leader more friendly, and proficient in the undertakings of her sex. In either sex the leader is characterized by initiative and fertility of ideas; he suggests things to do and gets things going.

Various circumstances may play a part in becoming a leader. One of the writers remembers the summer during his boyhood when a relative gave him a fine patrol wagon; for some weeks afterward he was leader of a group that wanted to play with his unusual new toy. The son of an ex-governor of the state was consistently a neighborhood leader; he combined natural vigor with confidence derived from his family's status, and was always ready with ideas for warlike games based on his father's stories of his military experiences.

Leader and isolate—these are two extremes. But in middle or later childhood there is another figure who is very important—the chum. The chum is an individual of the same sex and approximately the same age. He is likely to be in the same school class, to come from the same neighborhood, and to have the same socioeconomic status. That is, geographical, educational, and socioeconomic propinquity brings youngsters together and often seems adequate to account for a chum relationship. Some harmony of personalities is also involved; not all neighborhood classmates are chums. Some similarity of interests and coördination of traits is likewise necessary. Sometimes an active child may have associated with him a relatively quiet youngster whose personality complements his own. In any case, the chum relationship is usually very worth while, for each youngster gains in confidence, adaptability, and resourcefulness. It is the distinctive social relationship of middle childhood; the focus of social interest has now shifted from the parents to another of the same age and sex. Literature has many stories of chums—Tom Sawyer and Huckleberry Finn, for example.

Chum, leader, and isolate—these are the three major type figures in child society. But it must not be assumed that child society is without structure, except for the relationships thus implied. On the contrary, the structure is often complex. Yet the average teacher is often blind to these facts. Some concrete experimental data are of value here. Children in a sixth-grade class were told that the seating arrangements were soon to be changed; each was asked to write on a sheet of paper his first and second choice of classmate whom he would like to sit next to in class, and also to give his reason for wanting to sit next to that person. Fig. 6.1 shows some of the complexities of social interrelationship revealed by this simple inquiry.

Six children (*B, E, a, b, k, l*) were not chosen by anyone, even as second choice. They apparently were isolates. Girl *a* was herself so little acquainted that she made only one choice—girl *x* in another room. In contrast, boy *I* was chosen by six and girl *e* by five other children. The larger structure of the

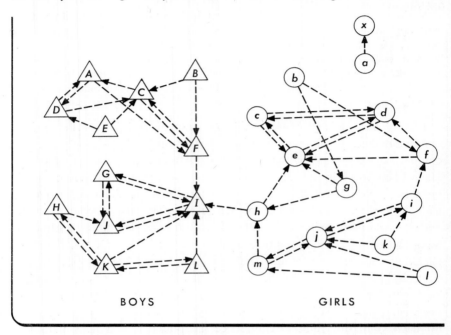

FIG. 6.1. Social structure of a small sixth-grade class resulting when each child was asked to name the two classmates whom he would like best to have sit next to him. The figure shows that boy *A* chose *D* and *F* and was chosen by *D* and *C*; boys *B* and *E* and girls *a*, *b*, *k*, and *l* were unchosen or isolates, but *l* and *e* were very popular, being chosen by six and five other children. (Method modified from Moreno [53].)

little society should be especially noted. The boys are in two distinct groups, the lower one in the figure having as its core the close-knit triangle *I-G-J*; the accessory chain is *H-K-L*, with *I* quite clearly the leader. The teacher considered that this group's character was not entirely healthy; the boys seemed on the way to becoming a mischief-making gang. The girls also formed certain groups, such as triangle *e-c-d*, but these groups seemed desirable on the whole. The big problem among the girls was to take care of the isolates.

On the basis of the seating chart and the children's explanations of their choices plus her own knowledge of them, the teacher proceeded with her change in the seating plan. Boys *F, I,* and *A* were put together to foster other groupings. Isolates were put with their choices if there was some compatibility of interest. The teacher tried to be the tactful hostess in fostering the relationships initiated by these classroom propinquities. As a result of her efforts, her class, instead of comprising two cliques, two other loose groups, and sundry outsiders, became one much more friendly group.

What, more generally, are the findings of such "sociometric tests"? Fig. 6.2 summarizes results for some 1800 children from kindergarten through

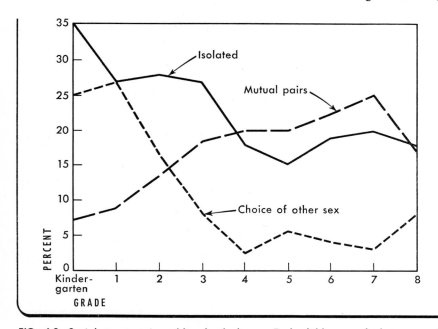

FIG. 6.2. Social structure in public-school classes. Each child was asked to name his first and second choice of the children he would like to have sit next to him. In the kindergarten 35 percent of the children were not chosen; they were isolates. A quarter of the choices were of the other sex. In only 7 percent of the cases did two kindergarten children choose each other. (1853 children in a Brooklyn public school, three months after school began.) (Data from Moreno [53], page 26.)

the eighth grade, obtained three months after school began, that is, after sufficient time for the children to become acquainted with and appraise each other. Isolates are most common in kindergarten simply because the children are too young to know each other well, but even in the upper grades about a fifth of the children are not chosen. The number of mutual pairs (these may be called chums) increases, but the majority of the children in every grade are without such friends or at least without a

chum in the same class. Choosing the other sex practically disappears in
the middle grades but appears again in the eighth. Here indeed is a perspective in social trends and problems.

The remarks of the children in explaining their choices often gave exceedingly valuable insights regarding levels of social development and values in
child society. Consider, for instance, the following (53, pages 378, 393):
1st grade (age 6–7 yrs.). Marion chooses Claire: "I like her because she
always gives me some candy when I eat with her. She lends me crayons when
I have lost mine."
6th grade (ages 11–12 yrs.). Madeline chooses Marietta: "She is about my
size and age. I like to walk with her 'cause I think we look nice together.
She isn't noisy or rude. She is willing to play games that are gay and with a
lot of action. She is truthful. Also if you ask her to bring you something, she
will bring it even if she has a lot of other things to carry just the same."
Joel chooses Gunther: "I keep tropical fish, and I collect stamps, and Gunther likes to see my things. That's what I like about him. He isn't only always
wanting to play baseball. I don't see very well so I like to do other things
than play sports."
8th grade (ages 13–14 yrs.). David chooses Marie: "She's better-looking
than the majority. Curly brown hair, blue eyes, same height as I am. She's my
idea of what a girl should be like."

Clearly a child's problem in finding his place and status in the society
of his fellows is neither simple nor easy. A teacher must study both the
children and the group. As suggested in the preceding section, she must
help each child make good in some way. She must see each class as a total social pattern, with a given child fitting well into some parts of it but
not at all into others. There is hardly any greater service she can give him
than helping him find his place and status.

The preceding paragraphs have dealt with child society in the schoolroom for the obvious reasons that there is where it is both most available
for study and of greatest concern for the teacher. But it should never be
forgotten that child society exists chiefly outside the classroom, and that
status and structure may vary in different groups and situations.

When one of the writers was in the fifth grade his chum (this because he
lived next door, had similar mechanical interests, and lived with kindly grandparents who indulged both boys in numerous minor ways) was in the grade
above. A second frequent play companion went to another school, but the
families were friends and the children became well acquainted through family
and church gatherings. A third pal was in the same class in school, but this
companionship was based more on the friendship of the two families. An
occasional fourth companion was an older slightly lame boy who was liked for

his good nature and his pluck and who, because of his physical handicap, found his play level with younger boys. If the Moreno sociometric test had been applied to the fifth grade in the Murray school so many years ago, this somewhat heterogeneous group of boys might never have been discovered.

Furthermore, choice of any companion depends on the situation. Harry was a good person to have sit next you because he was excellent in his school work and was anxious to obtain the other children's regard by helping them. But he was also stout and clumsy, and hence no one to choose for your side in a game. Art was biggest and strongest; Jim had the best stamp collection; Will's athletic older brother gave him prestige and taught him athletic skills; Sidney was best in certain handicrafts.

Isolates were rejected because of similarly diverse factors. Henry showed off in the classroom and was considered a teacher's pet. Algernon was affected and sissified. The children in the big Jones family stayed by themselves. The Smiths had recently moved into the neighborhood and nobody seemed to know them; their only son was quiet, shy, and offish.

Clearly such larger understanding of child society requires knowledge of home and community, and the use of community resources—church, boys' club, playground, summer camp—in dealing with any problems that may be discovered. Before we specifically consider the influence of the home on the elementary-school youngster, it is desirable to stress that such resources as club and camp should more often be made a part of the total program for handling problems of child society. Suggestive of possibilities here is an experiment in which thirteen shy and socially maladjusted children 6 to 10 years old spent several weeks in a small camp where there were no other children. At first each played alone; but gradually they became acquainted, asserted themselves more, achieved confidence in the group. When they returned home they showed distinct improvement in poise and status (45). One member of a child group—boaster or crybaby or cheat—may be disciplined to good purpose by the others, or the group may tease or ignore in a way which accentuates the social maladjustment. In such cases the playground or camp director can perhaps discover and feature some ability the misfit does have and thus raise his status, or get some other child to befriend him (56). In any case, constructive social thinking is called for.

Home

Up to the time he goes to school the child has lived primarily in only one social world, the home. In that home there may be conflict, or at least disharmony. But when he goes to school he enters two other social worlds: school and child society. There may be conflicts or disharmonies between these worlds. And gradually he becomes aware of any conflicts between his family and the adult world they live in. Examples will clarify each type of difficulty.

After much bitter quarreling and charges against each other, often in the presence of Mildred, their only child, her parents obtained a divorce. Mildred lives part of the time with one parent and the remainder of the time with the other. Spending part of her time in one neighborhood and school and part in another, she makes few friends in either place. In no one of her three social worlds—home, school, or child society—does she feel established or secure.

Mediocre Marjorie's younger sister is brilliant and exceptionally attractive. In a mistaken effort to urge Marjorie to do better work, she is constantly and disparagingly compared with this sister. The younger sister is now in the same grade with Marjorie. An unwise teacher in a moment of irritation threw this fact at the older girl, and the other children have shown that they sense the situation. Marjorie's lack of status makes her timid and seclusive, and so upsets her that her work is even less effective than it might be.

Mary's ignorant Kentucky mountaineer parents are puzzled and defensive about the school's efforts to help her. The mother resents well-meaning but blunt suggestions from the school nurse regarding better diet for her children, and a visit from the nurse antagonizes even more, for it is sensed as being critical. Mary's school work is poor; a note from the teacher, asking the mother's help in improving it, shows a painful lack of awareness of the parents' near-illiteracy and poverty; the mother's scrawled reply is shown to the principal with a comment which Mary overhears. The girl is increasingly absent, and inquiries from the school are met with evasion and antagonism. Home and school societies are in conflict. Mary senses that her family lacks status in the community, and that she herself does in child society.

Mrs. Johnson's oldest son was struck by an automobile while at play, and after six months of pathetic struggle he died. Albert is now the only remaining child; he is frail and frequently ill. Lest some misfortune come to him, he is given little opportunity to play with other boys, is kept home from school at the slightest sign of bad weather or indisposition; he has become a timid little hypochondriac. In contrast, the minister's little red-haired son Lester, reacting against the dreary decorum of his home, has become the neighborhood brat, his group's leader in mischief. And Henrietta, trained in elocution by her once stage-struck mother, is featured in every school or church affair—and scorned by the other children as a conceited little show-off.

One vicious "home" consists of a father, three children by a divorced wife, and a stepmother. The stepmother dislikes the children because they are a constant reminder of the former wife, and the children are bitter toward her. A conservative neighborhood regards the divorce and remarriage with disfavor and ostracizes not only the two adults but also the children; neighborhood youngsters are not allowed to play with them. The children lack affection and security in their own home and are social outcasts in the community; in class they are emotionally preoccupied and indifferent. No wonder they are suspicious in their attitude toward teachers and other adults, defensive and irritable in their relation with other children in the school, and belong to a delinquent gang "across the track"—it is the only group which will accept them.

What generalizations may be drawn from these instances? One should be obvious: that children cannot be understood without some knowledge of their homes. Yet a teacher may have no knowledge of the homes of most of her children. What are the essentials of a psychologically good home? Two are outstanding. First, the home should give the child affection and security. Second, it should help, not hamper, the child in achieving belonging and status in child society. Whatever its other shortcomings, if a home does these two things it is almost certain to be a psychologically good home.

It should be made clear that a home which is psychologically good may be very modest—even poverty-stricken—as far as material things are concerned. Poverty makes it harder to give the child a sense of security and it handicaps in other ways; but kindly and sensible parents may make a home that is poor economically an admirable place for child development, whereas a domineering successful businessman and a butterfly mother may make a wretched home for a child.

The influence of the home is pervasive and often shows itself in ways that have no apparent relationship to the home situation. Thus a study compared children whose parents were decidedly fond of them with children whose parents showed lack of affection or rejection. Children in the first group more often slept soundly, kept their clothes neat, worked well with others, were attentive and popular, liked school; the "rejected" children smoked, sought attention, boasted, were classroom nuisances, had younger companions, were emotionally unstable and antagonistic. Children of dominating parents were neat, courteous, docile; children of over-indulgent parents had food fads and poor table manners, were aggressive and disobedient, lacked interest in school, but were self-confident and expressed themselves well (71).

The Social Triumph of Later Childhood

The child who enters the first grade is little more than a baby. He must learn his way around in school. He must get along in his home, but socially and emotionally he must escape from it. He must find his place and his status in child society. What an overwhelming lot of problems! Yet such are the vitality and adaptability of those years that the average person attains in later childhood what is often the most adequate social adjustment of his entire life. He has a nonchalant sophistication about his teachers and school. He associates with easy confidence with others of his own age and sex. His family now accords him the independence of boyhood, and he has not yet asked for the anxiety-causing freedoms of adolescence. The socioeconomic stratifications and stresses of adult life have determined the neighborhood he lives in, and he is not unaware of such matters; but among the children with whom he has contact he associates more freely and democratically than he ever will again. The other sex does not trouble him; he scorns it. This is the period of happy, self-sufficient, carefree childhood.

THE SOCIAL PROBLEMS OF ADOLESCENCE

Even though later childhood may be a period of comfortably assured relationships with almost everyone in the youngster's social world, problems such as the following usually appear in almost all those relationships, perhaps in a relatively short time.

Achievement of Heterosexuality

The formidable phrase, the achievement of heterosexuality, means simply the attainment of normal, healthy interest in and relationships with the other sex. This outcome of biological maturing might seem so natural as to present little difficulty. On the contrary, many people never achieve a satisfactory adjustment to the other sex; as a result, there is lack of normal participation in adult social activities, possible difficulty in marriage, and a warping of the whole life. Adolescence is the crucial time for this sex-social readjustment.

It must not be inferred from the above that there are no sex problems before puberty. Curiosity on the part of children regarding sex is healthy; it should be met with matter-of-fact, straightforward answers so that the child does not worry about such matters or dwell upon them. Episodes of mutual curiosity and sex play between children may not be entirely desirable but are relatively common. They also should be met calmly, with such explanations as seem called for and then diversion of attention to other interests and other companions— not by horrified moralizing which increases the attention given them.

Occasional childhood anticipation of the thrill of interest in some member of the other sex is entirely normal, as when a little boy discovers that a curly-headed little girl is really a surprisingly attractive person. In healthy child society, however, the rapidly changing manifold interests and the teasing of other little boys soon dispose of the matter. Demonstrativeness between girls is common. In a considerable number of such situations there is at one time or another some sex feeling and more or less sex play (41). But again no harm ordinarily results, unless from an adult's clumsy handling of the situation. In almost every respect portentous moralizing is the wrong approach; the child's attention is centered on the undesired acts rather than distracted from them. More or less homosexual episodes may also occur among boys; they should be similarly regarded and calmly dealt with. Occasional masturbation is an almost universal phenomenon that most commonly begins in childhood. It usually causes no harm unless bungling adults foster feelings of shame and guilt that are in themselves harmful and cause the youngster to dwell morbidly on the act, which in turn tends to its excessive recurrence.

What are the important points in understanding youngsters who are going through this exciting experience of discovering the other sex? At first, because this experience is so exciting and so new, the boys and girls do not know quite what to make of each other or how to get along together. The boy now sees even the neighbor girl in a new way that gives her an interest she never had before. She really is, in subtle ways, a different person from the leggy kid he knew when they both were 12. There may be many complicating circumstances. The early adolescent boy may have recently entered a big high school where there are many girls he never knew as children; these new feminine associates seem even more glamorous. Furthermore, there may be many situations, in this big school and with these attractive girls, in which he doesn't know what to do. Social occasions—dances, for instance—call for new social skills and graces, as well as clothes and money, that he may not have. More intimate problems arise. How about petting? How far should or can he go safely? The youngster wishes he knew more about sex.

These are questions aplenty for youngsters still in their early and middle teens to deal with. Failure to deal effectively with them may take either of two directions. Disconcerted and timid in the face of all these manifold difficulties, a youngster may avoid them by withdrawing from association with the other sex. Or he may become too interested or go too far. The latter may occasionally create scandal. But from the point of view of mental health the withdrawing reaction is more serious. The introvert youngster who has no normal healthy association with the other sex, whose sex interests are either stifled or find only indirect satisfaction, has so limited an acquaintance with and understanding of the other sex that marriage is either improbable or likely to be unhappy.

John was small, awkward, and shy. His parents were "good plain folks." He helped in the little family store afternoons and Saturdays, and had little leisure and little money. "Society" was a phenomenon of which his family was hardly aware. At first he tried, awkwardly, to get acquainted with some of the high-school girls. Some of them snubbed him; others were friendly enough, but he didn't know what to do. He didn't dance. He was too shy for even a minor friendship. Gradually he came to accept and continue the role of social outsider.

Ruby was the pretty, youngest daughter in a large Italian family. Her father was a tavern owner. What with her older brothers and sisters and her father's hard sophistication there wasn't much she didn't know. She knew her family didn't rate. But in social competition she had much to offer—her dark vivacity, her racy "line," and a willingness to go further than most.

As girls go into adolescence they increasingly do things to get the attention of the boys. At first the girls may be more active in this than the boys because of their earlier sex-social maturing. Another frequent outcome of this earlier maturing is the fact that many girls find the boys of their own age immature and unresponsive and hence seek attention from older boys. The entire situation is still further complicated by the great individual differences in the age at which this sex maturing occurs. Little wonder that many youngsters have trouble making this new social adjustment in such a complicated and rapidly changing social situation.

Madge, who is sexually mature, tries to get the attention of Jimmy, a late-maturing classmate who is still preadolescent and doesn't quite know what to make of the situation. Still boyish in size, figure, and voice, Jimmy is worried about his immaturity and the fact that he is being left out of the new groups of boys *and* girls that are being formed among his classmates. For him to find a place in heterosexual groups later may be a bit awkward; if he does, it may be with a group chronologically though not physiologically younger.

Rose presented largely the opposite problem. She developed feminine contours and an interest in boys two years earlier than her chums, and got a reputation for being oversexed and sophisticated as a result of her association with older boys.

Many factors may complicate these first efforts of boys and girls to get acquainted with each other. Thus Betty, in high school, is rebuffed three times by boys she invites to school parties and accordingly resolves never to go out with boys again (7). She soon breaks this resolution and becomes interested in a college student, partly because his greater maturity and assurance give her a feeling of security and partly because she admires and feels comfortable with her older brother and hence with young men like him. But college students pay little attention to her. She becomes greatly concerned about her appearance and distressed about a mole on her face.[5] She also gives much thought to her manners—a remark made by another college student suggested that she would be more attractive to men if she were sweeter and more demure—and her conversation. Her ignorance and timidity regarding sex tend to make her feel insecure and self-conscious with boys; her information is vague, and her feelings are so new and strong that she is afraid of what they may lead her into.

Gradually most adolescents find activities, such as dancing, which facilitate girl-boy association. And they find other people of both sexes who are congenial in these new interests and activities. This new group, the "crowd," is the typical adolescent social unit. A crowd is usually composed of a dozen to twenty youngsters, about half of them boys and the other half girls, who go around together. Its influence is great. The members wear the same kind of clothes, use the same catch phrases, dance with one another at parties, and tend to form a definite clique in any social relationships. A boy or girl is either in a crowd or not in it; a youngster no longer rambles from one group to another as in early childhood. The members of the crowd may criticize one another in private but they present a united front to the world. Much of the friction between parents and adolescents arises from conflicts in behavior standards between the home and the crowd.

As there is a shift in the composition of the social group from the childhood gang of one sex to the adolescent crowd containing both sexes, so there is a shift in the center of social interest from the chum of the same sex to the "girl friend" or "boy friend" of the opposite sex. Since this interest in the other sex is so new and so strong, and since unfortunately the average adolescent has so little understanding of himself or of sex or the other sex, he may blunder about to a great extent. There may be puppy-love episodes which seem very silly. The object of a boy's affection may be some scatter-brained little girl whose sex appeal is based on the very superficial elements of appearance and conversational line. But members of a lively heterosexual adolescent society soon become acquainted with many members of the other sex, who are constantly discussed and appraised, with increasing shrewdness, in the interminable talk that goes on in one sex group about the other. The present-day frank-

---

[5] Acute sensitivity about even slight blemishes is common. The adolescent whose appearance is handicapped by acne, banded teeth, adenoidal features, or cross-eyes may become so self-conscious and shy as to affect his whole personality. Correction of such defects, before adolescence if possible, may pay manifold returns psychologically.

ness among adolescents is healthier than the awkward unfamiliarity with the other sex that was common fifty years ago.

Frequent casual contact with the other sex is also healthier and more productive of real understanding than the ready-made pseudoexperiences provided by movies or TV or pulp magazines or the self-manufactured pseudoexperiences made possible by daydreaming. As has been pointed out, current movies, TV programs, and magazine stories are false in their emphasis on impulsive romanticism in relations between the sexes, an expensive and feverish social life, and standards of attractiveness and attracting that are unrealistic. The desired standards of social life and companionship thus set are likely to lead to extravagance and to dissatisfaction with things as they are. Nevertheless, as was also pointed out earlier, movies and radio and TV may be helpful in informing about manners, conversation, and dress; and they set the style in make-up, dress, catch phrases, and amusements.

Readjustment to Associates of One's Own Sex

As was brought out in the preceding section, the social psychology of later childhood is primarily the story of relationships with others of one's own sex. Ordinarily many of these acquaintanceships carry over into the adolescent period, and much that was said about childhood society is applicable here. However, there are important differences, certain of which have already been touched upon.

The family's socioeconomic status becomes much more important in adolescence than it is in childhood. Thus when high-school youngsters in the little midwestern city of Elmtown were asked to list their best friend, 78 percent of the girls and 71 percent of the boys named someone in their same socioeconomic class. No "upper"-class girl or boy named anyone in a "lower" class, or any out-of-school adolescent. But a third of the friends of "lower"-class high-school pupils were out-of-school youth (34, pages 216–217).

Since adolescent society is dominated by heterosexual interests, associations with the same sex are affected; thus the girl who is not popular with boys does not maintain close friendships with girls who are. As already pointed out, the time of maturation greatly affects social relations. Two boys who develop slowly or fail to make heterosexual adjustments may find pleasure in companionship, perhaps working at a hobby. For the typical adolescent, sex and the other sex are perennial topics of conversation. Warily, affecting sophistication, each trying not to betray ignorance, they learn or try to learn from each other and often they do help each other. A girl said that when "we find one of us knows practically nothing of what she should know, we try to explain the best way we can." Help is given with social difficulties. According to another girl, "Maizie was so shy with boys . . . but we told her how to act, and now she's able to be herself with them" (77, page 534).

We saw earlier that childhood "society" has some structure; the occasional child who is not popular does not "belong." As might be expected, such problems are both more common and more distressing in adolescence. For instance, a study of over 600 adolescent boys showed the friendship of 13 percent almost entirely "unrequited"; that is, the boys whom a given lad rated as his best friends did not regard him as their best friend. And the investigator said of these boys with unreciprocated friendships: "Their deep and eager longing for the companionship of understanding friends denied, they feel the dejection and loneliness of those who are in the social group but not of it. . . . With shriveled ego and punctured self-esteem they seek by devious ways to convince themselves that they possess a worth and a social status that their world of associates cruelly denies" (19, page 125).

What can be done for such youngsters? Or, more generally, what factors and traits particularly affect popularity? The topic has been investigated. Thus teen-agers have been asked what they especially like in their friends or dislike in those they reject. In general, the people who are liked seem to be lively, cheerful, humorous, willing to enter into things, and to have ideas about what to do. Those disliked are quarrelsome or unduly sensitive, not to be depended upon. Untidiness, fidgeting, and other nervous habits may be elements making for avoidance, and the moodiness, resentfulness, and shyness resulting from social rejection may increase the difficulty (38, pages 210 ff.). We shall return to this topic later.

Readjustments to and Conflicts with the Family

The adolescent, progressing to maturity as he is, wants increasing independence. He wishes to enlarge his acquaintance with the other sex. He may make mistakes, and his family worries lest he do so. Customs change. Obviously there are many possibilities for conflict or misunderstanding.

An obvious direct way to get at such problems is to ask adolescents and parents—one or the other or both groups—about difficulties they have with each other. In one excellent inquiry of this type (6), some 500 adolescents were asked about conflicts with their mothers. Being pestered about table manners was mentioned by 75 percent of the boys and 65 percent of the girls, having a sister or brother held up as a model by 67 and 76 percent, being refused permission to use the car by 86 and 71 percent, objections to going for automobile rides at night by 66 and 87 percent, being scolded for low school marks by 82 and 86 percent, having to account for the money they spent by 80 and 81 percent. There were numerous other complaints, but the above were most frequent. However, this study, made some years ago, had one important feature. The results were presented at a parent-teacher meeting, discussed there and in many of the homes, and taken up in conferences between adviser and parent or pupil. After a year of such efforts, it was felt that all concerned understood each other better and got along better than before. More important than any single effort such as this are indications that, as a result of many similar investigations and discussions, parents and adolescents are in general adjusting better to each other. Thus, according to a survey in 1955, "It would appear from the response that the majority of the parents interviewed had an understanding of the emotional needs and development of teen-agers" (*14*).

In some instances, however, the difficulties between parent and adolescent are much more complex. Some special experience a parent has had, or a personality trait, may result in an unfortunate dominance of the child which comes to a head in adolescence. The following four youngsters all came to a college counseling office.

Helen was the large, awkward, easily embarrassed daughter of a divorced and emotional mother. The mother had married impetuously, unwisely, and too young, was lonely, and was determined that Helen should not make the same mistake she had made. She laid down strict rules about Helen's social life; if the girl rebelled, the mother wept and sometimes became ill. Helen never chose her own clothes and had never been away from her mother overnight. She had little companionship with others of her own age and sex, and lost out completely in social affairs with the other sex.

Even more unfortunate is the situation when the youngster acquiesces in or even prefers dependence. Archie's mother was prominent, attractive, vigorous, very fond of her slight, languid son. He was fond of her and found it easy to let her indulge him, do things for him, look after him. In high school he seemed little interested in girls of his own age but enjoyed being in the company of older women; his favorite teacher was somewhat like his mother.

Very different was the case of Irene, whose mother, having had few good times in her own girlhood, tried to give her daughter all the pleasures she had missed. Attractive clothes, more spending money than the family could spare easily, and a pushing into social life that Irene sometimes resented led to over-stimulation and irresponsibility.

June's mother had given up her hopes of a career as a pianist to marry. In her daughter she saw the possibility of her own unrealized ambitions being achieved. Piano lessons and interminable practice were June's lot. During childhood she was reasonably docile. But her music interfered more and more with her desire to live her own life. Seeing her plan in danger, the mother insisted all the more on lessons and practice and tried to block off conflicting social activities. To June her music became a hated thing, and she insisted on going to a college in a distant state to "get as far away from mother as possible."

Difficulties in the general pattern of social behavior are more often related to socioeconomic class, or associated therewith. Thus a popular Elmtown high-school girl remarked as follows about another girl from a conservative family: "Judy doesn't go out. She would like to, but her folks won't let her. . . . You can't be tied to your mother's apron strings and be told you have to be in at ten o'clock and you can't wear lipstick, and can't do this, and you can't do that, and be popular" (*34*, page 253).

A working-class father of a very bright boy complained, with good reason, that "the School Board's children and children of prominent people . . . seem to be in everything, and it's difficult for other students to get into activities and offices" (page 182). A girl who had left school said, "The kids looked down on us . . . because Dad drove the oil truck. . . . They had a club . . . we didn't belong. . . . Some of the girls who thought they were somebody used to snub me when I waited tables in high school. . . . The day I was 16 I walked out of that high school" (page 344).

The School and Adolescent Social Development

The typical adolescent is trying to escape, psychologically, from his home. But economically and vocationally he is not yet able to leave home. He needs a way point. This the modern American secondary school supplies—and does this socially perhaps better than intellectually or vocationally. It provides a place where he can be away from home regularly and with the full approval of his home and community, and it creates many additional occasions for being away from home. It affords constant association with other adolescents—going to and from school, in the corridors and classrooms and study halls, and in athletic and social affairs. Class and extraclass activities furnish topics of conversation and foci of interest. Classes in modern schools are increasingly informal, and social and special projects and trips are coöperative social ventures. Beyond the educational procedures and more interesting to both students and community is "school life."

What is there of special social significance that happens *in* school?

First of all, it is well to remember that not only are adolescent students markedly social in their interests, but the staff are also human beings (often young) with their own social interests and problems. Put these two groups together and sundry situations always develop.

Affable, unmarried Mr. Smith, the young physics teacher, is inevitably an object of interest to adolescent high-school senior girls who are naturally more attracted by males somewhat older than their classmates. And Mr. Smith can hardly be totally unaware of these attractive girls.

Miss Andrews, the physical education teacher, is a vigorous young woman who would like to marry, but somehow—perhaps partly because of her somewhat masculine manner—men of her own age have passed her by. Martha is a shy appealing little girl who has not made satisfactory associations with boys. She greatly admires this vigorous, self-confident woman, who in turn enjoys having someone pay her devoted attention. It is very natural that these two should enjoy being together. But when, at long last, a man becomes interested in Miss Andrews, she finds her ever-present young admirer a nuisance, shows this none too tactfully, and leaves the girl isolated and miserable.

When sex-social interests are lively, it is only natural that they should hold a youngster's attention at the expense of the conventional subject matter. In fact, much that goes on in a class cannot be rightly understood unless the social undercurrents are appreciated.

Unusually insightful is a high-school girl's account of a session of a class taught by a young man. She admits that languor and boredom and unpreparedness are a pose to compete with another girl in the class who shows off. By her own display of ignorance and her appearance of malaise she finally gets the attention of the instructor. He inquires solicitously about her as she rises with elaborate weariness and leaves the classroom, conveniently and ostentatiously last (77).

Striking indeed may be the contrast shown by different classes in the extensiveness and naturalness of social experiences. Miss Henry in Spanish gives no opportunity for direct social relationships between students. She asks a question of Mabel or Tom or Jane and they in turn speak to her. Or they translate, addressing their translation to her; and she in turn, when a correction is necessary, calls upon someone to make it. The students could hardly be more isolated from each other if each were in a separate stall. Contrast this with what has been going on in home economics. The girls have been planning the banquet they are giving for their parents. They are working in committees, and thus each chairman has an opportunity for leadership. The committees have visited stores and got the prices of what will be needed. They have consulted with their parents about the program. The youngsters work together informally, chattering as freely as they would after school. School undertakings such as the latter could hardly be more social and informal if they were neighborhood affairs initiated and carried out by the girls themselves.

A variety of "activities" provide obvious socializing experiences. Some, adult-sponsored and guided, go their decorous way and often are socially very valuable, though sometimes flat. A club holds meetings in which students learn rules of order and the procedure followed in a debate or an election; they also may gain some poise in speaking to a group. Col-

TABLE 6.1. Participation in Various High-School Activities by Children from Different Socioeconomic Classes[6]

| | Social Class | | | |
| | | | Wage | |
	Upper	Middle	Earners	Lower
Percentage distribution of student body	9	37	47	7
Percentage composition of student council	22	46	32	0
Percentage seldom missing or attending most				
Evening plays and parties	89	56	12	0
High-school dances	77	47	13	0
Games	94	75	44	0
No participation (%)	0	25	43	73
Number of cases	35	146	163	26

lege alumni frequently refer to such experiences in high school and college as having been very valuable in preparing them to participate in business meetings or public affairs. These clubs are more democratic than the typical adolescent crowd. If wisely directed, they provide opportunities for leadership that the quieter youngsters might not otherwise have. There are the assemblies, the games, rallies, dances, and other school affairs. The typical school has a fever of these goings-on. The newspapers feature them, they are talked about in town. To those at their center they are life. But for many others, on the outside enviously looking on, they mark the beginning of a lifelong jealousy of the have-nots for the haves. Such unfortunate outcomes are especially likely if they are tied in with and are in part due to handicaps arising from family status.

Table 6.1 shows the situation in this respect in Elmtown. The 9 percent of the high-school student body whose families were upper class had over twice their proportion on the student council; 89 percent attended most of

[6] Adapted from Hollingshead (34, pp. 193–202).

the evening plays and parties and 77 percent went to most of the high-school dances; almost all went to most of the games. But none of the lowest socioeconomic group were on the council or went often to any of the social affairs; 73 percent of them did not participate at all.

Another investigator found that 8 percent of the senior girls in a large high school had never belonged to any club, team, committee, or other group; 35 percent had belonged to no social group; 30 percent had been to no dances or parties; and 15 percent had had no "dates" within the past month.[7]

AN APPLIED SOCIAL PSYCHOLOGY FOR TEACHERS

The preceding paragraph commented on the "extracurricular" problems of high-school senior girls, and the chapter itself extended back to the "social" responses of infancy. Are there any largely common problems for teachers from the nursery school on, and basic approaches to these problems?

In any typical class from the elementary grades through college (consider the students in your own classes to see whether this is not true) there is someone who is too anxious to have the teacher's favorable regard; he raises his hand too often, takes part too much. Another is a smart aleck who tries to get laughs and attention from the other members of the class. Still another is overactive, restless, mischievous. A pretty girl plays up to the boys, and some of the boys pay too much attention to her. One girl could participate in what is going on, but never does unless asked. Another does little but sit, apparently daydreaming. A fourth girl is sensitive, critical, unsocial. In a given class, only eight or nine out of the entire thirty students really take much part in things. Three or four are disturbers; they may be impertinent, cheat, play truant. There are about a dozen ordinary, somewhat colorless, reasonably well-behaved youngsters who have so little classroom personality, good or bad, that the teacher is likely to forget them.

It is only natural for the teacher to encourage the youngsters who act in accordance with the school program, and to call little upon those who contribute little. She bluntly snubs the persistent seeker of her attention. If she is of a vigorous nature she may counter the aggressive youngster with aggressive behavior of her own. If she is kind, she may hesitate to disturb the shy, sensitive child; at any rate he presents no obvious classroom problem. In all these instances she may be doing exactly the wrong thing. The boy who too persistently bids for her attention is compensating for his failure to make good with the other boys outside of school; he needs to be helped with that problem, not cut off from the one source of favorable attention he has found. The overactive

[7] Unpublished data of Dr. Richard Wilkinson.

boy needs to be given responsibility and things to do, not challenged to even more aggression. The daydreamer and the sensitive girl are really the most serious problems in the class; somehow the teacher must bring them out of their isolation and into the social group. The colorless nonparticipators are the ones who most need experience in participation.

Evidently such insightful understanding of such various social problems presented by such different youngsters requires appraisal of their social liabilities and assets, their position at home and in their social group

TABLE 6.2. Where Midwest Children Under 12 Spent the Greatest Amount of Time[8]

Setting	% of Total Hours Spent in Community
School classes	30.9
Traffic ways	7.4
Indoor entertainments	6.4
Open spaces	4.3
County jail and sheriff's residence	3.9
Hotels, rooming houses, and nurseries	3.6
Sunday-school classes	3.2
Indoor athletic contests	3.0
Shoe repair shop	3.0
Drug, variety, and department store	2.5
Rest rooms	2.4
Classrooms: free time	2.3
Dining and lunch rooms	2.3
Music education groups	2.1
Out-of-door athletic contests	1.9
Church services	1.6

as well as at school. Special attention should be given to the quiet, commonplace individuals who are so often overlooked because there is nothing special about them to catch the attention. Not very attractive, not very vigorous, coming from drab homes, socially isolated or with a chum like themselves, socially they lead a half-starved existence. They are the forgotten youngsters. What steps can be taken to understand them better and help them? The following suggestions may help.

1. *Know settings and backgrounds.* Teachers should know more than they do about the community and neighborhood in which they teach. Of interest in this connection is Table 6.2, showing where children in the little town of Midwest spent most of their time. In fifth place is the county

[8] Adapted from Barker and Wright (3), p. 107.

jail. But when it is known that the mother of three of these children was the sheriff's wife and that apparently she was a good cook and indulgent of children, the situation is understandable. Still it is worth noting that these children spent considerable time in the jail.

There was a gap in the social understanding of an Elmtown teacher who did not realize that, for some of the high-school students, the community rarely included the public library or a local church but often included the country club or the cloverleaf night spot. A teacher in that smug little city would have been socially blind not to see how socioeconomic status dominated high-school society and pervaded teacher attitudes—but some of the teachers saw these realities of the local social scene only dimly.

2. *Make a social appraisal of each pupil.* As mentioned in the earlier description of a typical class, even casual observation shows many differences between pupils in their classroom social behavior. Also pointed out in that connection was the fact that any understanding of those differences requires some knowledge both of each youngster's relationships with other youngsters and of his family. A perceptive elementary-school teacher can obtain a little of this understanding from observing her pupils in the classroom and on the playground, and she will understand much better in proportion as she gets acquainted in the neighborhood and with the parents. In a secondary school, especially a large one, the task is both more difficult and more important. Notations regarding each student's activities should be as much a part of his record as the courses he takes and the grades he obtains. An occasional request that pupils list the groups they belong to and the things they do will yield helpful information.

Such data practically always show that many students do not participate at all and a few others too much. A sample finding from a high-school senior class of 211 further emphasizes the first statement—62 percent had never belonged to any subject club and 37 percent had never been in any kind of social club either school-connected or otherwise; 8 percent said that they had never belonged to any team, club, society, or even a committee connected with church, school, or other organization.

Quite clearly, gathering such material is a special task; and interpreting it may involve even further inquiry, as of parents. So special and so important is such work, and the special skills required for it, that later chapters are given over to discussion of it.

Thorough appraisal should include possible constitutional elements, such as the vivacity and physical appeal mentioned early in the chapter as sometimes being evident even in infancy and recognizable years later. In the chapter on physical growth, early or late maturing was mentioned as often influencing social status, particularly at adolescence. As has been brought out elsewhere, the family's socioeconomic status may be of extreme importance. How good is the youngster's equipment of socially useful skills—for example, in popular sports and, in adolescence, dancing? How well does he conform to the code of his group—in childhood, not to tattle, and in adolescence, to be loyal to the crowd? What also has been the range and nature of his social experience? For instance, how much visiting has he done, for, as we saw earlier, visiting can entail socially very significant experiences (10)?

3. *Plan a social program that is broad enough to include all the pupils, and use it so that the needs of all are met.* A resourceful elementary-school teacher can do much by herself in the little subsociety of her classroom. For example, two girls of foreign-born parents, who at first felt shy and out of place, became centers of interest when their teacher featured a discussion of their parents' homeland. Children present very different problems, and a teacher must be both resourceful and clever in social maneuvers—as well as understanding each child. But the able teacher realizes that social problems that are evident in school involve after-school hours and vacation time too, and she tries to coöperate with the neighborhood playground, the summer camp, and other agencies that foster desirable companionship.

A secondary school usually has various activities, but they are too limited and conventional in nature and in range of membership; the major problem is to serve the "outsiders" and make the activities more significant. Will providing for informal dancing in the school at noon help some socially marginal pupils? Do very inexpensive boy-girl sports like ping-pong and paddle tennis have possibilities? Would a science club or a junior academy reach able but shy youngsters who have special interests and abilities, and bring them special attention because of possible state and national affiliations of such groups? Could the school combine forces with the community recreation department—perhaps a men's service organization such as Rotary—to serve youth not only during but after school hours—and out-of-school youth—through the year? Clearly such programs go beyond the work of one teacher, but she should be an understanding coöperator. (Various types of special work with young people will be considered later in this volume, and also their important relations with problems of adult life.)

The preceding statements might seem to imply that the secondary-school teacher is concerned in class only with history or math—not with her students' social development. On the contrary, the writers believe that in both secondary school and college a constructive social program should begin in class. Certainly every class should have a good-humored, relaxed, friendly social climate where every student can have the com-

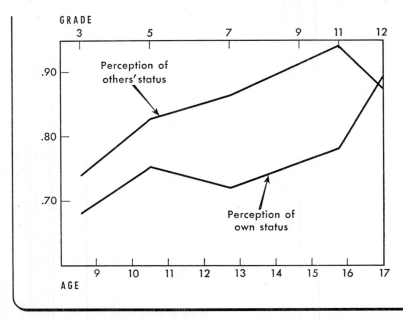

FIG. 6.3. Prediction of own and others' sociometric status at various grade and age levels. Correlation between mean sociometric or friendship rating of each pupil in a class in Grades 3, 5, 7, 9, 11, and 12 in a midwestern area, and each pupil's mean estimate of his popularity with his classmates. Average class size, 49; average ages of the classes, 8.5, 10.5, 12.7, 15.8, and 17.0. (Adapted from Ausubel and Gasser [2].)

fortable feeling of belonging. But the writers' experiments in university classes in educational psychology have shown that acquaintance among students can be doubled and its nature greatly enriched over that usual in the average class, when there is a socialized activity program in which students work freely together around tables and take trips to schools and playgrounds with an instructor who is a practicing "social psychologist" (60, 61). High-school teachers, who teach in their pupils' home community, have far greater opportunity to understand and further the social development of their pupils, and also to further the improvement in both learning and community-school relations, as was illustrated by the home economics class described earlier. This is another topic so important that it will be discussed more fully in a later chapter.

4. *Directly or indirectly, teach an informal applied social psychology.* The preceding discussion has this serious fault, that it may apparently imply that only a teacher or other adult, and often only a specially trained school psychologist or counselor, can understand and provide for handling problems of social maladjustment. Actually, of course, youngsters learn from their joint social life how John and Harry and Ruth rate, and what their faults and merits are, and also something as to how John and Harry and Ruth regard them. Fig. 6.3 shows that perception of self grows more slowly than that of others; by later adolescence, however, there is a fairly accurate self-estimate.

An experienced teacher recently said that the social problems presented by a junior-high-school girl had completely baffled him. Finally he mentioned his difficulties to two fine youngsters in whom he had confidence, and they helped him in both understanding and dealing with her. Obviously discussion of one pupil with others must be extremely guarded. But a variety of evidence suggests that, at least by junior high school, social understanding and social adeptness have grown sufficiently that a school might well attempt somewhat to guide and advance their development. Secondary-school courses in home economics now usually include something on grooming and often—perhaps in connection with the discussion of family life—a variety of material on interpersonal relations. As will be mentioned at several points in this book, psychologists are becoming increasingly interested in the possible values to be found in teaching an informal psychology in high school (20). The writers believe that even elementary-school children may be helped to a better understanding of both others and self, and to progress in social adjustment in which they participate understandingly.

SUMMARY

This chapter deals with what is in many respects the central problem of development over the school years, and indeed throughout life—learning to get along satisfactorily and effectively with other people.

In the first six years, the preschool years, the child's major task is to become adjusted to his family; his parents are at the center of his social world. His physical constitution and health, his parents' attitudes and discipline, and his relations with any siblings all combine to develop in him confidence or assertiveness or timidity, good nature or passivity or irritability. The children who are so fortunate as to go to nursery school have professional guidance in much of this developing and in their first adjustments to both adults and children outside the home.

Major social contacts outside the family do not begin for most children until they enter elementary school. There the teacher enjoys great prestige as parent-surrogate, source of knowledge, wielder of authority, bestower of favors. And the social climate and the modes of social behavior in the classroom may have considerable influence on the development of the child's personality. Even more important in this respect is how at this time he finds a place for himself—belonging, and a role and status—in the society of his fellows. He associates primarily with others of the same sex and about the same age, and especially with his chum.

The most distinctive and most important feature of social development during adolescence is the change in attitude toward the other sex, from indifference or scorn to great interest—a shift vital for emotional health and normal social life and, later, a happy marriage. Social relations with one sex are affected and change; sensitivity increases, with leaders becoming more prominent, and isolates more unhappy. Desire for independence of the family increases, and conflicts are likely. Differences in socioeconomic status and in codes of social behavior become prominent. The school usually tries to moderate or arbitrate these differences and to work for desirable social development.

To foster intelligently the social development of its pupils, the writers believe that a school should take four steps. (1) Know physical and social settings and backgrounds that may significantly influence its pupils' social development; (2) make an appraisal of the social assets and liabilities of each pupil, and his social status; (3) formulate a social program that is broad enough to serve all its pupils and use it accordingly; (4) directly or indirectly, teach a simple applied social psychology so that the youngsters will have some intelligence concerning their social growth.

BIBLIOGRAPHY

1. Austin, Mary C., and Thompson, G. G., Children's friendships: a study of the bases on which children select and reject their best friends, *J. Educ. Psychol.*, 1948, *39*:101–116.
2. Ausubel, D. P., Schiff, H. M., and Gasser, E. B., A preliminary study of developmental trends in socioempathy: accuracy of perception of own and others' sociometric status, *Child Devel.*, 1952, *23*:113–128.
3. Barker, R. G., and Wright, H. F., *Midwest and Its Children*, Evanston: Row, Peterson, 1954.
4. Baruch, D. W., A study of reported tension in interparental relationships

as co-existent with behavior adjustment in young children, *J. Exp. Educ.,* 1937, *6*:187–204.

5. Berger, E., Relation between expressed acceptance of self and others, *J. Abnorm. Soc. Psychol.,* 1952, *47*:778–782.

6. Block, V. L., Conflicts of adolescents with their mothers, *J. Abnorm. Soc. Psychol.,* 1937, *32*:193–206.

7. Blos, P., *The Adolescent Personality,* New York: Appleton-Century-Crofts, 1941.

8. Bonney, M. E., A sociometric study of relationship of some factors to mutual friendships on the elementary, secondary and college levels, *Sociometry,* 1946, *9*:21–47.

9. Bonney, M. E., Sociometric study of agreement between teachers' judgments and student choices, *Sociometry,* 1947, *10*:133–146.

10. Bossard, J. H. S., Process in social weaning: A study of childhood visiting, *Child Devel.,* 1951, *22*:211–220.

11. Bossard, J. H. S., *Parent and Child,* Philadelphia: Univ. of Pennsylvania Press, 1953.

12. Bossard, J. H. S., and Boll, Eleanor S., Personality roles in the large family, *Child Devel.,* 1955, *26*:71–78.

13. Bretsch, H. S., Social skills and activities of socially accepted and unaccepted adolescents, *J. Educ. Psychol.,* 1952, *43*:449–458.

14. Briggs, Vivian, and Schulz, Lois R., Parental response to concepts of parent-adolescent relationships, *Child Devel.,* 1955, *26*:279–284.

15. Christensen, H. T., Dating behavior as evaluated by high school students, *Amer. J. Sociol.,* 1952, *57*:580–586.

16. Connor, R. T., Johannis, T. B., Jr., and Walters, J., Parent-adolescent relationships. I, Parent-adolescent conflicts: current and retrospect, *J. Home Econ.,* 1954, *46,* 183–186.

17. Cox, F. N., Sociometric status and individual adjustment before and after play therapy, *J. Abnorm. Soc. Psychol.,* 1953, *48*:354–356.

18. Crist, J. R., High school dating as a behavior system, *Marriage and Family Living,* 1953, *15*:23–28.

19. Dimock, H. S., *Rediscovering the Adolescent,* New York: Association Press, 1937.

20. Engle, T. L., and Bunch, M. E., The teaching of psychology in high school, *Amer. Psychol.,* 1956, *11*:188–193.

21. Foshay, A. W., The teacher and children's social attitudes, *Teach. Coll. Rec.,* 1951, *52*:287–296.

22. Fox, W. H., and Segel, D., The validity of the choice of friends: Method of measuring social adjustment, *J. Educ. Res.,* 1954, *47*:389–394.

23. Frenkel-Brunswik, Else, A study of prejudice in children, *Hum. Rel.,* 1948, *1*:295–306.

24. Gough, H. G., Harris, D. B., Martin, W. E., and Edwards, M., Children's ethnic attitudes: I, Relationship to certain personality factors, *Child Devel.,* 1950, *21*:83–91.

25. Green, E. H., Friendships and quarrels among pre-school children, *Child Devel.*, 1933, *4*:237–252.
26. Greenberg, Pearl J., Competition in children: An experimental study, *Amer. J. Psychol.*, 1932, *44*:221–248.
27. Gronlund, N. E., The accuracy of teachers' judgments concerning the sociometric status of sixth-grade pupils, *Sociometry*, 1950, *13*:197–225.
28. Gronlund, N. E., Relationship between the sociometric status of pupils' and teachers' preferences for or against having them in class, *Sociometry*, 1953, *16*:142–150.
29. Guest, H., Adolescents and parents talk it over, *Understanding the Child*, 1955, *24*:98–102.
30. Hanley, C., Physique and reputation of junior high school boys, *Child Devel.*, 1951, *22*:247–260.
31. Hattwick, B. W., Interrelations between the pre-school child's behavior and certain factors in the home, *Child Devel.*, 1936, *9*:27–47.
32. Havighurst, R. J., and Taba, H., *Adolescent Character and Personality*, New York: Wiley, 1949.
33. Himmelweit, H. T., Halsey, A. H., and Oppenheim, A. N., The views of adolescents on some aspects of the social class structure, *Brit. J. Sociol.*, 1952, *3*:148–172.
34. Hollingshead, A. B., *Elmtown's Youth*, New York: Wiley, 1949.
35. Horrocks, J. E., and Buker, M. E., A study of the friendship fluctuations of preadolescents, *J. Genet. Psychol.*, 1951, *78*:131–144.
36. Jennings, Helen H., *Sociometry in Group Relations: A Work Guide for Teachers*, Washington: American Council on Education, 1948.
37. Jersild, A. T., Self-understanding in childhood and adolescence, *Amer. Psychol.*, 1951, *6*:122–126.
38. Jersild, A. T., *The Psychology of Adolescence*, New York: Macmillan, 1957.
39. Jones, H. E., *Development in Adolescence*, New York: Appleton-Century-Crofts, 1943.
40. Jones, H. E., Physical ability as a factor in social adjustment in adolescence, *J. Educ. Res.*, 1946, *40*:287–301.
41. Kinsey, A. C., Pomeroy, W. B., and Martin, C. E., *Sexual Behavior in the Human Male*, Philadelphia: Saunders, 1948.
42. Kuhlen, R. G., and Bretsch, H. S., Sociometric status and personal problems of adolescents, *Sociometry*, 1947, *10*:122–132.
43. Lewin, Kurt, Lippitt, R., and White, R. K., Patterns of aggressive behavior in experimentally created "social climates," *J. Soc. Psychol.*, 1939, *10*:271–299.
44. Lewis, Claudia, *Children of the Cumberland*, New York: Columbia Univ. Press, 1946.
45. Lowenstein, P., and Svendsen, M., Experimental modification of the behavior of a selected group of shy and withdrawn children, *Amer. J. Orthopsychiat.*, 1938, *8*:639–653.

46. Mallay, H., Study of some of the techniques underlying the establishment of successful social contacts at the pre-school level, *Ped. Sem.*, 1935, 47:431–457.
47. Martin, W. E., and Stendler, Celia B., *Child Development: The Process of Growing Up in Society*, New York: Harcourt, Brace, 1953.
48. McGraw, L. W., and Tolbert, J. W., Sociometric status and athletic ability of junior high school boys, *Res. Quart. Amer. Assn. Health, Phys. Educ., and Recreation*, 1953, 24:72–80.
49. McGuire, C., and Clark, R. A., Age-mate acceptance and indices of peer status, *Child Devel.*, 1952, 23:141–154.
50. McKee, J. P., and Leader, Florence B., Relation of socio-economic status and aggression to the competitive behavior of school children, *Child Devel.*, 1955, 26:135–142.
51. Mead, Margaret, and Calas, N., *Primitive Heritage*, New York: Random, 1953.
52. Mead, Margaret, and McGregor, Francis D., *Growth v. Culture*, New York: Putnam, 1951.
53. Moreno, T. L., Who shall survive? *Nerv. Ment. Dis. Monog.*, No. 58, 1934.
54. Neilon, Patricia, Shirley's babies after 15 years, *J. Genet. Psychol.*, 1948, 73:175–186.
55. Olson, C. M., The adolescent: his society, *Rev. Educ. Res.*, 1954, 24:5–10.
56. Osborne, E. G., *Camping and Guidance*, New York: Association Press, 1939.
57. Page, Marjorie Lou, The modification of ascendant behavior in pre-school children, *Univ. Iowa Stud. Child Welfare* No. 3, 1936.
58. Parten, M. B., Social participation among pre-school children, *J. Abnorm. Soc. Psychol.*, 1932, 27:243–269.
59. Patti, J. B., Elementary psychology for eighth graders? *Amer. Psychol.*, 1956, 11:194–196.
60. Pressey, S. L., Teaching in the ivory tower, with rarely a step outside, *Psychol. Bull.*, 1955, 52:343–344.
61. Pressey, S. L., and Hanna, D. C., The class as a psycho-sociological unit, *J. Psychol.*, 1943, 16:13–19.
62. Radke, M., Trager, H. G., and Davis, H., Social perceptions and attitudes of children, *Genet. Psychol. Monog.*, 1949, 40:327–347.
63. Reader, N., and English, H. B., Personality factors in adolescent female friendships, *J. Consult. Psychol.*, 1947, 11:212–220.
64. Roff, M., and Brody, D., Appearances and choice status during adolescence, *J. Psychol.*, 1953, 36:347–356.
65. Scodel, A., and Mussen, P., Social perceptions of authoritarians and non-authoritarians, *J. Abnorm. Soc. Psychol.*, 1953, 48:181–189.
66. Shirley, M. M., *The First Two Years: A Study of Twenty-five Babies*, Minneapolis: Univ. of Minnesota Press, 3 vol., 1931–1933.
67. Shirley, M. M., Common content in the speech of pre-school children, *Child Devel.*, 1938, 9:333–346.

68. Sowers, Alice, Parent-child relationship from the child's point of view, *J. Exp. Educ.,* 1937, *6*:205–232.
69. Spivak, S. S., A study of a method of appraising self-acceptance and self-rejection, *J. Genet. Psychol.,* 1956, *88*:183–202.
70. Stendler, Celia B., and Young, N., The impact of beginning first grade upon socialization as reported by mothers, *Child Devel.,* 1950, *21*:241–260.
71. Symonds, P. M., *Psychology of Parent-Child Relationships,* New York: Appleton-Century-Crofts, 1939.
72. Thompson, G. G., and Horrocks, J. E., A study of the friendship fluctuations of urban boys and girls, *J. Genet. Psychol.,* 1947, *70*:53–63.
73. Trow, W. C., A child who feared teachers, *J. Educ. Sociol.,* 1930, *3*:590–601.
74. Tuddenham, R. D., Studies in reputation. III, Correlates of popularity among elementary school children, *J. Educ. Psychol.,* 1951, *42*:257–276.
75. Walsh, Elizabeth, Relation of nursery school training to development of personality traits, *Child Devel.,* 1931, *2*:72–73.
76. White, M. A., and Williams, H. M., The approach-withdrawal pattern in the social behavior of young children, *Ped. Sem.,* 1939, *54*:73–84.
77. Zachry, C. B., and Lighty, M., *Emotion and Conduct in Adolescence,* New York: Appleton-Century-Crofts, 1940.

PART II

The Nature and Fostering of Learning